OTTO WAGNER 1841 1918

OTTO WAGNER 1841 1918

THE EXPANDING CITY THE BEGINNING OF MODERN ARCHITECTURE

By HEINZ GERETSEGGER and MAX PEINTNER

Associate Author WALTER PICHLER
Introduction by RICHARD NEUTRA
Translated by Gerald Onn

RIZZOLI
NEW YORK

The jacket illustrations are prints 36 and 38 from Otto Wagner's *Einige Skizzen, Projekte und ausgeführte Bauwerke* (Some Sketches, Designs and Buildings), Vol. III, Vienna, 1906, and they show the front and rear elevations of the Church Am Steinhof. The frontispiece shows one of the two acroteria on the projecting face of the Post Office Savings Bank.

Acknowledgements are made for the use of the quotations which appear in the text:

Comte de Lautréamont, *Maldoror*, translated by Guy Wernham. Copyright 1943 by Guy Wernham. Reprinted by permission of New Directions Publishing Corporation, New York.

Robert Musil, *The Man Without Qualities*, translated by Eithne Wilkins and Ernst Kaiser. Reprinted by permission of Coward-McCann, New York.

Arthur Rimbaud, *Illuminations*, translated by Louise Varèse. Copyright 1946 and 1957 by New Directions Publishing Corporation, New York. Reprinted by permission of the copyright holder.

Published in the United States of America in 1979 by
RIZZOLI INTERNATIONAL PUBLICATIONS, INC.
712 Fifth Avenue/New York 10019
Copyright © 1964 Residenz Verlag Salzburg

English language edition copyright © 1979 Academy Editions

Library of Congress Catalog Card Number: 78-68493
ISBN: 0-8478-0217-5

Printed and bound in Hong Kong

FOREWORD

The authors and publishers of this book have performed the extremely difficult task of preserving the life's work of a great and unusual man from the dusty annals of history. Unfortunately, the popular belief that a man's work is better understood and appreciated after his death is a fallacy. I am quite convinced that no Gothic cathedral has ever been so appreciated by posterity as it was at the time of its conception. It is the first manifestation of a new work which is most readily imprinted on men's mind.

In this detailed biographical and pictorial study illuminating parallels are drawn between Otto Wagner's world of thought and our own times. We are also shown the provocative attitudes adopted by this man who stepped with a supreme lack of diplomacy on so many toes, even when their owners stood 'on the steps of the throne'. Such attitudes, incidentally, would not be out of place today. In a period of transition Wagner opposed clichés. Some, which were important, he revitalised with the sure touch of a master only to discard them as a mature man, when he became intoxicated with the future, which is merely to say that he became 'rational'.

Often, when investigating the scene of other people's deeds, the historian believes that he is able to detect fingerprints which had been overlooked by his predecessors. The architect, on the other hand, sees and experiences the deeds themselves. As for myself, all I can detect in the dark recesses of my being are a few hidden fingerprints which serve as pointers to the past.

For two generations now my being has drawn strength from the memory of Otto Wagner and has clung to him with affection. My memoirs*, which were written far from the land of my youth, contain many references to him. English-speaking readers may well have been surprised to learn of an eight-year-old Viennese boy who fell in love before the turn of the century with the stations on the underground and high-level railways of his native city. Such heartfelt relationships to public transportation systems are more than rare in New York or Chicago and it is difficult for people there to identify with this Viennese enthusiasm. When I recall that very intricate project, which extended over 40 kilometers of track, when I think that Wagner worked so long and so hard on this great municipal scheme for such an incredibly small fee, it seems to me that this cannot be explained in terms of his personal wealth alone. Another, far more important, factor was his absolute obsession with art and architecture.

This tremendous enthusiasm of his, which he communicated to his students and colleagues, also made an impact on me, although to the best of my knowledge my work took on none of the formal characteristics of the 'Wagner School'. Nor, for that matter, did I adopt the arts and crafts approach favoured by Adolf Loos, who continued to work within the Chippendale tradition. And yet, at a deeper level, I was influenced by both of these men throughout my life. It would not have been surprising if such divergent influences had triggered off a conflict but, as it happens, they did not. Somehow the antithesis was resolved.

When you really think about it, interpersonal relations are quite fantastic. The way in which mental attitudes are passed from an older to a younger man is often more mysterious than the processes of chromosome transmission which are now being investigated on an ever increasing scale by the geneticists.

* *Life and Shape.* New York 1962.

Wagner was still a child when he first decided to become an architect. He tells us that on the day on which he was confirmed his godfather—who was himself a successful architect—took him for a ride after the ceremony in an elegant carriage. Impressed by such opulence, the boy decided there and then to enter this lucrative profession. It is strange to reflect that childish opportunism should have been the prelude to the triumphs and tribulations which marked Otto Wagner's splendid career.

I heard in my parents' house and from my grown-up brothers—and understood in part—something of the never ending struggle which this great man conducted with such heroic patience. Feeling-toned empathy (whatever it may be) plays a special part in memory formation, which is a product of childhood. So too does the perception of architectural forms or the gentle, lazy ascent of a flight of Wagner steps, which has remained imprinted in my leg muscles for the best part of seventy years. But I first heard of Otto Wagner as a human being and even in those days I conceived the idea that to be a human being was part of 'being an architect'. He regarded his gifted pupils as members of a 'superior minority' which he distinguished (with perhaps a hint of intolerance) from the 'inferior majority'. People who were once close to him never left him. His daughters remained devoted to him, each in her own way, long after his death and he loved them, as he loved his disciples. Once, when Wagner was in his bedroom, he was heard saying to his wife through the half open door: 'Wouldn't it be wonderful if Louise could marry Olbrich and Christl Hoffmann!' He loved his students, his wife, his two close friends (Gustav Klimt—whom I also met and admired in Klimt's studio—and Koloman Moser) with an intensity that is rare in a man so engrossed in his work.

I already knew as a child that he had the ability to win friends in widely different camps, from Lueger to Lux: the first a great mayor and the highly original popular leader of a great party which he himself had created, the second a faithful publicist—for Lueger's opposition—and also the first and, until now, the only biographer of Otto Wagner. But I also knew that much had miscarried for my hero, although it was not until sixty years later that I discovered, at the shattering retrospective exhibition staged in the Wiener Stadtmuseum, that as many as forty of his large-scale projects, on which he had worked so hard, had come to nothing.

The middle finger of Otto Wagner's right hand had been injured by a shotgun pellet, but nobody who saw him wield a 4-pencil ever doubted his powers. And when he spoke to people, they believed him. Nowadays his general plan, his vision of the 'expanding city', is frequently misconstrued. There are many who regard it as a product of Imperial Baroque, whereas in point of fact Wagner lost the commission for the Wiener Museum because he simply disregarded the royal command that the building should be 'marietheresian'. But, having lost it, he did not lose heart. As always, he set to work on the next rationally optimistic project.

Towards the end of his life Wagner lost his wife, after which he became completely estranged from the world. Like Louis Sullivan, whom I saw die in Chicago six years later, his closing years were clouded by berceavement and loneliness.

At first I sensed and later I realised more and more vividly that here was a truly excellent man who, after mastering the growing doubts which assailed him throughout two whole generations of the last century, led the way forward through the *fin de siècle* into a new era which, for all his plans, remained unpredictable.

R i c h a r d   J.   N e u t r a
Vienna, 1969

CONTENTS

LIFE

Otto Koloman Wagner was born on July 13, 1841 in the Viennese suburb of Penzing, then still a country village. His father, Rudolf Simeon Wagner (1802-46), a notary to the Royal Hungarian Court, was the son of a master smith and as such socially inferior to his fiancée, Suzanne von Helffenstorffer-Hueber (1806-80). Suzanne's father, who was archivist to the Imperial Court and Army, opposed the match throughout his lifetime and it was only after his death that the couple were at last able to marry.

Eight years later, when Otto was five, Rudolf Simeon died of a chest complaint, leaving his wife and two sons three houses on the Göttweihergasse, which were then modernised and converted into a single residence with a view to increasing their investment value. But this project, which was planned by Theophil von Hansen,[1] was threatened by the revolution of 1848 and it was only with difficulty that it was brought to a successful conclusion. Nor was the family's financial crisis greatly ameliorated by the precipitate disposal of its personal effects. None the less, Otto Wagner was educated by private tutors and French governesses up to the age of nine; he then attended the Akademisches Gymnasium in Vienna for two years before joining the boarding school run by the Benedictines at Kremsmünster. His mother had decided that her son, 'a well-built, fair-haired boy with eyes of an intense blue',[2] was to be trained as a lawyer. But Otto hated the life at the boarding school. On one occasion he even ran away and made his own way to Vienna, where his mother had the greatest difficulty in persuading him to return. Much against his will he completed the humanist education which was later to stand him in such good stead as a source of useful slogans. When he was sixteen he studied at the Polytechnic Institute in Vienna, where Stummer von Traunfels[3] gave a class in civil engineering. In view of his excellent reports at the Polytechnic Wagner was exempted from military service and was able to proceed at once to the Königliche Bauakademie in Berlin, a step advocated by Hansen. The classes in Berlin were given by C. F. Busse (1802-68), who had once been assistant to Karl Schinkel (1781-1841). In 1861 Wagner returned to Vienna, where he attended the Academy of Fine Arts, finding in August Siccard von Siccardsburg and Eduard van der Nüll (who were shortly to acquire such unhappy fame[4]) two teachers whom he was able to respect at all times. He described Siccardsburg as the man who had inculcated the 'utilitarian principle' in his 'artistic soul' and van der Nüll as an 'incomparable draughtsman'.[5] In 1863 Wagner completed his studies and won his first competition: for the casino in the Wiener Stadtpark. (The finished building, however, departed from Wagner's design.) At this point Wagner worked briefly in the studio of Ludwig von Förster, the Ringstrasse architect. In the same year Wagner married Josefine Domhart by whom he had three children, Otto, Robert and Susanna. The marriage was unsuccessful and in 1880, shortly after his mother's death,

Wagner divorced his wife. In the next year Wagner married Louise Stiffel.

In the final period of his first marriage Wagner wrote to Louise: 'No matter where I spend my evenings, even when I am engaged in a passionate discussion of artistic questions in the "Künstlerhaus", I am always dissatisfied when I return to my moral prison, otherwise known as my home.' But he went on to assure her: 'You will find in me all that a true gentleman is capable of.'[6] Louise, who was eighteen years younger than himself, Wagner described as 'a creature whom I adore and revere and who, I feel, loves me (loves me as I wish to be loved)'. In 1884 his son Stefan was born, followed in 1885 and 1889 by his daughters Luise and Christine. Wagner transferred the 'religious' reverence which he had felt for his mother to his young wife. A paradise began for him. Wagner thanked 'a gracious fate' for having shown it to him and expressed the hope that he would be allowed to enjoy it. The paradise lasted thirty-four years. Wagner's 'romantic intoxication' which, to quote his own words, was compounded of 'interest, sympathy, friendship and love' was both relieved and intensified by his work, as is evident from the following letter to Louise: 'I would have written to you last night, but the work which I began was so interesting, and then—yesterday above all—it was so delightful just to think of you that there were times when I simply sat in a reverie for minutes on end without moving a finger. This work of mine, this gradual compiling and arranging of ideas, all of them permeated by my incomparable love for you and by the bliss of knowing myself to be loved in return, really did afford me a divine joy, which could only have been increased if you had been sitting nearby playing the piano and had come in from time to time to kiss me.'[7] In 1915, when his wife was taken ill, Wagner started a diary and later that year, after she had died of cancer, his entries gradually took the form of letters; eventually every entry was addressed to his dead wife and closed with 'Your Otto' or a similar phrase. One aspect of Wagner's relationship to his wife was the belief that she understood him; this served to strengthen him in his conviction that the turning point in his professional career had also come in his fortieth year.[8]

Wagner's earliest buildings include numerous apartment houses, at least thirty of which are now unknown to us, due to his subsequent endeavours to conceal all trace of his connection with them. The houses which can definitely be attributed to him are: Bellariastrasse 4 (1869), Schottenring 23 (1877), Rathausstrasse 3 (1880-81), Stadiongasse 6-8 (1882-83) and Lobkowitzplatz 1 (1884), all of which are in Vienna's 1st district. During his early period Wagner also contributed to Otto Thienemann's Grabenhof (1873-74), while the theatre on the Wasagasse (1864-65),[9] the synagogue in Budapest (1871, *Ill. 248*) and the conversion of the Dianabad (1878) all added to his growing prestige, as did his decorations for Hans Makart's

1. Otto Wagner im Alter von 26 Jahren.

2. Susanne Wagner, die Mutter.

3. Otto Wagner, Altersbildnis.

4. Louise Wagner, die zweite Frau.

procession on the occasion of the Emperor's silver wedding anniversary in 1879 (Ill. 11) and for the reception in 1881 of Princess Stephanie of Belgium (Ill. 10) who married Crown Prince Rudolph. Wagner proudly asserted that these decorations had given the *coup de grâce* to 'the fairground style with its eternal fir branches'.[10] From the very outset Wagner's buildings were interlarded either with competition designs for specified projects; e. g., the Palace of Justice (1874) which was to be built as part of the Ringstrasse development, the Landtag building in Lemberg (1875) and the Rathaus in Hamburg (1876, prize-winning entry); or else with studies; e. g., for a private museum (1876) or a church in Soborsin (1879). In 1880, Wagner created his 'Artibus', an immensely comprehensive design for a museum enclave (*Ills. 201, 202*), in which he applied on a far larger scale the same elaborate, 'jigsaw' method which had already produced a number of established European architectural forms. Joseph August Lux believes that it was due to the public and professional reaction to this design that Wagner was appointed professor at the Academy of Fine Arts some fourteen years later.[11]

In 1880 Wagner also produced his first (competition) design for a bank, the Giro- und Kassenverein (Deposit and Credit Account Banking Association, (*Ills. 163, 164*). This incorporated the semicircular counter used in the Länderbank (Provincial Bank) which was built in 1883-84 (*Ills. 165-8*). In the 1880 competition Wagner came third, in the competition for the Länderbank he came first; he also won prizes in the competitions for the Reichstag building in Berlin and the parliament building in Budapest (both 1882, *Ills. 237, 238*). The rather conventional front façade of the Länderbank conceals a well-conceived internal structure which, however, is clearly indicated both by the smooth semicircular rear façade (which is unfortunately difficult of access) and the 'inner façades' encircling the 'light trap' above the counter section. Wagner repeated the clear-cut, functional lines of the Länderbank in the design which he made in 1884 for a building for the Bodenkreditanstalt (Land Credit Association, *Ill. 169*). In the same year he submitted a competition design for the Exchange building in Amsterdam (*Ills. 170, 171*), which failed to reach the final round; the building which was eventually completed in 1903 was based on a modified version of the design by Hendrik Petrus Berlage (1856-1934), which had won fourth prize in the competition.

After completing the Villa Hahn in Baden (1885-6) Wagner built the villa at Hüttelbergstrasse 26 as a summer residence for his new family, which by then included two children. This symmetrical building (*Ills. 5, 110-17*) with its double flight of steps leading up to the entrance door and its twin pergolas (one of which was fitted out as a conservatory) now stands side by side with the smaller villa, a flat-roofed building with smooth walls and rows of narrow high windows, which Wagner built in 1912-13. Although he organised a comprehensive exhibition of his designs in the Künstlerhaus, for the time being Wagner had to content himself with building further houses on a speculative basis. These were then followed by a further apartment house, Universitätsstrasse 12 (1888, *Ill. 118*) and a group of three houses on Rennweg (1890-1). Wagner always sought to live in an environment which reflected his current architectural thinking and he built one of these houses (Rennweg 3, Palais Wagner or Hoyos, *Ills. 119-22*), for his own use. It incorporated a new studio to replace the old one on the Stadiongasse and was designed to meet his personal requirements in every way: each floor was divided into two sections—one for the master, the other for the servants—which ran parallel to each other and so afforded easy access.

In 1890 the first volume of Wagner's *Einige Skizzen, Projekte und ausgeführte Bauwerke* (Some Sketches, Designs and Buildings) appeared in a *de luxe* edition as a private publication.

It was just before he evolved his plan for the regulation of the city of Vienna that Wagner first tried to apply his motto (taken from Gottfried Semper) *Artis sola domina necessitas* to religious buildings. It must be conceded, however, that his design for the parish church in Esseg (1890) and his study for the Berliner Dom (1891, *Ill. 249*) were more concerned with problems of technical construction than with functional considerations. But then the competition for the general regulation of Vienna (1893, *Ill. 22*) gave him ample scope to follow his motto. The new general plan was expected to bring the unending and fruitless debate concerning the Stadtbahn to a successful conclusion, to solve the pressing problem of regulating the river Wien and the Danube Canal, to remove the confusion wrought by the dangerous growth in road traffic and resolve the administrative and supply difficulties facing the individual districts.

Wagner's ideas on municipal planning, which he developed within the framework of his plan for the general regulation of Vienna[12] were later reproduced in his 1911 study *Die Grossstadt* (The Big City). In this publication he reviewed the problem, first in general terms, then with particular reference to Vienna. Wagner received one of the two first prizes awarded for the general plan and, although he did not win the prize for the regulation of the Stubenviertel, his plans were certainly drawn on for this project. In 1893 Wagner also submitted an unsuccessful design for the Royal and Imperial Ministry of Trade building. But the outcome of the various competitions was not what really mattered. The fact that Wagner was made artistic adviser to the Viennese Transport Commission and the Commission for the Regulation of the Danube Canal was of far greater significance: this led to the construction of the Stadtbahn (1894-1901, *Ills. 13, 23-67*), the Nussdorf Dam (1894-98), *Ills. 69-88*), the quayside installations on the Danube Canal and the Kaiserbad Dam (1898-1908, *Ills. 89, 93-109*). Wagner owed these splendid commissions which brought him great fame if little money, to the recommendation of the Künstlerhaus (1894).

Following Karl von Hasenauer's (1833-94) death the professorial body at the Academy was also able to make the happy suggestion that Wagner should be offered the vacant chair and placed in charge of a special school of architecture.[13] This received official approval at the highest level and Wagner was speedily promoted from *Baurat* to *Oberbaurat*.[14] He also inherited Hasenauer's assistant, Joseph Olbrich (1867-1908), and his prize student, Josef Hoffmann (1870-1956), who was then in his final year. He thought so highly of these two men that ten years later he recommended Olbrich for the director's post at the Academy's second school of architecture (which had just fallen vacant) and Hoffmann as his own successor. Olbrich worked in Wagner's studio for five years, chiefly on the Stadtbahn project, before accepting an invitation from Grand Duke Ernst Ludwig of Hesse to join the artists' colony at Darmstadt. Hoffmann, after finishing his studies and spending a year in Italy on a travelling scholarship which he had won during his final year, worked for twelve months in Wagner's studio. (In the busy years of the 1890s Wagner is said to have employed a staff of seventy, consisting of architects, engineers and draughtsmen; in the period preceeding the outbreak of the First World War he made do with a staff of ten.)

'Having been invited to join the foremost art school in the Empire', Wagner felt 'obliged to define, substantiate and defend the theses', which he had established in 'the practice of his art', so as to 'further his task as a teacher'.[15] In 1895 he published his *Moderne Architektur* (Modern Architecture), which was reprinted in 1899, 1902 and 1914, the 1914 reprint appearing under the title *Die Baukunst unserer Zeit* (Architecture Today). In the prefaces to the first two reprints Wagner was justifiably optimistic, for in addition to his great municipal building projects, he had also been asked to execute two private commissions, one for the Neumann department store on the Kärntner Strasse (1895, *Ill. 123*), the other, for Der Anker, the insurance building on the Graben (1895, *Ills. 124-7*). Both of these buildings were fitted with a curtain wall of glass extending from street level to the top of the first floor and the Anker building also had a remarkable glass superstructure, which was specified as a photographic studio.

But only a fraction of Wagner's designs were actually executed, although it should perhaps be pointed out that, in view of his prolific output, this could hardly have been otherwise. Those rejected were the designs for a Museum of Plaster Casts (1896); for a national monument (1897, *Ill. 251*); for a new Academy of Fine Arts with studio pavilions 'in which there are no light-absorbing pillars'[16] and museums, including one for plaster casts (1898, *Ills. 203-5); for the Capuchin church and imperial crypt (1898, *Ills. 253-5*); and for the parish church in Währing (1898, *Ill. 252*) which was intended as a riposte to the adjudicators of the competition for the Jubiläumskirche. Wagner had the courage to point out that, if a man were dealing with buildings consecrated to God, he had to proceed quite as logically as if he were dealing with God himself. His attitude to religious architecture is shown in his comment: 'Although, to the best of the author's knowledge, the Church liturgy allows this position [with the priest facing the congregation] only in cathedrals, aesthetically it seems so desirable that it has been incorporated into this study.'[17]

The second volume of Wagner's *Einige Skizzen . . .* appeared in 1897 and, like his *Moderne Architektur*, it was translated into foreign languages. As successive volumes of this work appeared its influence grew, and it was increased still further when the 'Wagner school' brought out its collective publications; Antonio Sant'Elia (1888-1916), for example, was well-acquainted with these works. In 1898, when the Academy presented the Emperor with a loyal address on the occasion of his Jubilee, Wagner found himself in a difficult position. On the one hand he was one of those responsible for this act of homage to a defunct system, while on the other hand public attention of a most unpleasant kind was being directed towards him because of his new group of houses on the corner of the Wienzeile and Köstlergasse (1898-99, *Ills. 128-38*) and because of his decision to join the Secession, which naturally meant withdrawal from the conservative Künst-

lerhaus.[18] Although Wagner's anxious biographer Lux predicted that the 'madly Secessionist trend' of the Wienzeile houses (especially the Majolica House) would soon be discarded as a 'foreign body'[19] he was not blinded by this development to Wagner's fundamental method, which was strictly additive.

In his design for the Moderne Galerie (1900, *Ills. 208-10*) Wagner completed only the façade of the building. The interior was purposely left unfinished for he proposed that works of art by twentieth-century artists should be installed gradually over the coming decades and that the decor should be chosen as and when the various rooms came into commission.[20] For his arrangements at the Paris International Exhibition in 1900—'Group VI. Engineering' and the exhibit for the directors of the Hofgarten (*Ill. 228*)—Wagner was made a member of the *légion d'honneur*. By contrast, his design for the Emperor Francis Joseph Municipal Museum on the Karlsplatz— a scheme which he launched on his own account—brought him nothing but disappointment. The same was true of a whole series of projects, for which the organisers constantly laid down new conditions. Wagner had already dealt with the Karlsplatz in detail in his plan for the regulation of the city; at that time he had proposed a series of open areas with rectilinear borders affording direct access to a further open area in the east. While he was engaged in his great controversy with the reactionary Friedrich Schachner (1841-1907)— which had been sparked off by the open competition of 1901 (for Wagner's design see *Ill. 212*) and the limited competition of 1902 (*Ill. 226*)—Wagner evolved a compact design for the square, in which the whole of the eastern side was to be occupied by the museum, whose level roof would provide a uniform border throughout (*Ills. 211, 213-5*). In all subsequent studies for the Karlsplatz he retained the principal features of this design. Wagner's rival, Schachner, who was of the same age and had also studied under van der Nüll and Siccardsburg, committed a number of errors, which Wagner avoided: 'The architectural motifs of the [neighbouring Karl's] Church, e. g. columns, portals, pediment, dome, *etc.*, must on no account be introduced into the Museum, for the only way to enhance the Church is to use contrasting forms.'[21]

The battle over the Municipal Museum on the Karlsplatz dragged on until 1912, when the theatre of war shifted to the suburban district of the Schmelz. During that time Wagner designed a department store for the Karlsplatz (1904) to mark its southern limit and a monumental fountain (1903; 1905, *Ill. 293*). The museum designs with a reception hall immediately in front of the main building were supplemented by a number of single-unit designs, the last of which was made in 1909 (*Ills. 216-21*) and incorporated the "Culture" statue (*Ill. 6*). The only things that Wagner was allowed to build on the Karlsplatz were the Stadtbahn station and a canvas mock-up of his museum, which aroused little enthusiasm. (Between 1954 and 1958 a museum was erected on part of the site selected by Wagner. It is in the post-war Austrian modernistic style which has proved so tenacious.) Wagner was never allowed to build a museum, because he refused to make the building an exhibit in its own right: 'The exhibition halls in a museum are there for the exhibits, not vice versa.'[22] Wagner considered that it was not for the architect to predetermine the arrangement of the objects on show. On the contrary, the architectural organisation of the building had to allow for the future expansion of the museum's collection while at the same time providing

Ill. 5. First Villa Wagner, Hüttelbergstrasse 26 (built 1886-8): Side view of the pergola, which was converted into a studio in 1900. Window by Adolf Böhm: "Autumn landscape in the Wienerwald".

subtle forms of orientation. For example, the main staircase should be built in such a way 'as to afford the visitor an unimpeded view at all times', i. e., with the 'flights of stairs next to and not on top of one another'.[23]

In 1902 Wagner defeated one of his own students, Leopold Bauer (who had just won a competition for a small country church), in the three-man competition for a church for the Lower Austrian Sanatorium and Institution Am Steinhof. In the competition for a new Post Office Savings Bank held in 1903 his design was chosen from a total entry of thirty-seven because it was the one best calculated to meet the requirements of the Royal and Imperial Post Office. In the same year he entered the competition for the Greek Orthodox cathedral in Patras, while in his design for a 'little theatre' he created the basic layout of the theatre wing which was subsequently incorporated into his design for a "Palace for Viennese Society" (Ills. 243, 244; with concert hall Ills. 245, 246; both designs 1906). Another design which Wagner made in 1903 was for an exhibition building.

The Post Office Savings Bank (Ills. 14-17, 172-200) was built in two stages. The first section was erected between 1904 and 1906 on the wider side of the trapezoid site which had been created when Wagner regulated the surrounding Stubenviertel. If we allow for the difficulties encountered in laying the foundations and the delay caused by a three-month strike of building workers, the first stage of the work was completed in record time. The second section was erected between 1910 and 1912.

The early completion date was due entirely to Wagner's simplified construction methods: e. g., the ceiling cavities were not filled with sand and, although the Post Office had asked for 'maximum solidity'—a requirement which it was generally believed could only be met by building with massive blocks of natural stone—Wagner fulfilled this condition by facing his building with sheets of marble (and to a lesser extent glass) which were fixed to the walls with metal bolts. He used similar components for the façade of the Church Am Steinhof (1905-7, Ills. 257-91) and the control building of the Kaiserbad Dam (1906-7, Ills. 94-106). In the Post Office building he repeated the technique he had first used for the entrance door to the telegraph office of Die Zeit (1902, Ill. 9) by introducing aluminium instead of relying on more traditional metals. He also produced quite spectacular effects with aluminium by using it for the heads of the bolts on the façade, the corner acroteria and the hot-air ducts in the glass-roofed counter section. His use of space was quite exemplary. Although it has since become possible to reduce the Post Office personnel from 2,700 before the First World War to only 1,900 today, the demands made on the building have actually increased. And yet senior Post Office officials have stated quite categorically that the building is still completely adequate for their purpose. Opposite the Savings Bank stands the Ministry of War designed by Ludwig Baumann (1853-1936), the last of the Ringstrasse architects, who was the leading light in a professional association which regarded the setting up of architectural chambers as its highest aim. Significantly enough, Wagner was bitterly opposed to such chambers.[24] The commission for the War Ministry project was awarded on the results of a competition (1907-8, Ill. 247), for which both Wagner and Adolf Loos entered but whose conditions neither was able to accept.

The Church Am Steinhof stands on the highest point of a complex which contains more than sixty flat-roofed buildings. These were all built at the same time as the church but do not bear comparison with it, even in purely functional terms. The Lower Austrian Provincial Council commented on the extreme pains Wagner took over this church project: 'The two holy-water fonts at the entrances have been fashioned as fountains so that, instead of placing their fingers in a basin, the members of the congregation hold their hand under a thin jet of water, which is kept running throughout the service. This helps to prevent infection.'[25] Despite the positively pedantic concern accorded to the special character of the church it still made a considerable impact on those present; Archbishop Dr Piffl, who officiated at the consecration, assured Wagner that he was 'really gripped by the monumental character of the building'.

Wagner was assisted in the execution of both the Church Am Steinhof and the Post Office building by two of his students, Otto Schönthal (1878-1961) and Marcel Kammerer (1878-1959), who were later associated with Emil Hoppe (1876-1957) and acquired considerable fame as members of the 'Wagner school'. Among other things they designed the stand for the Vienna Trotting Stadium and the spa installation in Abbazia. At the turn of the century Hevesi, the chronicler of the Viennese Secession, had triumphantly pointed out that Wagner's students were so sought after both at home and abroad that it was only the master's personal prestige that kept them chained to Vienna and to his studio.[26] After completing his studies and spending a brief period in Italy Jan Kotěra (1871-1923), who later founded the Czech arts and crafts association, returned to Prague, where he soon collected enough material for a book on The Works of Jan Kotéra and his Students. As were most of Wagner's writings, Kotěra's book was published by Schroll. Jože Plečnik (1872-1957), who first worked as a free-lance architect in Vienna, where he built the much under-rated Zacherlhaus, was soon asked to work in Prague and subsequently in Ljubljana. Rudolph M. Schindler (1887-1953) studied under Wagner in 1910-1 and 1912-3 and was then offered work in America just before the outbreak of war.[27] Apart from Olbrich and Hoffmann, he was the only representative of the 'new race of architects'[28] trained by Wagner to acquire international prestige. Ernst Lichtblau (1883-1963) was another representative of the 'Wagner school' in America. (Whether Adolf Hitler, after failing to gain admittance to the school of painting at the Academy, was rejected as a student of architecture by Wagner or by Friedrich Ohmann (1858-1927), the head of the second school, remains an intriguing historical mystery.)

The great buildings which Wagner erected around about 1905, his prodigious efforts to get his plan for the Karlsplatz accepted, his competition entry for the Palace of Peace in The Hague (1905, Ills. 236, 239-42 with an alternative design), which suffered the same fate abroad as the Karlsplatz project had undeservedly suffered at home, all these large-scale activities have tended to overshadow a few smaller designs, which Wagner made at this time and in which he came to grips with various problems of pure engineering. These were the designs for the Vindobonabrücke (1904, Ill. 90), the Ferdinandsbrücke (1905, Ills. 91, 92) in which he finally used a suspended deck type of construction, and the Interimskirche (1905, Ill. 292), which was structurally a replica of Bernhard Maybeck's Hearst Hall at the University of California (1899), but in

Ill. 6. "Culture". Projected statue in front of the Emperor Francis Joseph Municipal Museum on the Karlsplatz (1909). Concrete base faced with glazed tiles. Figures in gilded bronze and porcelain.

DIE KVLTVR DENKMAL VOR DEM KAISER FRANZ JOSEF STADTMVSEVM

which Wagner used unfaced iron instead of wood for the arches.

In 1905 the group led by Gustav Klimt (1862-1918) walked out of the Secession to a man. Wagner, who was a friend of Klimt's, was one of the eighteen members of this group, which also included Hoffmann and the painter Kolo Moser (1868-1918), the leading lights of the newly founded Wiener Werkstätte. Moser and the sculptor Othmar Schimkowitz (1864-1947) were Wagner's favourite collaborators in this circle. The members of the Viennese Secession had established important contacts with many leading European artists. Wagner was on personal terms with both Charles Rennie Mackintosh (1868-1928) and Henry van de Velde (1863-1957). He was also acquainted with Loos, who was one of his admirers,[29] but he made no attempt to develop this acquaintance, although he supported the unornamented house on the Michaelerplatz.

In 1905 Wagner designed a small villa (*Ill. 144*) for his wife to retire to in the event of his own death; this house was built in 1912-3 in a somewhat modified form (*Ills. 145-51*). By then Wagner had sold his Palais, which was extremely costly to run, to the 'Variety King', Ben Tiber, and after his wife's death he sold the villa as well. In 1906 his competition design for the Karlsbad Colonnades, which featured a 'roof promenade', won a third prize. But neither of the designs

which he made for a "Palace for Viennese Society" (which was to have introduced its guests to the more presentable pleasures of big-city life at the Parkring) was executed. In fact, Wagner never was commissioned to build a palace.

In 1908 he was made president of the International Congress of Architects, which was about to meet in Vienna, and at the time it was considered 'very probable that the Congress would develop into an act of homage to him and his work'.[30] On the other hand the municipal authorities did not proceed with the conversion of the Zedlitzhalle, which had been chosen for the Congress exhibition, although this had in fact been envisaged. Wagner's design had won the small closed competition, in which each architect had been judged by his fellow-competitors. Later, when it was decided to use the Zedlitzhalle as an exhibition building for craft products, Wagner submitted a second design, which also came to nothing (1913, *Ill. 235*). The mysterious "House of Glory" (*Ills. 229, 230*), which was probably intended for San Francisco, never saw the New World. The adjudication of the competitions for the War Ministry building and the Technical Museum for Industry and Trade (1909), for which Adolf Loos also entered, gave the impression that criteria of architectural excellence played an even smaller part here than in the altercation over the Karlsplatz and the Municipal Museum. This affair ended in victory for the immutable forces of prejudice, which had operated with great skill throughout, capitalising on each new misunderstanding.

Ill. 7. Otto Wagner. Reproduced from a pastel drawing by Kempf (1896). The following description of Wagner appeared on page 60 of a publication entitled *The Royal and Imperial Academy of Fine Arts in Vienna from 1892 to 1917:* 'Otto Wagner, Architect, Royal and Imperial *Hofrat,* Royal and Imperial *Oberbaurat,* member of the Francis Joseph Order, the Order of the Iron Crown (IIIrd Class), Ritterkreuz member of the Imperial Russian Order of Stanislaus, member of the Serbian Takowo Order, the French *légion d'honneur,* honorary president of the Association of Austrian Architects, honorary president of the Association of Austrian Artists, honorary member and correspondent of the Royal Institute of British Architects in London, the Société Centrale des Architectes in Paris, the Imperial Society of Architects in St Petersburg, the Imperial Association of Architects in the City of St Petersburg, the Société Centrale d'Architecture de Belgique in Brussels and the Society for the Promotion of Architecture in Amsterdam, honorary member of the Institute of American Architects, the Societade des Architectes Portugueses, honorary member of the Association of Hungarian Architects and of the Architectural Institute of Canada. Appointed Artistic Adviser to the Viennese Transport Commission and the Commission for the Regulation of the Danube in 1894, made a permanent member of the Art Commission and Art Council in the Ministry of Culture and Education in 1895 and elected to the board of the Austrian Museum for Art and Industry in 1898.' The obituarist added to this list the honorary doctorate conferred on Wagner by the Technical College in Dresden, his honorary membership of the Society of International Culture and the 'golden Salvator medallion' awarded to him by the municipality of Vienna.

Ill. 8. Left to right: The painter Wilhelm List, the sculptor Othmar Schimkowitz, Otto Wagner and Josef Hoffmann.

When Wagner's museum project was banished to the Schmelz he tried to promote a project for a hotel (1910-1, *Ill. 161*) on the open eastern side of the Karlsplatz, which was then threatened by residential development. Since a museum and a hotel, especially if they appear within a single complex, must necessarily have somewhat similar façades Wagner's opponents were able to frustrate this project by asserting that the only difference between the two buildings was the sign. Wagner had created his first design for an Academy of Fine Arts in 1898. He created his second (*Ills. 206, 207*) in 1910 for the site on the Schmelz, since conditions in Hansen's building on the Schillerplatz—which had been designed with little regard for student requirements—had grown steadily worse during the intervening twelve years. He retained his original layout, which was based on individual pavilions, but enlarged the 'head' of the installation centred on the aula. The most distinctive feature of this conception was provided by the unbroken wall surfaces, which had been made possible by using glass roofs. Later in 1910 Wagner made a modified version of the second design, in which he placed the banished Municipal Museum in front of the school (*Ills. 222, 223*). Then, in 1912, the museum project was again thrown open to competition, although Wagner might have been excused for feeling that he had already done enough to earn the commission. However, it is to this competition that we are indebted for Opus IV (1912, *Ills. 224, 225, 227*), which was subsequently reviewed in the *Illustrierte Zeitung:* 'Wagner of course avoided building a "mediaeval castle"; but it seems that, if his design should be executed, then, despite his unquestioned artistry, we might find that our projected museum had been transformed into a commercial building.'[31] Although Opus IV was awarded one of the two first prizes, thanks largely to the persistent advocacy of Peter Behrens, one of the adjudicators, there was no question of its being commissioned.

Wagner's last buildings—the two apartment houses on the corner of Neustiftgasse and Döblergasse (1909-12, *Ills. 139-42*), which housed Wagner's flat and studio, Hoffmann's studio and part of the Wiener Werkstätte; the Lupus Sanatorium (1910-3, *Ills. 152-7*), and the new villa—all had a simple cube construction and a smooth floated finish relieved by decorative strips of glass tiles. The austere ground-plans of Wagner's maturity are seldom, if ever, at variance with present-day architectural practices; the only technique which he failed to develop was the curtain wall, which he had introduced into his commercial buildings in 1895.

The designs for the hotel on the Ringstrasse (1910, *Ills. 158-60*) and for the university library, a twin structure with walls and skeleton framework of reinforced concrete (first design 1910, *Ills. 231-3*) were prominent features of Wagner's 'Ideal Design for the XXIInd Viennese District' (1910-11, *Ills. 18, 20, 21*), which he used to illustrate his study *Die Grossstadt*. The study was prompted by an invitation which Wagner received from Columbia University to address the International Congress for Civic Art in New York. In Austria, of course, it produced no reaction whatsoever, but in 1914 Wagner was asked 'to plan a capital city for Australia and to design all the important public buildings. At 72 years of age he was seriously contemplating this great journey . . .'[32]

Wagner went on teaching his pupils until 1915, first in rented classrooms, then in his own studio. Upon reaching retirement age at seventy he had been asked to stay on for an extra year. It was not until 1912, when he was awarded the honorary title of *Hofrat*,[33] that he went into permanent retirement, and that too was deferred for a while because the professors at the Academy were unable to agree on his successor. Eventually they settled their differences and appointed the opportunist Leopold Bauer, who had studied under Wagner but who was not averse to borrowing on occasions from the historical repertoire. When he first came to take up his post the students prevented him from entering the Academy building.

In 1914 Wagner made a second design for the university library (*Ill. 234*) and also a design for the "Palmschloss", a mountain sanatorium for open-air and sunbath treatment near Brixen (*Ill. 162*). These were followed by designs for a group of huts for the use of convalescent soldiers and subsequently of tubercular patients, a statue of the emperor (which was rather conventional by comparison with his monumental fountain or his "Culture" statue), a forest school in the Wienerwald (1916), a conversion of the Brigittabrücke (which was to have been called Heeresbrücke or Armeebrücke) and a Friedenskirche (Armistice Church; 1917, *Ill. 294*).

In the autumn of 1915 Wagner's wife died. He wrote in his diary at the time: 'fate cruelly snatched her from me . . .'[34] Why, if I had been able to bury Louise as I would have liked, I would have had a temple requiem with columns of incense 1,000 metres high ascending to heaven and the music of the spheres would have softly told the furnace of the feelings in my heart.'[35]

Wagner knew that these diary entries were monologues. It was not as a conversationalist that he missed his wife, but as an audience. And, when she had gone, there was no one to take her place for, although there were many whom he regarded as his friends, only very few of them actually were. In the majority of cases these so-called friends were either protegés, whose reverence precluded the possibility of genuine friendship, or fellow artists with whom he had built up a mutual admiration society. The admiration was genuine enough, but it was hardly calculated to produce an enduring human relationship. Olbrich, for example, had written to Wagner on the occasion of his sixtieth birthday: 'I know full well, my dear *Oberbaurat* . . ., that this dear work [of ours] is the most beautiful and the finest of our birthrights. And who could be more envied than a man like yourself who has enjoyed these fruits to the full for a period of sixty years. And I am supposed to congratulate you!'[36]

After his wife's death Wagner lived very quietly. By then the war had even crept into his studio, for draughtsmen were in short supply: 'I am greatly oppressed by the lack of an assistant. Herr Günther has almost stopped coming. How am I to finish the church? So far only one design has been inked in and the two perspectives have not even been started.'[37] His son, Otto, also a professional architect, was not an ideal assistant: 'I have never seen anybody with so little artistic flair and with so little taste. This worries me greatly, for what are all my buildings going to look like if it is left to him to complete them. During the past year I have been considering whether to join up with Kammerer.'[38] A few days after making this diary entry Wagner wrote to Kammerer suggesting an association. Kammerer declined and Wagner was somewhat shaken: 'Although I had not counted on Kammerer his refusal has left me with an unpleasant feeling.'[39]

As a true patriot Wagner was not prepared to buy food on the black market and for long periods he was prone to minor illnesses: 'Today I have nothing to eat for my breakfast. And I am supposed to put on weight! I am just skin and bones.' These words were written by the greatest architect of the old and the new Austria and a man accustomed to leading the life of a *grand seigneur*, on July 31, 1917. By then he weighed 130 lbs., compared with 186 lbs. before the war. But, despite the wartime difficulties, Wagner persevered with his designs. 'I have been working on the bridge like a black', he wrote in 1917. 'It is coming along very well.'[40] He had great hopes for the Friedenskirche and was confident that he would be able to interest Archbishop Dr Piffl, who had been so impressed by the Church Am Steinhof, in this project. 'I have the feeling', he wrote, 'that the Friedenskirche is the best thing I have ever done and my sense of taste persuades me that no architect has ever created anything like it.'[41] For a while it was even proposed that Wagner should be commissioned to build the Viennese underground, starting, it seems, with the Währinger Strasse line. Commenting on this, Wagner wrote: 'this really is a triumph for, despite all the hatred these gentlemen have . . . now realised that an architect should be judged by the quality of his work.'[42]

Ill. 9. Telegraph Office of *Die Zeit* (built 1902): Entrance door in aluminium with iron framework covered with aluminium.

On February 6, 1918 Wagner wrote morosely to his dead wife about a lecture due to be given by Behrens in a few days' time: 'I find these lectures objectionable, because people take offence if I don't go and I know perfectly well that I can learn nothing from any of them; all I am likely to get out of it is a cold on my way home.' Later the same evening he once more took up his pen: 'I have to write to you again. Something terrible has happened. Klimt is dead. If this stupid world only knew what it has lost today!' Kolo Moser also fell ill at this time and on October 11, 1918 he died of cancer of the mouth. Meanwhile, however, Otto Wagner himself had died of erysipelas on April 11. He was buried in the family vault, which he himself had built, in the Hietzing cemetery.

If I am successful with the church I shall be recognised as the foremost architect in Austria as well. If only I live to see it.
Diary entry for July 28, 1917.

THE EXPANDING CITY
THE BEGINNING OF MODERN
ARCHITECTURE

THE PERIOD from 1848 to 1914, which covered virtually the whole of Wagner's life, opened with a series of bloody revolutions in Paris, Berlin and Vienna; Italian and Hungarian nationalists within the empire were also active and had to be suppressed by the Austrian government. Before 1914 there were fourteen major wars in various parts of the world and countless disturbances, crises and revolts. As a result certain states became great powers; others such as Germany and Italy achieved internal unity, while the apparently lethargic Austria eventually provided the spark which set off the First World War. But the Austria of those days was a strange place. The personal war, which Otto Wagner was obliged to wage in order to force through his architectural revolution was typical of this land, whose people found it so difficult to arrive at clear-cut decisions. Robert Musil has analysed this complex psychological structure in his *The Man Without Qualities:*

'There, in Kakania,[1] that misunderstood state that has since vanished, which was in so many things a model, though all unacknowledged, there was speed too; but not too much speed . . . Of course cars also drove along those roads—but not too many cars! The conquest of the air had begun here too; but not too intensively. Now and then a ship was sent off to South America or the Far East; but not too often. There was no ambition to have world markets and world power. Here one was in the centre of Europe, at the focal point of the world's old axes; the words 'colony' and 'overseas' had the ring of something as yet utterly untried and remote. There was some display of luxury; but it was not of course as over-sophisticated as that of the French. One went in for sport; but not in madly Anglo-Saxon fashion. One spent tremendous sums on the army; but only just enough to ensure one of remaining the second weakest among the great powers. The capital, too, was somewhat smaller than all the rest of the world's largest cities, but nonetheless quite considerably larger than a mere ordinary large city. And the administration of this country was carried out in an enlightened, hardly perceptible manner, with a cautious clipping of all sharp points, by the best bureaucracy in Europe, which could be accused of only one defect: it could not help regarding genius and enterprise of genius in private persons, unless privileged by high birth and State appointment, as ostentation, indeed presumption . . .

'All in all, how many remarkable things might be said about that vanished Kakania! For instance, it was *kaiserlich-königlich* (Imperial-Royal) and it was *kaiserlich und königlich* (Imperial & Royal); one of the two abbreviations, k. k. or k. u. k., applied to every thing and person, but esoteric lore was nevertheless required in order to be sure of distinguishing which institutions and persons were to be referred to as k. k. and which as k. u. k. On paper it called itself the Austro-Hungarian monarchy; in speaking, however, one referred to it as Austria, that is to say, it was known by the name that it had, as a State, solemnly renounced by oath, while preserving it in all matters of sentiment . . . By its constitution it was liberal, but its system of government was clerical. The system of government was clerical, but the general attitude to life was liberal. Before the law all citizens were equal, but not everyone, of course, was a citizen. There was a parliament, which made such vigorous use of its liberty that it was usually kept shut; but there was also an emergency powers act, by means of which it was possible to manage without Parliament, and every time when everyone was just beginning to rejoice in absolutism, the Crown decreed that there must now again be a return to parliamentary government. Many such things happened in this State, and among them were those national struggles that justifiably aroused Europe's curiosity and are today completely misrepresented. They were so violent that they several times a year caused the machinery of State to jam and come to a dead stop. But between whiles, in the breathing spaces between government and government, everyone got on excellently with everyone else and behaved as though nothing had ever been the matter. Nor had anything real ever been the matter. It was nothing more than the fact that every human being's dislike of every other human being's attempts to get on—a dislike in which today we are all agreed—in that country crystallised earlier, assuming the form of a sublimated ceremonial that might have become of great importance if its evolution had not been prematurely cut short by a catastrophe.'[2]

The immediate cause of the catastrophe, the assassination of Crown Prince Francis Ferdinand and his wife Sophia at Sarajevo, removed one great obstacle from Wagner's path; he had always regarded the crown prince as his principal enemy: 'The Archduke Francis Ferdinand represented the Emperor at the inauguration of the Church Am Steinhof. I was called upon to explain the building to him, whereupon he delivered an address, which closed with the words: "The style of Maria Theresa is still the most beautiful." I pointed out to him that at the time of Maria Theresa it had been customary to decorate the barrels of the cannon whereas today they were left completely plain. He turned away from me with overbearing arrogance and, despite various intercessions made on my behalf, his hatred continued to pursue me to an extent that I lost a number of commissions for which I had been considered . . . The municipality was far too timid to oppose the archduke's machinations, which were truly spiteful. I consider that the death of the Crown Prince has removed the greatest single obstacle to the practice and further development of modern architecture . . . in Austria.'[3]

The archduke's congenial subjects were also able to voice their opposition to Wagner by means of the surveys organised by the Royal and Imperial Central Commission for the Preservation of Artistic and Historical Monuments. They had opposed him since 1899 when Wagner had provoked the hatred of the entire city by going over the Secession. In the public mind this move had stamped the popular architect of the 1879 and 1881 festival decorations as a malicious, dangerous fool. The Nussdorf Dam and the Stadtbahn had been greatly admired—although possibly for the wrong reasons. But then came the turning point. Josef August Lux, who tells us that he stood 'at Wagner's side as his literary champion during the hectic days of his new struggle', described the psychology behind this public reaction: 'There is nothing a Viennese would sooner read about in his morning paper than some new scandal involving a really great man. Scandal is the only thing that can bring him closer to the newspaper reader. When he has been humiliated, when his name has been dragged through the mud, the reader is able to understand him, for then there is common ground between them, then the great man is no better than anyone else.'[4]

The apartment houses on the Wienzeile certainly annoyed the public, especially No. 40 with its magnificent flowered façade, which was felt to be hideous beyond measure. Whenever one of Wagner's designs came up for discussion the experts, who included many of his colleagues, would condemn it out of hand in accordance with the blatant protectionism practised by the members of the architectural establishment. These men treated Wagner with complete cynism over the Karlsplatz and Schmelz projects, constantly giving

Ill. 10. Decorations for the reception of Princess Stephanie of Belgium on the occasion of her marriage to Crown Prince Rudolph in 1881.

Ill. 11. Square in front of the Burgtor decorated for the Makart Procession, which was staged on the occasion of the emperor's silver wedding anniversary in 1879.

him grounds for hope and constantly disappointing him. His comprehensive designs for these projects included nine separate designs for a municipal museum, a hotel design, a design for a new Academy of Art and a composite design, in which the museum and the academy were accommodated on a single site. Not one of these designs was executed. The competition prizes and the commissions for both the War Ministry building and the Technical Museum went to ungifted eclectics. The Palace for Viennese Society was never built, nor was the hotel on the Ringstrasse or the university library. In his study for the hotel Wagner said that the rooms must be built more along the lines of hospital wards than 'living rooms'. He also stipulated two basic types of room for the whole building and insisted that 'each type should be capable of conversion within a matter of minutes into a sort of salon (living, reception and work room) by changing the furniture and introducing tapestries'.[5] Small wonder that this scheme should have met with opposition! Certain features of the library design, which also dates from 1910, were even more ahead of their time: the storerooms for the books, for example, were to have been constructed from reinforced concrete and fitted with automatic doors, which would have rendered them both air-tight and fireproof. But the proposed height of these storerooms—2.22 metres—is more striking still. Le Corbusier's Modulor I, which was completed and patented in 1945, gives 2.16 metres as a suitable ceiling level for an average human height of 1.75 metres, even in a living room. The improved version of the Modulor II, which was geared to human height of six feet, and therefore gave a figure of 2.26 metres.[6]

The editors of the *Technischer Führer durch Wien* (Technical Guide to Vienna), a publication issued in 1910 by the Association of Austrian Engineers and Architects, painted a positively grotesque picture of the architecture of the past fifty years and adopted a superior and patronising attitude to the 'so-called modern trend': 'The Secessionist movement was led by Otto Wagner . . . It soon rejected Renaissance forms in its quest for a more primitive and a purer style . . . The experimental buildings designed by the members of this group—some of which are interesting, some merely problematical—are too disparate to reveal common characteristics. We can only wait and see whether this radical movement really does produce the new contemporary style which its protagonists are hoping for.'[7] This criticism was of course entirely unfounded. All types of traditional architecture gave, of course, indications of common and, what is more, desirable characteristics.

Not surprisingly the Association's chronicler felt happiest in the sphere of traditional architecture:

'Hansen[8] has created his own personal view of art. Greece became a second artistic home to him; he made no attempt to distinguish between the different impressions which he received there and so absorbed both the classical temple style and the Greek Christian style of a later age . . .'

'When the Votive Church' was consecrated in 1879 Vienna acquired a Gothic Cathedral . . . in which the German and French traditions were welded . . . into a harmonious whole.'

'Vienna is also developing her own brand of Renaissance architecture, which features motifs of Italian and French origin and reveals a marked penchant for opulence and a happy flair for contrasting decorative schemes: "Viennese Renaissance" '!

'When Friedrich von Schmidt[10] came to build his modern Rathaus in the Gothic style he was faced with the same basic problem as Hansen, who had already designed his classical building for the Reichsrat. The formal treatment of the Rathaus is undoubtedly Gothic but in its general character it bears the personal stamp of its creator, who is essentially a product of the modern school but who also knew just what the Renaissance had to offer for his own Gothic system."[11]

Before turning unwillingly to 'modern architecture' the chronicler dealt with the transition from the Renaissance to the Baroque, which he attributed partly to the 'belief' that the Renaissance forms had been exhausted and partly to local tradition. Wagner knew that no architect, wherever he lives, is required to come to terms with a local tradition but merely with his impression of the locality and his impression of the tradition. This was the whole point of traditional architecture. To describe the Stadtbahn stations on the Gürtellinie as an example of 'free Renaissance with predominantly Dorian proportions'—a popular contemporary label—would be a very superficial assessment. It was not even possible to apply this label to the great light well above the counter section of the Länderbank, which was built by 1883.

But despite his many enemies and his many disappointments Wagner was an extremely successful architect. Even during the Secession, which was a difficult time for him, he received important public commissions. In 1904 he built the quayside installations for the Danube canal and started work on the control building for the Kaiserbad dam and the Post Office Savings Bank. Then, in the following year, he began the Church Am Steinhof. His object in life was to put up buildings and in order to achieve this object he constantly presented his views to the reading public. His most important designs appeared in four large volumes,[12] but he also published numerous pamphlets in which he pleaded his cause. On April 7, 1917, a year before Wagner's death, the *Neue Freie Presse*, one of the most influential contemporary newspapers, published his article "Vienna after the War", in which he listed the most important projects for the immediate post-war period.

This article, which was featured on the front page side by side with the report of America's entrance into the war, called for the following new buildings:

1. An art centre with exhibition halls to be financed by the Austrian government and the municipality of Vienna.
2. A monument commemorating the unity of the Central Powers.
3. A 'victory church' for a congregation of 10,000 in iron and reinforced concrete incorporating a crypt and a porch and flanked by a boarding school and mission museum.
4. A monument in memory of Austrian heroes on the square facing the Votive Church.

Ill. 12. Gothic Revival in Vienna, latter half of nineteenth century: The Rathaus (foreground) and the Votive Church (background).

5. A complex of artists' studios with a gallery and a Museum for Plaster Casts.

6. A 'Modern Gallery' (which Wagner envisaged as a 'hundred year' building in twenty sections, the sections to be filled successively—one every five years—by contemporary artists of all disciplines so that 'both their successes and their failures should remain on display for posterity'.)

7. A gateway for the Danube-Oder canal.

8. Co-operative stores, which would meet the needs of the various Viennese districts and cut out the middle man.

9. Two sanatoria for middle-class patients, each with 300 beds arranged in single rows.

10. A hospital for female syphilis patients of 300 to 500 beds, also arranged in single rows.

11. A monument to Emperor Francis Joseph; extension of the Burg; extension of the Viennese museums.

12. A Habsburg museum with an imperial crypt.

In addition Wagner called for sporting stadia, swimming baths, regatta installations, children's playgrounds, army drill grounds, an airfield,

Ill. 13. The Alserstrasse station on the Gürtellinie of the Stadtbahn, which was opened in 1898.

tuberculosis sanatoria with fifty to one hundred beds (to be sited near major towns and subsequently used for other types of patients), hostels for young men and women and finally a state library, which would incorporate the existing university library.

In his article Wagner repeatedly referred to the war as a mentor; he spoke of the value of art—especially of architecture—to the national economy and gave the reader grounds for hope that art too would emerge victorious from the war.

Wagner had also prepared a brochure containing forty drawings to illustrate his twelve-point programme but, because of the paper shortage, this could not be published. It was intended as a corollary to the publication issued by the permanent commission for the architectural development of Vienna, a subcommittee of the Austrian Engineers' and Architects' Association, which had annoyed Wagner by restricting its observations to purely technical problems.

It had long been Wagner's practice to draw attention to pressing social problems, which called for a speedy solution. He had done so in his study for the "Conversion of the Capuchin Church and Monastery with the Imperial Crypt",[13] composed as early as 1899: 'Certainly there are many who find it distressing that the mortal remains of the members of our dynasty should have been interred in such an undignified fashion.—The present crypt is a cellar, whose walls have been eaten away by saltpetre and which is far too small for its purpose.—The author of this study was prompted to approach the competent authorities in this matter several years ago, and, in view of the subsequent decease of so many members of the Imperial family, he now feels constrained to raise this question again and to suggest that the new building drawn up in the enclosed study should be undertaken in conjunction with a worthy monument to the Queen and Empress, which would stand in the interior of the Church.' The queen and empress was Elizabeth of Bavaria, the wife of Emperor Francis Joseph, who was stabbed to death by an anarchist in 1898.

After this spirited introduction Wagner quickly turned to the details of the projected works with a view to convincing potential patrons of the practicability of his designs. The monastery garden was to be flanked on all four sides by vaults, which would be covered by a continuous pergola. These vaults would accomodate some of the coffins permanently, others until such time as the new building was ready to receive them.[14] Wagner stressed the fact that, in his installation, neither the pallbearers nor the officiants, would have to negotiate any corners. He also pointed out that the onlookers, including the musicians, would have an unimpeded view of all stages of the funeral ceremonies. This sort of argument was typical of Otto Wagner. In his study, "The Modern Movement in Church Architecture"[15], he worked out the cost of the high altar in four of his church designs per head of the 'viewing' congregation. This fluctuated between 150.95 and 480.67 florins, the cheapest building being the parish church in Währing, whose circular form combined good visibility with economical construction. In this respect Wagner insisted that the modern gasometer had radically proved the efficacy of building in the round and he cited the Pantheon in Rome as an early example of 'gasometer' design.

UNSYMPATHETIC AND ASSIMILATED TECHNOLOGY

In the same study Wagner commiserated with the architects of 'all earlier epochs', who had been able to produce only relatively modest spatial effects due to the rigidity of their techniques. With his knowledge of modern engineering he was able to develop the idea that such effects depend primarily on the amount of uninterrupted space that can be created—uninterrupted, that is, by weight-bearing structures. The 74-metre span of St Pancras railway station in London, which W. H. Barlow[1] had built as early as 1863-65, was more than one-and-a-half times as big as the maximum spans achieved by the Renaissance architects, while the triple-jointed arches in the machine shop at the 1889 International Exhibition in Paris, which was designed by Dutert and Contamin,[2] spanned a full 117 metres. At the same time Wagner was strongly opposed to the practice of introducing 'abnormal' height factors to compensate for the lack of true space and, by way of example, he cited 'the visitors to St Peter's in Rome . . . who stand with mirrors in their hands, trying to study the ceiling of the church'.[3] Consequently, when he came to build the Church Am Steinhof, he incorporated only a fraction of the space in the dome into the interior of the church: the structure of this building is not just a thin shell separating the interior from the exterior; on the contrary, the church is constructed in such a way that its internal and external proportions are quite different and the two parts exist independently of one another as separate entities.

Wagner was quick to realise that the new materials and structural methods were beginning to lead a life of their own in the hands of contemporary engineers. He formulated this criticism in the first edition of *Moderne Architektur* in 1895 and was still pressing it in the fourth edition, which appeared in 1914.[4] But it was in his study, *Die Grossstadt,* of 1911 that Wagner passed final judgement on the engineer: 'In the regulation of every big city the most important thing will be to ensure that the artist has his say, that the power of the engineer, whose influence in aesthetic matters is quite pernicious, is broken and that "speculation", the vampire which renders the autonomy of our present cities virtually illusory, is kept under strict control.'[5] But, although he castigated the engineers, Wagner appreciated engineering. He claimed that 'neither the Renaissance nor antiquity had produced anything comparable to the great architectural creations' of his own day, which had been made possible by the tremendous advances achieved in the engineering sciences.[6] But he wanted the engineer to be a scientist, *i. e.*, a man who provided the architect with new techniques; he did not want him to be a builder in his own right.[7] Although he may not have foreseen the obnoxious routine of the method builders (whose usual buildings' now provide a whole repertoire of classical mediocrity, which is distinguished only by its lack of imagination, its complacence and the evident desire on the part of those concerned to take the easy way out), Wagner was repelled by the great zeal of contemporary engineers who, with nothing but their methodology to guide them, were obliged to solve all new problems by recourse to ready-made answers. He knew that their methodical approach was extremely useful when it came to solving specific technical problems, but he also knew that it was likely to mean they would prejudge a problem when they tried to synthesise their partial solutions. This danger was all the more real since they tended to regard their prejudices as an integral part of their method. In the Nussdorf Dam and the Stadtbahn bridge over the Zeile Wagner left the engineer's design for the iron trusses unaltered, adding nothing of his own, for the structure and the shape were interdependent. But this was not the case with the abutments for the dam. All that the engineers could insist on there was a specific mass. Nor could the engineers determine the shape of the pillars on Wagner's bridges if the deck was to be supported by independent trusses. In such cases the most that the engineers were able to do was to stipulate the design for the fixed and freesliding platforms on the abutments. The individual structural elements in modern architecture are conceived of as parts of an entire corporate whole; for example, we speak of bridges and buildings made of prestressed concrete. But the situation is still confused. Many engineers, tired of their complex calculations (which are based on over-simplified theories), are now turning to the idea advanced by Wagner in order to 'ensure that the pernicious power of the engineer is broken': that structure is also an intuitive undertaking. Wagner said: 'The basic conception underlying every structure is not to be sought in . . . statistical calculations but in a certain natural ingenuity; it is an inventive faculty.'[8]

Writing in 1959 Félix Candela made a similar analysis: 'The erection of a Gothic cathedral, although executed without the aid of differential calculus, presupposed a high degree of refinement in the use of stone, a material whose limitations are so obvious. By contrast, our modern techniques—which have of course been quite overwhelmed by the tremendous impact of mathematics—have enabled us to achieve comparable structural refinements only on rare occasions despite the availability of a far more complete material, namely reinforced concrete . . . Although this assertion may appear blasphemous to many scientists, let us pause for a moment to consider what the outcome of our modern techniques would have been if they had been combined with the intuitive and experimental outlook which produced such splendid results in the Middle Ages and the Renaissance. It is quite possible that, if our architects had been encouraged to use their inventive faculty, they would have made better use of their material, because then they would have tackled their problems with a more open mind, *i. e.*, without the preconceived idea that all problems have to be solved mathematically. It was not without good rea-

Ills. 14, 15. Post Office Savings Bank (second stage, built 1910-12). Above: Shutters for pillars and roof beams. Below: Pay office for securities and bonds.

Ill. 16. Post Office Savings Bank (first stage, built 1904-6): Corner acroterium above the main projecting face executed in aluminium by Othmar Schimkowitz.

son that architects came to be know as engineers. Since the most appropriate and logical forms do not normally lend themselves to mathematical analysis, they were discarded in favour of less appropriate forms which were, however, capable of straightforward mathematical analysis.'[9]

But the newly discovered intuition of the modern engineer, his refusal to formulate problems in an oversimplified form, do not make him an architect by Wagner's standards. For that he would have to 'select, determine, perfect or invent the structure which would fit in most naturally with his conception and was best suited to its emerging artistic form.'[10] Inspired by Darwin, Wagner even developed an architectural theory of evolution, in which structure fulfilled the role of the 'original cell': 'Every architectural form has arisen from a structural form and then developed by successive stages into an artistic form.'[11] But Wagner had one advantage over Darwin and Lamarck. He knew the end object of his evolutionary process: 'although these forms [those based on modern structures] have not all been perfected or generally accepted as artistic forms, their adaptation for artistic purposes is now being promoted by utilitarian considerations. In this connection it bears repeating that every formative process takes place slowly and imperceptibly.'[12]

In his use of the new structures Wagner was always at pains to show the interaction between the various functional elements: he allowed them to permeate one another, he contrasted them by empha-

Ill. 17. View of corner acroterium showing the construction of the wings.

sising one at the expense of the other, but he never allowed them to merge. The pillars supporting the glass roof of the Post Office Savings Bank ran up through the ceiling of the counter section. By constructing the ceiling from glass Wagner was able to indicate the real functional purpose of these pillars, namely to support the roof. In fact, he purposely avoided a smooth union between pillar and ceiling, since it would have concealed this purpose. The central section of the control building on the Danube Canal housed a crane installation, which extended beyond the outer surface of the building in the form of a balcony on one side (above the sliding door) and in the form of a buttressed projection on the other side (on a level with the driver's cabin). These two sections and the glass panel above the door, which was also fixed to the crane installation, were capable of independent movement, because the installation was allowed to slide freely on its abutment to prevent the generation of heat stresses. Consequently, the control building actually consisted of two distinct structures which, while combining to form a unified whole, nonetheless retained their individuality. Wagner did not allow one design to impinge on the other. This project also showed that he had both the courage and the ability to use a large number of different materials within a single building, a practice which posed quite as many problems in his day as it does in our own. These materials included granite blocks, granite and marble sheets (which were fixed to the walls with bolts), glazed tiles, wood, glass, rolled-steel joists (some of them riveted), sheet metal, corrugated sheet copper and renderings. Similar structures erected today do not have the same carefree air or the same vigour. But then, of course, it is foolish for the modern architect to pretend that he is still treading a revolutionary path when the revolution to which he lays claim was fought and won fifty years ago. Is it really necessary for him to go on, in the words of Rimbaud, 'making himself ridiculous, proving to himself over and over again something which is already perfectly clear to everybody else and doing nothing else with his life?'

Wagner carried the 'imperceptible' development of 'artistic forms' into the sphere of industrial building practices. This was why he insisted on what he called the 'division of work, *i. e.,* the simultaneous execution of different structural units in order to speed up the work programme'[13] This synthetic method, which lies at the heart of all genuine building, was extremely characteristic of Wagner's work. When an observer studies one of his buildings and follows the logical development of its intersecting structural patterns he will probably think that his principal object is to understand the work. In point of fact, however, understanding is only secondary. What is far more important is the visionary process: the observer finds himself in a state of mental tension, which appears to be quite amorphous but from which new temporal and spatial relationships may emerge at any moment. This process, which is self-renewing, is of course the way in which we experience all art. We start with a given system which leads us via work, tension, restlessness and formlessness to a new system, which we ourselves have created and which consequently soothes us.

When Wagner introduced the new engineering structures into his theory of the evolution of artistic forms he knew that he would not be able to modify them, but he was confident that he would be able to combine them more intelligently than the engineers themselves. In order to show that his combinations were capable of providing a genuine artistic stimulus he used them on public buildings, *e. g.,* for the acroteria on the corners of the main projecting face on the Post Office Savings Bank. These angels, which stand twice life-size, hold wreaths in their hands, through which the viewer is able to see heavens from street level. Their wings, which are attached to massive blocks, describe an angle of ninety degrees. The angels are of course counterfeit symbols. But, although they have quite evidently been stripped of their traditional significance, they still posses the power to attract the viewer's attention and direct it to other parts of the building. The viewer's reaction to these symbols, which he thinks he understands, draws his attention to the structural technique. The decorative wreaths on the walls of many of Wagner's buildings serve a similar purpose, as do the ornamental flowers on the iron arch in front of the Hofpavillon, which form a raised surface on the upper face.

THE DEMYSTIFICATION OF ART
On Polemics

Art Historians tell us that in past times art was created in a hundred different ways which are no longer viable today. They also tell us that, when we try to recreate a work by a past artist, we should do so in the particular way in which it was originally conceived. True, they concede that 'history is changed when touched'.[1] But the concessions is worthless: once a thing is past we can no longer touch or change it.

The history of art is a history of coteries and of unconscious plagiarism. As such it is, of course, superfluous for those who assume the inevitability of plagiarism in any intellectual pursuit. It is in the nature of things that art historians should have more to say about the hardy perennials which clutter our unhappy history than about the mutations which have somehow contrived to take place in spite of them. They record the lives of stillborn offspring with an impartiality that is quite sublime. Of many things, which are unquestionably dead, they ask the extremely perplexing question: why are they still living? And they do not hesitate to ask the same question of living things, in which case, of course, they receive no answer. But they do have the wit to offer a justification of art, one which is based largely on its historical development and in which art is presented as one of the necessities of life. In this way they are able to set themselves up as the defenders of art *vis-a-vis* the masses (or a certain section of the masses). In actual fact, of course, art cannot be justified. Nor does it need to be. It does not impose obligations. And it was not created in a hundred different ways.

Otto Wagner had to deal with a particularly pernicious branch of the history of art, namely a 'creative' of art whose protagonists regarded works of art as 'the fruits of archaeological studies.' He said of the neo-Gothic Votive Church: '999 out of every 1,000' city dwellers will recognise the style at sight, 'which . . . will help to keep them happy'.[2] The fact that the present-day American architect Minoru Yamasaki is still able to manipulate the prefabricated complex of feelings inspired by the Gothic is of course quite ludicrous. But Yamasaki, who was born in Japan in 1912, was able to predict his success in America with absolute certainty. Generally speaking, what has happened today is that the minds of the viewing public have been taken over by the art historians, who have replaced the actual works, to which people should be reacting, by historical information about the works. They have indoctrinated people by persuading them to think in terms of certain human types, certain lines of development; they have inculcated a respectful attitude of mind and a genteel desire to conform to standard taste, which is merely to say that they have created phantom values and denied the basic factor underlying all art—the need to come to terms with the vicissitudes of the human condition.

Otto Wagner created a style which not only embraced 'but clearly manifested a distinct change in traditional sensitivity, the almost total breakdown of romanticism and the emergence of purpose-built structures in every sphere of architecture'.[3] In his polemical writings he attacked the adaptation of literary experiences for architectural purposes; in other words the adaptation of experiences culled either from the interpretations of art historians or from religious symbolism. In Wagner's view the 'character and symbolism' of a building emerged 'of their own accord' provided 'lies' were avoided, provided the external appearance of the building reflected its inner structure etc.[4] In point of fact, since symbolism can never emerge of its own accord, *i. e.*, without the aid of conventional signs, what Wagner is actually saying here is that architects should not attempt to gratify man's desire for symbolism, which is grounded in sloth. The effect of architecture is non-specific: we do not have different kinds of architecture corresponding to different kinds of feeling. There is no such thing as serene, carefree, serious or gloomy architecture, there is no architecture which leads man to God. (On the other hand, it is conceivable that men will come to believe that buildings—even present-day and future buildings—are gods in their own right, just as the practising Christian believes that the blessed sacrament is God or the members of the Cargo cult in New Guinea that the aircraft which fly over the island are the souls of their departed ancestors, who are returning briefly from paradise and have temporarily strayed on to the white man's runways.)

Wagner stubbornly resisted the idiotic idea which 'culminated in the rigid postulate: Churches and town halls must be Gothic, parliament buildings and museums Greek and private houses Renaissance'.[5] Although Wagner's buildings were intended to 'manifest the emergence of purpose-built structures', this does not mean that he first designed a functional church and then tried to stamp it with the concept of 'the church' or a functional town hall and tried to stamp that with the concept of 'the town hall'. On the contrary, he insisted that the character of his buildings 'emerged of its own accord'. In any case, such concepts have no real significance, for they cannot even be expressed in language, let alone in architecture, which by its very nature is incapable of communicating ideas or sentiments.

Otto Wagner insisted that architects must have 'a thorough grasp of functional requirements and fulfil them completely (down to the smallest detail)'.[6] He was one of the first scientific architects. Above all, he recognised the importance of statistics, which offer the only means of assessing functional needs in the modern world. But the acceptance of statistics in the social sciences for example, presupposes acceptance of the fact that 'the concepts which determine systematic connections have nothing to do with emotional experiences. There is just a "So-Sein" [a given condition], but no intention, no evaluation, no good and bad, no end object.'[7]

And yet those who regard the further development of civilisation as desirable in itself are surely entitled to regard the means, whereby they pursue it, as an end: 'All things created today must reflect the new materials and the new requirements of our time: if they are to meet the needs of modern man they must express our improved, democratic, self-confident, clear-thinking selves and do justice both to our colossal technical and scientific achievements and to the practical bent which remains one of our chief characteristics—that much is quite clear!'[8]

But even for those who do not regard the further development of civilisation as something fundamentally desirable, the means whereby this end is to be achieved might still exercise a considerable fascination.

Once he has fulfilled his role as scientist the architect has also fulfilled all conceivable obligations *vis-a-vis* the people who are going to use his building. Having collected and evaluated all available information about them, his task is finished as far as they are concerned. No matter what he does, he cannot improve on the solution which he has arrived at. Apart from comfort and hygiene the only specifically human requirement that the architect is obliged to consider is that of his clients' way of life. He must, for example, make allowance for their 'lounge suits, their tennis and cycling costumes, their uniforms and their tweeds'.[9] But the architect is not required, nor indeed is he able, to express tangible ideas or 'meanings' in his buildings. Such things are incapable of logical analysis. No two men can explain to one another what they see when they look at the colour 'red'. The same holds true, of course, of more complex sense impressions. All such experiences are highly individual and do not lend themselves to comparison. We must tread warily when considering this question of the comparability of experience. Le Corbusier, for example, exaggerates when he says: 'Those who surrender themselves up to architecture body and soul will be rewarded with a condition of happiness, a kind of trance condition, which is produced by the labour pains of *the idea* and its shining birth. The power of invention, of creation, which enables us to give of our best in order to bring joy to others, in order to bring daily joy into their homes.'[10] This is mystification. Art is not 'service to one's fellow men', as Le Corbusier would have us believe. It is not created in a state of trance or altruistic ecstacy.

'It is my design to render it manifest that no one point in its composition [The Raven] is referable either to accident or intuition—that the work proceeded step by step to its completion with the precision and rigid consequence of a mathematical problem.'

Edgar Allen Poe[11]

Architects must have 'a thorough grasp of functional requirements and fulfil them completely (down to the smallest detail)'. They 'must make a happy choice of building material'—*i. e.* it must be 'easily worked, easily maintained, durable and economical' and they must select 'a simple and economical type of structure. Only after they have taken these three principal points into account should they consider the question of form arising out of these premises (which will present itself of its own accord and will always be easily understood). Works of art created according to this "recipe" will always conform to the artistic style of our period.'

Otto Wagner[12]

THE AVOIDANCE OF SIMPLIFICATION IN ART

On Work

'The artist must conceive and fully consider a good and great idea before ever setting pen to paper. Whether clarification comes in a flash or only very slowly, whether it is worth all the deliberation and mental effort, whether the solution arrived at turns out to be a hit or a miss in the first draft or whether the problem has to be tackled time and again is irrelevant. What is quite certain is that a good basic conception, which has been properly thought out, is an important factor today and contributes far more to the assessment placed on a work than the richest blossoms emerging from the artist's unconscious. The practical element in man, which is particulary pronounced at present, is evidently here to stay and every architect is going to have to come to grips with the postulate: "a thing that is unpractical cannot be beautiful".'

Otto Wagner[1]

'The most important thing is to have the vision. The next is to grasp and hold it. In this there is no difference whether you are writing a film script, pondering the plan of the production as a whole or thinking out a solution for some particular detail.

You must see and feel what you are thinking about. You must see and grasp it. You must hold and fix it in your memory and senses. And you must do it at once.

When you are in a good working mood, images swarm through your busy imagination. Keeping up with them and catching them is very much like grappling with a run of herring.'

Sergei Eisenstein[2]

Although Eisenstein describes the same basic process he goes further than Wagner when he says that the method is applicable, not only to a total project, but also to its component parts. However, both texts need to be elaborated if we are to understand the mechanism of creative activity. Wagner's peroration, which is a good example of his polemical writing, is blatantly one-sided. In point of fact there are only too many ways of avoiding an impractical structure and the solution of this problem cannot be defined in terms of function, which is the only known factor. Even assuming that the architect is not at liberty to choose between various types of structural systems there are still many ways in which he may utilise the particular system at his disposal. And as for his building material, he is explicitly told by Wagner that he must make a 'happy choice'. The truth of the matter is that materials and structure are interdependent variables. Moreover, there is no such thing as a single solution to an architectural problem. Every design consists of a number of smaller designs, which are first solved as individual problems and then joined together to form a composite whole. And Wagner's three principal points, namely function, materials and structure, do not always furnish adequate criteria by which to accomplish this combinative process.

According to Wagner himself the correct procedure is 'to align the specifications in accordance with the building schedule after the basic conception has been worked out and so produce a skeleton plan. This alignment must then be followed by . . . a detailed ground-plan, in which the architect—by experimenting empirically with the rooms and the shapes of the rooms—tries to find a clear, simple and axial solution . . .'[3] From this it follows that the ultimate solution is not determined by the detailed list of specifications either. But if the crucial impetus is not given by the existing conditions, where does it come from? If the architect is presented with various materials, structures and layouts, all equally appropriate, how does he avoid making a purely arbitrary decision? And if he is not to make an arbitrary decision, how is he to decide? He can make his decision by forcing himself to concentrate on the problem in hand. He will then find that his total experience—which is stored in his mind—will decide for him. In a general sense the human mind is of course a self-steering mechanism. But even in a more specialised sense, i. e., when it is dealing with specific problems, it retains its self-steering characteristics. In other words, it does not simply furnish predictable solutions reflecting man himself or, to be more precise, some part of the information stored in his brain.

However, the solution of the problem posed by artistic activity is not the end of the matter. There is also the question of the criteria by which that solution is to be judged; and insofar as these issues are interdependent, they have to be investigated simultaneously. Man is always trying to escape from the experiences of his normal environment, which he finds exhausting. (Sometimes when he is unable to escape, he will even try to intensify them in order to make himself more aware of his own identity.) The reason why he finds these experiences exhausting is that his feelings are subject to constant vacillation: sometimes they radiate outwards, sometimes they seem to bear in on him from outside. There are times when man's feelings try to take over his will and there are times when they reject this will; they fill his time for him and it is quite evident that they do no more. But, above all, they are unable to arrest the passage of time: 'All things are full of labour; man cannot utter it: the eye is not satisfied with seeing, nor the ear filled with hearing. The thing that hath been, it is that which shall be; and that which is done is that which shall be done; and there is no new thing under the sun.'[4] Somewhere in the background of life man feels the presence of a force, which would enable him to spread his own life out in such a way that things which he had already experienced would be preserved for him: his life is over-shadowed by the desire for simultaneity; he wants every conceivable object and event to exist at one and the same time. Religion meets this desire with an undertaking. The apocalyptic angel swears 'that there shall be time no longer'[5] and goes on to say that the body too will share in this condition. But man's impatience undermines his belief in this undertaking; slowly, almost imperceptibly, it gnaws away at its import:

'Up to my fifty-fifth year I believed in an unknown God. Later this God was forced to yield to an implacable fate until eventually the idea matured in me that man can have no faith and that after death his body simply returns to the earth . . . There is something extremely distressing about my theory concerning life after death but my reason obliges me to adhere to it.'

Otto Wagner[6]

'Thus disbelief crept over me at a very slow rate, but was at last complete. The rate was so slow that I felt no distress.'

Charles Darwin[7]

All works which enter into the sphere of intellectual life have been nurtured—like the Apocalypse itself—on impatience, doubt and disbelief, never on piety and patience. They are systems which their authors believe—at least while they are creating them—are capable of exercising a retroactive effect on their own lives.

More than any other system architecture constitutes an attempt to represent time itself, for the idea of a building or a section of a building when conceived as a self-contained whole, embraces within itself, from the very first moment of its conception and despite its own lack of movement, the whole sequence of movements which a viewer might execute in the actual building with his body, his eyes or his senses.[8] Although the process whereby this idea eventually enters into consciousness as a clearcut conception (or vision) is a sudden one, the conception is actually the final product of a number of processes, which have taken place in that area of the mind where unorganised experiences are stored. The man who wishes to make architecture has to acquire a clear conception of a structure which is quite as difficult to grasp as a waterfall. (Nor should it be thought that a clear conception is the same thing as a still photograph.) Wagner's absolute insistence on this point was based on the simple insight that a conception or vision which is not clear cannot be put down on paper. What this boils down to is that the final conception is formed before and not during the execution of the design. It may of course sink back into the unconscious, in which case it has to be worked on again until it finally 'springs to mind'.

Once a vision has been realised, either on paper or as a building, it is dead. Only the concentrated gaze of the viewer can revive it and, each time it is revived, it is likely to assume a slightly different form. Such concentration is prompted, partly by the building itself, partly by a suitable environment, which would consist of smaller houses of uniform shape, such as Wagner had envisaged for his 'Grossstadt' and such as the Incas and Mesopotamians actually built in their cities. But this uniformity should not be confused with the uniformity which is being introduced into our own cities by the use of millions of meaningless and enervating stylistic details. The architectural buildings of these earlier cultures, which were surrounded by densely packed, monotonic blocks of dwellings, attracted the attention of the inhabitants without recourse to mere pomp. They were inescapable and consequently provided the feeling of strength and security which the oppressed masses need. It is far better for them when the oppressive system under which they labour is openly manifested in visible symbols. Today, although oppression exists in every corner of the globe, it has no visible source, which would make it comprehensible to all levels of society. And, since it is widely held that the strength of a nation comes from its people, it is hardly surprising to find that the peoples of the world have no faith in the forces which impinge upon them, since they must consider these to be of their own making. As things are at present, architecture can have only a very limited effect, for it can reach only very few people.

Since a building is not a natural phenomenon but a system devised by human intelligence—Wagner defined it as 'a completely new structure based on human creativity'—it creates an impression which calls, first for analysis, then for synthesis. Even an apparently peaceful view is always charged with tension and movement. For example, if an observer has two separate objects in his field of vision, one of which is further away than the other, he has to decide which of the two he is going to focus on, since the adjustment of the crystalline lens and the parallax will be different in each case.

When a person walks towards, through or around a building he performs a highly complex mental act, in which he creates, at every stage along his path, a new image of the building, which then serves him as a system of reference for his movements. This process—which is in fact continuous—is promoted quite as much by the symmetry of the whole, or of parts, of the building as it is by its more prominent features. But, although the process helps to guide the person through the building, this is not its true purpose. If it were, it would not need to be nearly as complex. In fact, it has no purpose as such. It is a self-contained system built up from data provided by all the senses.

The human mind finds the sense perceptions which it tries to organise and bring into an orderly relationship more alien than those which it simply 'experiences' (and which are often the sole constituents of the mind). Thus, by focussing his attention on buildings, i. e., by making them an object of perception, man begins to dissociate himself from the external world. As a result of this partial dissociation his powers of perception are undoubtedly heightened but he himself is isolated and made aware of the narrow confines within which he has being. 'His thoughts are elevated, soothed, strengthened and set free . . . He knows: they are devoid of that which is not there, but what has remained, that is there.'[10] He then realises that he is living in a restricted present which, however, also embraces the real aspects of his past and future, i. e., those tiny parts of both which no longer reveal a temporal sequence. This is man's fundamental condition, which he must either look in the face without fear or bury beneath a daily round of diversions. 'In so far as spiritual beings recognise something outside of themselves they may be said to step out of themselves; but as soon as they recognise this act of recognition they begin to return to themselves: for recognition lies midway between the persons who recognise and that which is recognised.'[11]

THE EXPANDING CITY

Opinions differ widely as to how the problems of town planning ought to be tackled. Commenting on the final congress of the Congrès International d'Architecture Moderne (CIAM)[1] which was held in Otterlo in 1959, Reyner Banham wrote: 'It is clear from the records that a closed discussion of specific questions can be quite as trivial as an open discussion of general questions.'[2] Not surprisingly the CIAM foundered. Clearly, a living city, which functions badly, is one thing and a town planning programme, which functions well in theory but has yet to be put into practice, is another.

In planning a big city it would be entirely feasible for the architect to take as his point of departure the 'happiness' of the inhabitants. Only he must then be in a position to say what that happiness is. And there is surely nothing more desirable and nothing more worth fighting for than that man's happiness should remain undefined. Point 86 of the "Charter of Athens"[3] states: 'Permanent legislation will be passed to ensure that the inhabitants enjoy the comfort of their homes, the best possible working conditions and the benefits of leisure.' Under point 38 the authors elaborated: 'The weekly leisure periods are to be spent in places laid out with loving care, e. g., parks, forests, sporting installations, stadia and swimming pools.'[4] In fact, this charter laid down that the inhabitants of this city would be in one of four places: at home, at their place of work, at their place of leisure or travelling from one to the other. This was not a working hypothesis for a city but an attempt to regiment the lives of those who were to live in it. At their place of work they would play a useful and significant part in the life of the community, at home and at their place of leisure they would be 'happy', the rest of the time they would be on the move.

Otto Wagner's basic premise was quite different. He assumed that the majority of big-city dwellers preferred 'to disappear in the crowd, to become a "number"'[5]. The object of city life, as he saw it, was to make it possible for people to avoid social contact. He set out his view in the report, in which he explained his general plan for the regulation of Vienna (1893), and also in his study, 'Die Grossstadt' (1911). His principal concern was to ensure that the big city 'would be able to go on developing in the future'[6]. Consequently, he made no provision for checking its growth, although he made no attempt to induce it either and was opposed to overcrowding in any form. The inner city remained the focal point of his design but he insisted that any further demands which were to be made upon it must be carefully controlled, for he felt that the outer districts could and should become cities in their own right with a stipulated population density. Wagner considered that the whole city must remain a homogeneous structure and that the inner city should on no account become embroiled in constant strife with the individual outer suburbs.

His design for Vienna was based on ring and radial roads, which divided the entire city into districts,[7] each of which would be able to accommodate between 100,000 and 150,000 people: 'It goes without saying that, until such densities have been reached one, two or even three districts can come under a single administrative centre. —A population of 100 to 150 thousand will extend over an area of 500 to 1,000 hectares in each district, provided the dwelling houses are built to the maximum permitted height . . . If the city is to be regulated in a systematic way we must above all ensure that the main radial roads are wide enough to meet future traffic needs and that the ring roads are also able to cope with the as yet unknown demands which will one day be made on them. We can postulate a basic width of 80 to 100 metres for the ring roads. It will of course be extremely difficult to introduce these in the built-up areas of the city. It should, however, be possible to link them up with already existing roads and, if necessary, to reduce their width. —Since . . . the individual districts are to be spaced out at set intervals and will in fact form a group of smaller cities around the inner city it seems more appropriate to provide an adequate number of open air centres in the form of parks, gardens and playgrounds for

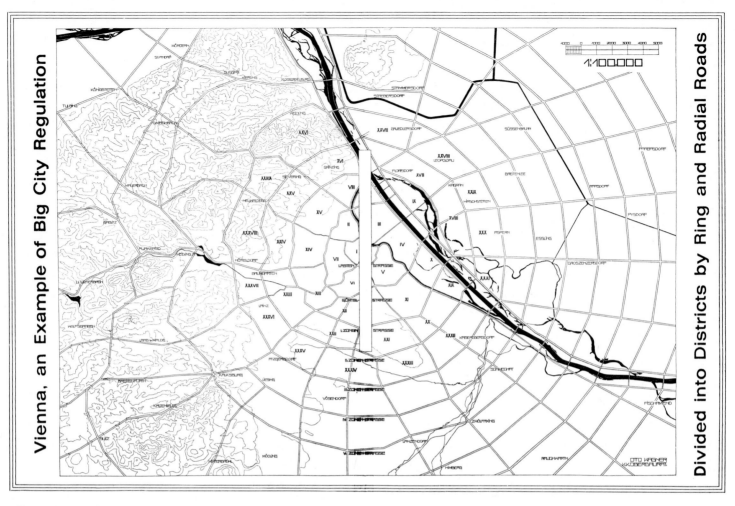

Vienna, an Example of Big City Regulation

Divided into Districts by Ring and Radial Roads

Ill. 18. Vienna, an Expanding City (1910-11). General plan published in *Die Grossstadt.*

each individual district than to allow for a green belt; the provision of a green belt around the whole city would simply be another kind of restriction, which must be avoided at all costs.'[8] Over and above this of course Wagner was aware of the disappointing outcome of Haussmann's[9] green belt project for the city of Paris, which was never put into effect. The Bois de Boulogne and Bois de Vincennes, which should have been linked by the green belt, remained out of reach of large sections of the population. Wagner also avoided the one-sidedness of the 'radical regulations'[10] carried out in the built-up areas of Paris by Haussmann, whose boulevards were intended 'to circulate, not only air and light, but also troops'.[11] He regarded them with admiration but reserve.

Wagner replaced Haussmann's 'théorie des dépenses productives'—which was based on the assumption that all expenditure must eventually produce a profit and which involved Haussmann in enormous expenditure in excess of his budget—by a far more cautious system of finance. 'The expansion of any city provides the civic authorities with a simple means of acquiring sufficient financial influence, for the municipality can buy up the undeveloped land surrounding the city, which will subsequently be used for the new districts, and hold on to it until the time is ripe. As soon as the land is bought it can be let out, either on lease or for rent, which should bring in an adequate interim return on the capital invested, while the long-term profit arising out of the subsequent building development would all go

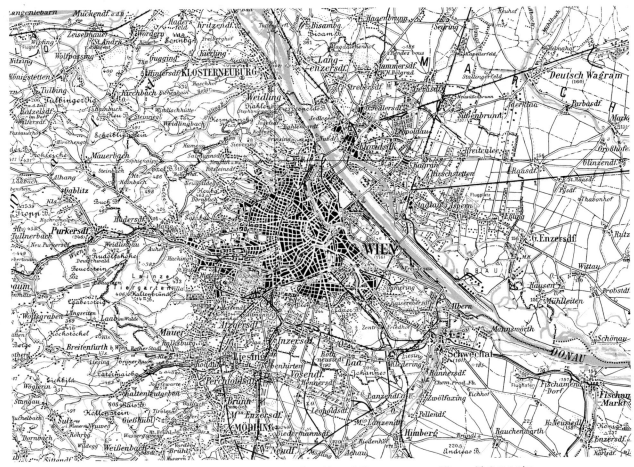

Ill. 19. Vienna today. Same area as in *Ill. 18.*

to the municipality.—But even if the initial return on the land were less than adequate we may certainly anticipate that within a very brief period its value would have increased to such an extent that it would far exceed the interest, the compound interest and the capital sum and that it might quite conceivably yield an additional profit of hundreds of millions.—It would certainly be true to say that the land surrounding all our big cities could be acquired for a relatively modest price. At the same time the increase in the population would suggest that part of this land will certainly be built on in the next fifty years, which means that any land acquired by the municipal authorities (presumably by compulsory purchase) would then return to private ownership. This process could of course be repeated over and over again. By controlling land prices, leasehold prices, etc., the municipality would be able to direct civic developments into specific channels, reserve the necessary public land for the various city districts, check land speculation . . . and use its profits to provide splendid institutions and civic amenities. It will be seen from the following sketch [*Ill. 20*] that the projected xxIInd district of Vienna will cover 5,100,000 square metres. If we subtract 50 per cent of this for public building there still remain 2,550,000 square metres which, if land prices rise by no more than 20 florins per square metre, would bring in a profit of 50 million.—It would not be difficult to realise an even higher profit since the municipal authorities, who would control the price of building land, could regulate the development of

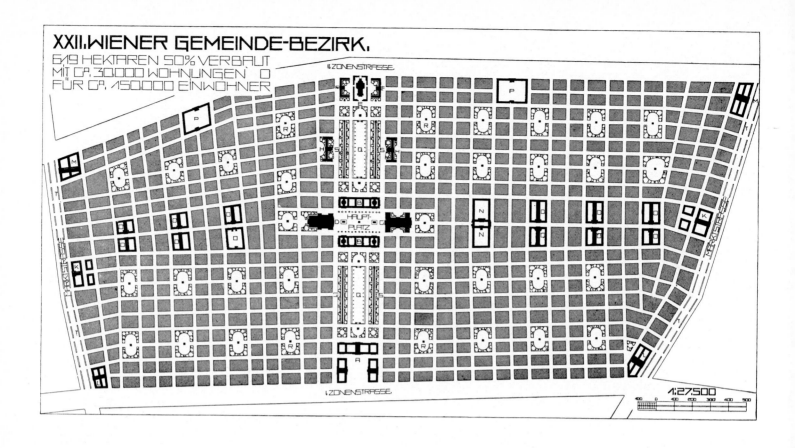

XXII. WIENER GEMEINDE-BEZIRK.

649 HEKTAREN 50% VERBAUT
MIT CA. 30.000 WOHNUNGEN
FÜR CA. 150.000 EINWOHNER

A. ÖFFENTLICHE GEBÄUDE B. HALBÖFFENTLICHE GEBÄUDE C. GESELLSCHAFTSHAUS U. AUSSTELLUNGSGEBÄUDE D. THEATER E. KIRCHE MIT CAMPO SANTO, PFARRHAUS U. LEICHENTRANSPORTHALLE F. VOLKSSCHULE G. BÜRGERSCHULE H. GYMNASIUM J. REALSCHULE K. WARENHÄUSER L. HOTELS M. LOGIERHÄUSER N. KASERNEN FÜR EIN BATAILLON O. WERKSTÄTTEN P. MATERIALHAUFEN U. LAGERPLÄTZE Q. GROSZE LUFT-ZENTREN 150.000 m² HAUPTPLATZ 43.500 m² R. GARTENANLAGEN MIT JE 2 KINDERSPIELPLÄTZEN TRINKHALLE U. ÖFFENTLICHEN ABORTANLAGEN S. WANDELBAHNEN T. VERKAUFSSTÄNDE IN DEN MARKTSTRASZEN ▨ 7-8 GESCHOSZIGE WOHNHÄUSER. K. K. OBERBAURAT OTTO WAGNER

Ill. 20. XXIInd Viennese district (1910-11): General plan published in *Die Grossstadt.*

the district so as to ensure that a large number of multi-storey dwellings were built, which would of-course increase the value of the plots.—If it were to adopt such methods the municipality could look forward to building housing estates and other lucrative installations—such as a civic plant for the manufacture of bricks—which would also provide a source of revenue.'[12] To facilitate the implementation of these measures Wagner recommended that the state should furnish its largest city, its 'biggest and most reliable taxpayer', with powers of compulsory purchase and he also proposed the setting up of a fund to enable the municipality to increase its building programme. 'If adequate funds are made available the municipal authorities will be able to erect public buildings, municipal dwellings, municipal sanatoria, exhibition halls and showrooms, promenades, monuments, fountains, observation towers, museums, theatres, "Wasserschlösser", Valhallas, etc., things which seem inconceivable today but which will undoubtedly form part of the big city scene in the future.'[13]

Wagner's method of finance was a logical development of his basic principle that 'it is improper for art to combat . . . economic trends[14] or to cloak them under a lie; on the contrary, it must contrive to satisfy such requirements'.[15] The vampire of 'speculation' had to be tamed and placed at the service of the community.

Ill. 21. XXIInd Viennese district: Bird's-eye view of the open air centre. Published in *Die Grossstadt.*

Although the population of Vienna remains more or less constant the city itself is now expanding and unquestionably needs at least one of the two outer belts[16] which Wagner had thought would be needed by 1930. He based this prediction on the belief 'that the populations of big cities would double every thirty to fifty years'.[17] He himself was not in the least perturbed by the prospect of these growing concentrations of people. On the contrary, he considered that the amenities of city life should be publicised in order to attract still more immigrants. Any attempt to check the spontaneous growth of big cities—which is a counsel of fear—must fail: greater Paris now has 8 million inhabitants and by the year 2000 it will have 15 million. The over-all length of the city of Tokyo has trebled in the past seventy years; in 1880 it measured ten kilometres from end to end, in 1953 it measured over thirty. In Wagner's general plan of Vienna, which appeared in his study *Die Grossstadt,* the length of the main diagonal roads was 50 kilometres, which is more than double the present diameter of the city. 'There can be no limits to the expansion of the big city if it is to accord with our modern outlook.'[18] This statement, which Wagner wrote in 1911, both reflects and parodies grandiose efforts of succesive generation to disseminate civilisation. Norbert Wiener rightly observed that 'our technical progress was mortgaged the future'. But he went on to say that our longing for the simple life 'should not blind us to the fact

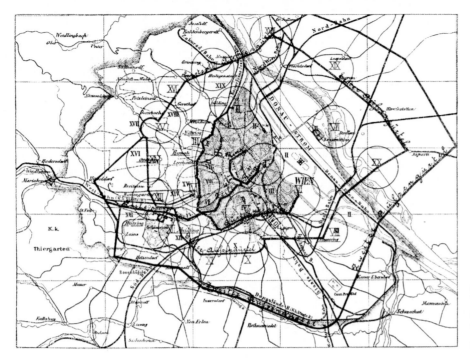

Ill. 22. Plan for the general regulation of Vienna (1893): Map showing the ring roads, the Zeile (from the centre westwards) and the 'centres', which are enclosed in circles 2 kilometres in diameter.

that we are not free to return to this original condition'.[19] Man is capable of renouncing his fixed and static longing, which produces nothing but symbols, religions, humanity and boredom. The right to work replaces and surpasses the right to hope. For us paradise is a building site. And it is not only the pressure of the mortgage which obliges us to go on working on it. It would become a hell on earth if we ever stopped. We could not endure a paradise which we were not at liberty to improve, one which precluded change. Our big cities are hotbeds of change because they are charged with information; and the lack of 'human contact' among city dwellers promotes an exchange of information, by which both men are able to influence, complement and encourage one another. Big cities also favour those types of work which, in their initial stages, are indistinguishable from sloth and remain so until such time as they produce results. This is more important than the freedom to choose one's place of work, one's flat, one's social circle, one's pleasures or one's enemies.

Numerous philosophies have opened with a justification of philosophy. This would seem to be a necessary practice, not only because the philosopher's goal is immutable, unattainable and unknown, but also because all attempts to approach this goal—although they may be undertaken along different lines—always have the same point of departure and always fall short of their objective. It is for this reason that the findings of different kinds of philosophical enquiry can never be combined, evaluated and grasped as a total entity. But they are still accepted by modern city dwellers despite the fact that they add nothing to their store of real knowledge and provide them with no articles of faith. Art is also accepted: as work, as movement, the categories embraced by this particular designation. Although he never defined it, Otto Wagner always insisted on 'art', art in 'the art treasuries of the big city',[20] art in the layout of streets, art in the townscape, art as the key to the distribution of works of art.

The expanding city will provide its own environment. City districts will fill every horizon. This new landscape, which is to replace the old countryside with its clusters of settlements, will be a new 'nature' in so far as it constitutes a natural condition, *i. e.,* one that is accepted without question. It will contain the 'concentrations of cells'[21] formed by the dwelling houses with their 'long and uniform façades flanking the wide streets, which raise them from uniformity to monumentality'.[22] The modern eye has lost its feeling for 'small and intimate proportions, it has grown accustomed to less varied images, longer and straighter lines, larger areas and greater masses . . .'[23] But it is thanks to this limitation, which is a consequence of 'the democratic condition that has been foisted on the great majority by the hue and cry for cheap and healthy flats and the enforced economy of their way of life'[24] that certain ostentatious buildings are able to exist at all. Wagner's expanding city was conceived as an enormous architectural warehouse (of Wagner buildings), which was to have housed an expanding population. Wagner seems to have been obsessed with the idea of educating the public to a better way of life by means of his architecture. In a city which has responded to the latest development of civilisation with cold-blooded parsimony people have come to regard architecture as an intermittent and 'fortunate disruption': they are forced to come to terms with it and, when they do, it disrupts their mundane and superficial stream of consciousness. They then realise how little they had seen, heard and understood and that, for the most part, their self-assurance had been a form of self-deception.

The great city, which Wagner envisaged as the background for his Viennese buildings, has never really materialised. Largely as a result of the First World War and the dissolution of the Habsburg monarchy Vienna did not develop to the point where it would have been obliged to 'transport its corpses by rail'.[25] Leopold Bloom describes this procedure in Joyce's *Ulysses:* 'Yes, Mr. Bloom said, and another thing I thought is to have municipal funeral trams like they have in Milan, you know. Run the line out to the cemetery gates and have special trams, hearse and carriage and all. Don't you know what I mean?'[26] Wagner had already drawn attention to the need for special funeral transportation in his explanatory report for the regulation of Vienna: '. . . and then there is the question of cheaper transport. I have now considered this and have made allowance for the transportation of corpses and their cortèges to the Central cemetery from the various mortuaries via a number of stations on the local rail network. These points of departure coincide with the principal centres in the outer belt . . .'[27] Once it is possible to reach these corpse reception centres in a maximum of fifteen minutes all other forms of transportation will . . . be eliminated.'[28] This project, which was mapped out in 1893, would have given to the dead of Vienna something which the living have yet to acquire: an efficient means of public transportation based primarily on the provision of an adequate number of diagonal routes. The Stadtbahn was only a fragment. For his 'big city' Otto Wagner proposed a series of express services running on high and low levels alongside the radial and ring roads so as to enable passengers 'to reach any desired point with only one change'.[29] But, of course, the way in which Wagner proposed to develop the different districts of Vienna, which was based on his design for the xxiind district, was ill-conceived even for his own day. His housing blocks, which were enclosed within a network of 23-metre-wide roads, were a glaring example of 'the force of economic factors': it is difficult to see how they can be justified by 'the constant fluctuation in the desires evinced by a population of many millions'.[30] The great open-air centres, which would have catered for the most important communal activities, were a valuable feature, but this is more than can be said for the smaller open spaces, which were created by the simple expedient of omitting occasional blocks of houses.

In his report Wagner cautiously wrote: 'The townscape of the future cannot be precisely established in advance since we have no catechism of municipal architecture. In many respects we shall just have to wait and see.'[31] As a result of our modern communications the whole world has become an expanding city. The question facing us today is not what we might reasonably expect from a big city but what we ought to expect, for this will lead us on to formulate new desires and new demands.

THE FUTURE

'Our modern way of life is going to bring many things to a head, of which we today have scarcely any conception, such as the house on wheels, the prefabricated house erected on a site rented from the municipality and much more besides'.[1] In recent times the prefabricated house, to which Wagner briefly refers in this excerpt from *Die Grossstadt,* and the 'division of work', on which he was always insisting, have become the mainspring of a new architectural programme, which appears to be taking his three principal points (functional requirements, material and structure) as its point of departure and is therefore calculated to promote the phasing-out of present-day standard architecture. Once the 'turning point in building' predicted by Wachsmann has been reached 'the support systems in a completed work will become so secondary that they will scarcely be noticed. Nor will they necessarily be recognisable as such since tensile bars, metal sheets and integrated weight-bearing systems will also be utilised . . . The weight-bearing components will recede more and more into the interior of the building. It will no longer be possible to look at the external surfaces of a building and determine the structural system in the sense of "form follows function".'[2]

Wagner's view was the exact opposite of this: 'We should be able to sense, even today, that the structural line, the tabular formation of large surfaces, the prominence of both structure and material and a conception of the utmost simplicity will be the dominant features of the art form of the future; modern engineering techniques and the procedures which we now have at our disposal make this necessary.'[3] According to Wachsmann the procedures which we now have at our disposal make it necessary 'to avoid the risk attendant on artistic intuition'[4]; in his buildings there 'will probably be less to see, but the little there is will become all the more significant'.[5] The components of such buildings are the products of automated production processes; even the erection and fitting is largely automated. It is of course perfectly true that only automation can bring about the necessary production explosion with which to counter our present population explosion. It is not difficult to work out how many dwellings will be needed for the 6 milliard people of the year 2000 or for the 25 milliard of the year 2070. The growth in the world population in the first half of this present century from 1.5 to 2.5 milliards has yet to be assimilated.[6] The planning, or, to be more precise, the invention of automated products is in many respects still in its infancy, but the complexity of the problems involved seems too great to be encompassed by the individual worker. Only teams of workers can be employed on such tasks, although these too offer no more than a temporary solution, for they are unwieldy and susceptible to error. However, since 'the complexity and ability of a machine is not, after all, limited in the long run by the intelligence of its designer'[7] cybernetic systems (*i. e.,* learning and self-steering but essentially inanimate systems) could take over this planning work for man.

Industry is getting ready for full-scale automation. Whole sections are being prepared, in accordance with the waste economy principle, for the mammoth production capacities which will be needed in the future. Utterly useless objects are being made. Gigantic factories are turning out radios which are not worth repairing, do-it-yourself geiger counters made up to look like fountain pens and even machines for producing such articles. Horrific sums of money are being invested in an endless sequence of exhibitions which seldom fulfil a useful purpose and for the most part merely serve to perpetuate each other. Like every other manifestation of wealth—the display of art for example—they create the illusion of possession (for a few) and the illusion of an exciting experience (for a few). To an ever increasing extent these exhibitions and the installations which are built for them the rôle previously fulfilled by genuine architecture. Although the layout of the buildings is determined in almost every case by a whole complex structure of interrelated specifications, these specifications are in themselves extremely simple. It would seem therefore that the viewpoint espoused by Adolf Loos is being borne out. Unlike Wagner, for whom every task came under the heading of art, he wanted to see all architectural buildings apart from tombs and monuments, *i. e.*, everything 'which served a purpose', removed from the 'sphere of art'.[8]

Building today is not yet entirely governed by ideologies which lie outside the architect's area of influence. And yet, the majority of architects are simply waiting for something to happen and are repeating standard solutions. The demise of architecture, if it should ever come about, is more likely to stem from this sort of attitude than from the introduction of automation.

PICTORIAL SURVEY

THIS PICTORIAL SURVEY of Otto Wagner's work has been divided into eight sections arranged as far as possible in chronological order. Each section is preceded by a brief introduction, which also serves to complement the information supplied in the captions. The quotations from Wagner's writings have been taken, with very few exceptions, from the fourth volume of *Einige Skizzen, Projekte und ausgeführte Bauwerke* (Some Sketches, Designs and Buildings). For pictorial sources the reader is referred to the list of illustrations at the back of the book.

Early Wagner buildings which have no apparent connection with his 'modern' or 'new style' have not been documented except where a given work has a special significance within its particular section. In view of the copious and consequently repetitive nature of some of the material (that dealing with unexecuted designs) it has been necessary to make a selection.

Wherever possible important buildings have been photographed in their natural sequence. In other words, the different views have been arranged in the order in which they would appear to the viewer if he were walking around the actual building. The best example of this method is provided by the photographs of the Nussdorf Dam and sluice installations, which proved to be particularly suitable subjects.

THE STADTBAHN

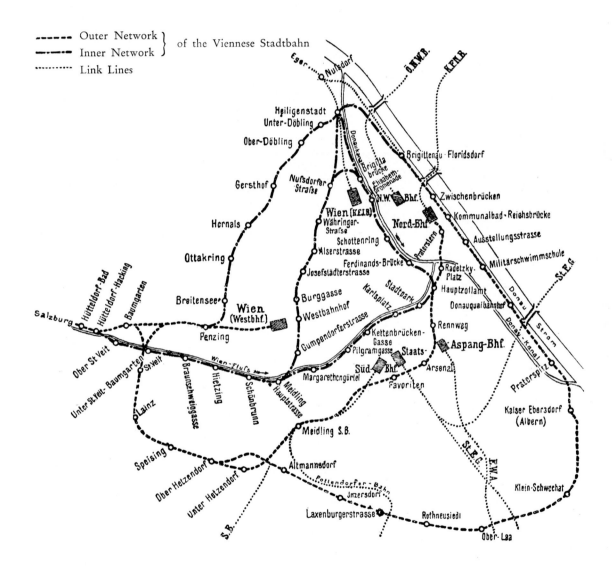

- - - - - - Outer Network ⎫
- · - · - Inner Network ⎬ of the Viennese Stadtbahn
········ Link Lines ⎭

Ill. 23. Stadtbahn plan showing the lines in service in 1910. Wagner was responsible for the architectural work on the following lines: Vorortelinie (Suburban line), Heiligenstadt to Penzing; Gürtellinie (Belt line), Heiligenstadt to Meidling-Hauptstrasse via Westbhnhof; Wiental-Donaukanallinie (Wien valley-Danube Canal line), Hütteldorf to Heiligenstadt via Hauptzollamt; Linie in den II. Bezirk (Line to the IInd district), Hauptzollamt to Praterstern. Most of these lines were on the 'Inner Network'.

Ill. 24. Unter-Döbling low-level station on the Vorortelinie (built 1895-6, now demolished).

Today the Gürtellinie and the Wiental-Donaukanallinie, which once formed part of a much larger network, carry 85 to 90 million people a year. On working days some 48,000 passengers pass through the busiest station—about 24,000 in each direction—while the next busiest handles some 36,000. In all Wagner built thirty-six stations to meet the needs of four separate lines: the two mentioned above, the Vorortelinie and the Line to the IInd district. He also built the viaducts, bridges, cuttings and open tunnels for these installations, which extended over some forty kilometres. Although he proceeded in accordance with the general guidelines laid down by the Imperial and Royal State Railways and although his plans were certainly comprehensive—he even provided scale drawings for tunnel porticos and retaining walls—his designs were not restricted to detail. On the contrary, they were highly imaginative. For example, the line of the gradient on the arched viaducts was offset by the staggered line of the railings while the gradient of the terrain through which the cuttings passed was reflected

by the line of the retaining walls, in which the whole of the top section was raised to form a parapet. In the case of the viaducts this linear relationship was emphasised by the upper section of the pillars, which rose above the level of the parapets.

With the exception of the station at Hütteldorf the Wiental section of the Stadtbahn ran through either cuttings or tunnels. The line was built in conjunction with the regulation of the river Wien, parts of which were vaulted over, and it was brought into commission in the year 1898-9. As a matter of fact, the Transport Bill of 1892 contained a clause to the effect that the construction of the Stadtbahn and the regulation of the river Wien and the Danube Canal must be undertaken simultaneously as a joint project. The famous Karlsplatz station (*Ills. 36-43*), which has two entrance buildings on opposite sides of the street, each serving a separate platform, is to be demolished when the new plan for the rebuilding of the Karlsplatz is put into effect. There were only two stations of

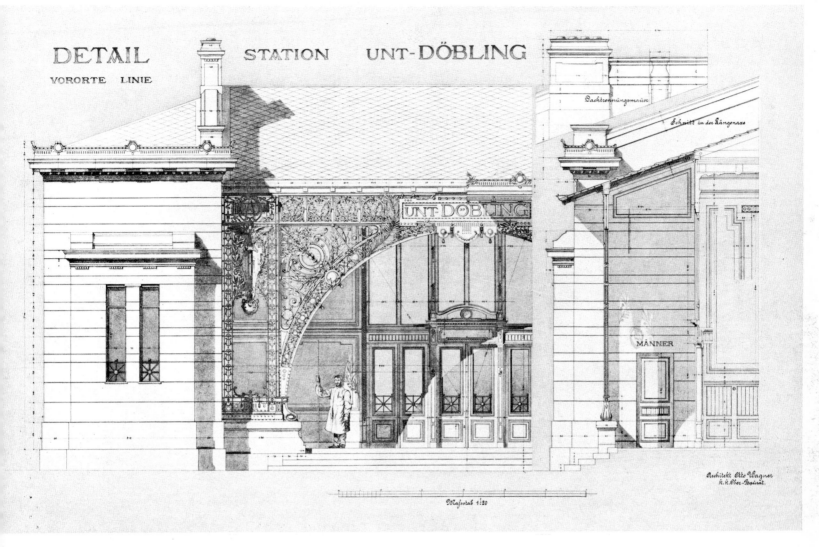

DETAIL STATION UNT-DÖBLING
VORORTE LINIE

Ill. 25. Unter-Döbling station: Front view and vertical section of entrance.

this type: Karlsplatz and Schwedenplatz (formerly Ferdinands-brücke). The station buildings on the Schwedenplatz have already been replaced.

The Donaukanallinie is a low-level line running from the Hauptzollamt to the Friedensbrücke (formerly Brigitta-brücke). For most of its length it passes through 'galerien', *i. e.*, special colonnades or tunnels, which are open on the canal side and whose iron pillars and girders were thought to be particularly impressive (*Ills. 44, 45*). It was of course only possible to build the line at canal level thanks to the con-struction of the dam in Nussdorf (*Ill. 68*). Originally it had been intended to make the last section of the line (from the Schottenring to the Brigittabrücke) a high-level installation but the plan was abandoned in the face of vehement public protest. This involved the municipality in additional expend-iture, for the cost of the new low-level line was greater, and in order to make good the deficit the projected link line be-tween Gumpendorf station and the Südbahn had to be aban-

doned. The Donaukanallinie and the loop line connecting it with the Gürtellinie, which were the last sections of the Stadt-bahn to be completed, were not brought into commission until 1901. This loop line and the section from the Friedensbrücke to Heiligenstadt are both high-level lines. On the Gürtellinie and especially on the Vorortelinie, both of which were opened in 1898, both high- and low-level lines were used because of the hilly nature of the terrain. On all the Stadtbahn lines the high-level sections run on support walls and viaducts while the open sections of the low-level lines are flanked by retaining walls. The only exceptions are certain parts of the Vorortelinie where, because the need to impress the public was felt to be less urgent, earth embankments and sloped cuttings were used. Before joining the Wiental low-level line the Gürtellinie crosses the Gumpendorfer Zeile by way of a bridge over 100 metres long (*Ills. 53-5*). The line to the IInd district was build on the site of an already existing railway.

The competition for thirty Stadtbahn projects was an-

Ill. 26. Breitensee low-level station: Vorortelinie. (built 1897, now demolished.)

nounced by the Viennese municipality in 1890. The city's transportation problem had become critical following the second large-scale building programme. Wagner's winning entry in the competition for the general regulation of the city (1893) provided for six lines in all, two more than were actually built. One of the two additional lines was to have run close to the Ringstrasse, the other along the projected outer belt.

Work started on the Stadtbahn in 1894 and was completed in 1901. The outer walls of the station buildings were rendered with an aggregate containing powdered marble. The iron structures in the entrance halls and ticket sections of the low-level stations were left unfaced. Unfaced I-beams were used as window lintels. The viaducts were built in yellow brick, but the sills, the socles, the facing on the viaduct pillars and the pillars on the bridges were made of natural stone. The station buildings on the Karlsplatz had special cavity walls; the inner surfaces consisted of sheets of stucco, the outer of sheets of marble, both of which were supported by unfaced iron frameworks. Originally the **Stadtbahn ran on steam but it was** electrified in 1924 with the exception of the Vorortelinie, which is no longer used for regular passenger services. The feasibility of incorporating this line into a new express network is now under consideration.

Many of the stations on the Stadtbahn have survived surprisingly well despite a general lack of maintenance, which often gives the impression of being almost intentional. Others, which have been subjected to partial modernisation, have fared less well. Those stations still in use are well able to accommodate the greatly increased number of passengers passing through them today. By allowing Wagner to build the Stadtbahn the Viennese municipal council saved the city from the tasteless design drawn up by the English engineers, Bunton and Fogerty, in which the Central Station looked more like a sarcophagus than a railway building, and also from the type of rail system proposed by the unimaginative architectural dilettantes of the International Association for Public Buildings in Paris.

Ill. 27. Ober-St. Veit station on the Wientallinie (built 1896-7). View from the bed of the river Wien.

Ills. 28, 29. Meidling-Hauptstrasse low-level station (junction for the Gürtellinie and the Wientallinie; three platforms; built 1897, now demolished).

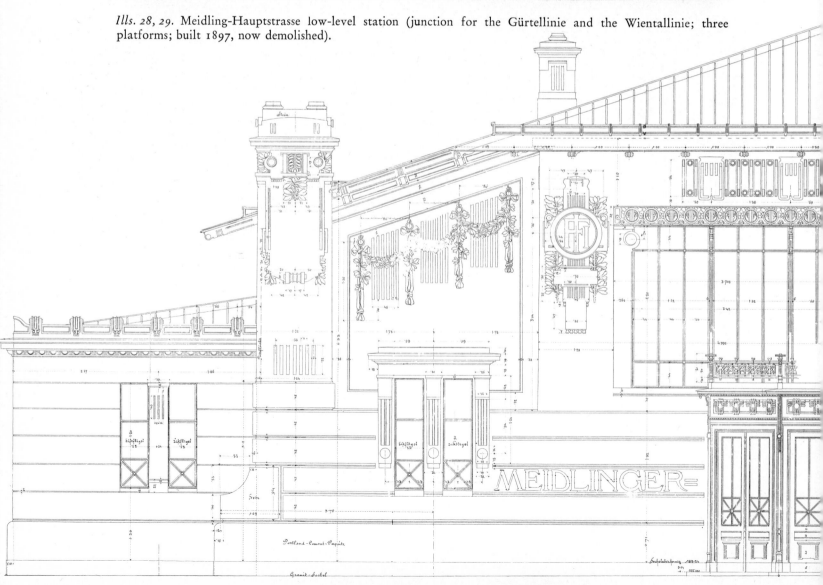

Ill. 30. Hofpavillon on the Wientallinie near Schloss Schönbrunn (built 1898). View from Hietzing station, which has since been rebuilt. The pavilion could be reached from the station platform. The river Wien is on the left.

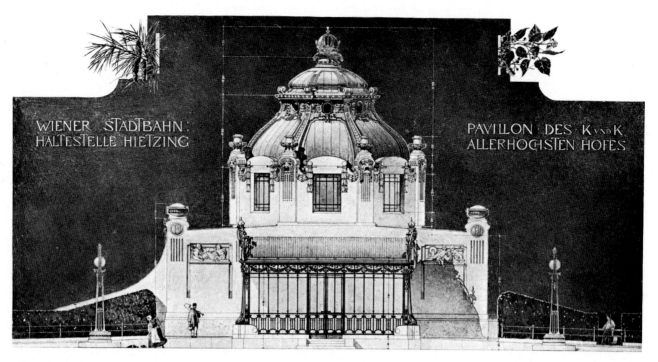

Ill. 31. Hofpavillon: Preliminary design (1896). View from the road with the stairs on the left.

Ill. 32. Hofpavillon: Arch covering the final section of the drive.

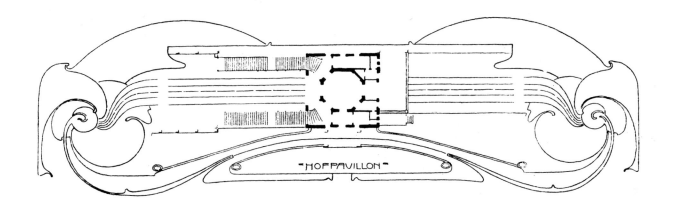

Ill. 33. Hofpavillon: Vignette based on the ground-plan and published in the Secessionist journal *Ver Sacrum.*

Ill. 34. Hofpavillon. View from the road.

Ill. 35. Hofpavillon: Waiting room with dome with silk tapestries in mahogany frames. The picture on the wall is a panoramic view of Vienna as it would appear from a height of 3,000 metres and shows the Stadtbahn network.

Ills. 36, 37. Karlsplatz station on the lower Wientallinie (built 1898-9). There were two station entrances, one on either side of the street, each serving a separate platform. The Karlskirche is on the right.

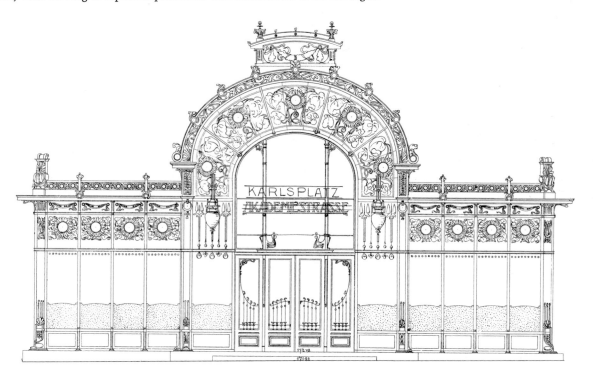

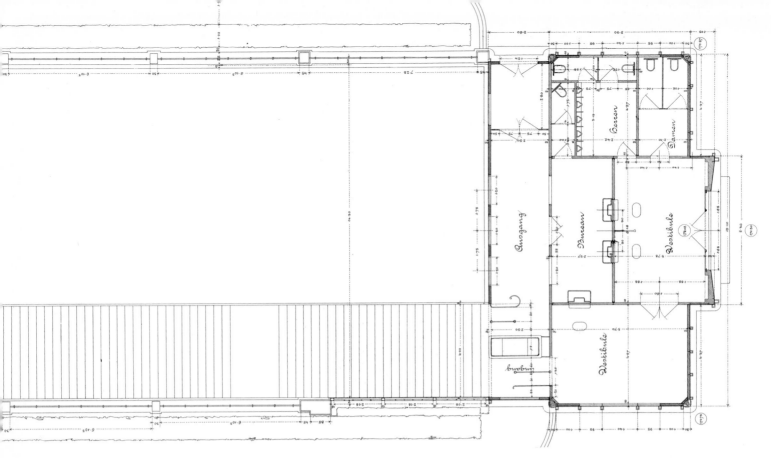

Ill. 38. Karlsplatz station: Ground-plan of one of the station buildings (street level). The prefabricated sections for the cavity walls, which were fitted into an unfaced iron framework, consisted of sheets of marble 2 centimetres thick and sheets of stucco 5 centimetres thick. The depth of the cavity was 3 centimetres.

Ill. 39. Karlsplatz station: Side view of one of the station buildings.

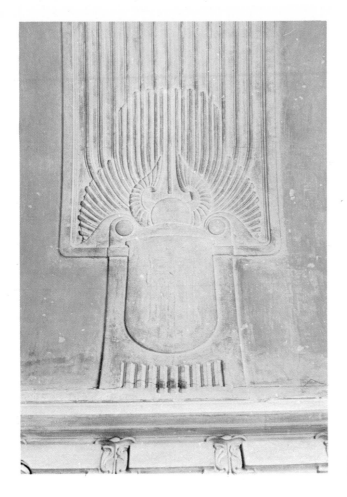

Ill. 40. Karlsplatz station: Detail of stuccoed ceiling in the ticket section.

Ill. 41. Karlsplatz station: Longitudinal section of one of the station building with flights of stairs.

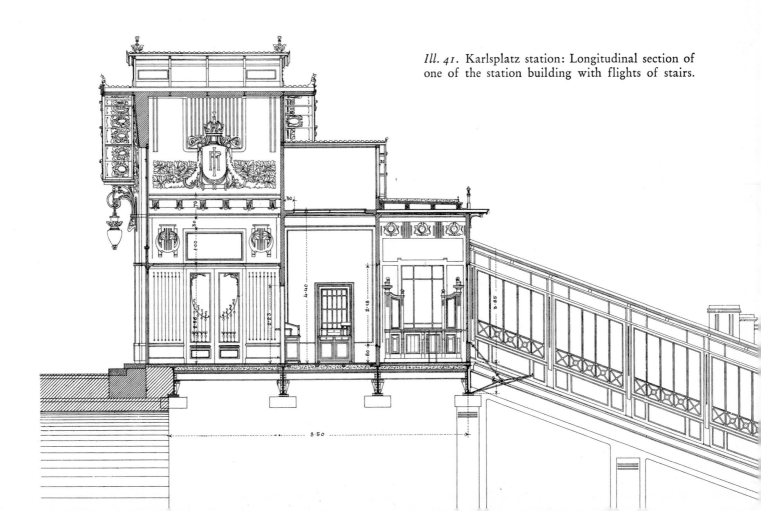

Ill. 42. Karlsplatz station: Roof above the ticket section. Rear view.

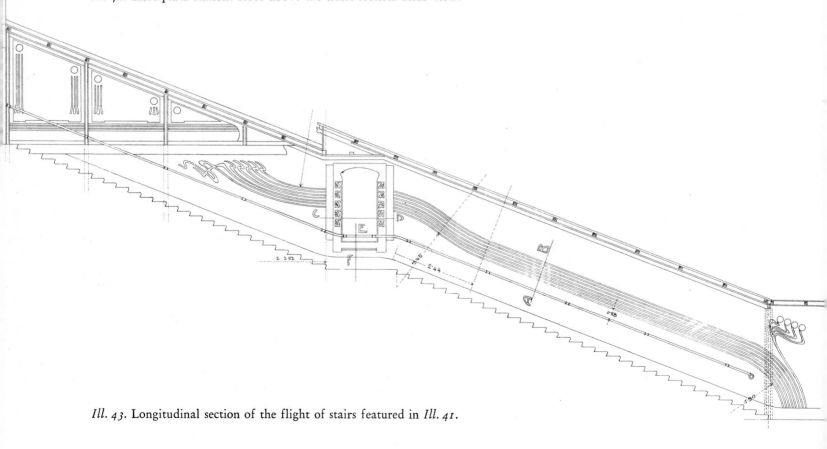

Ill. 43. Longitudinal section of the flight of stairs featured in *Ill. 41.*

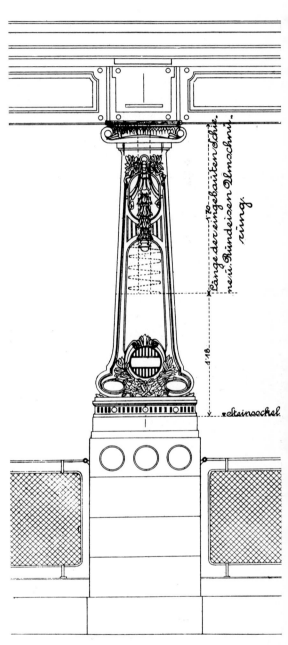

Ill. 44. Section of low-level line showing the open tunnel construction surmounted by a promenade (Donaukanallinie, brought into commission 1901).

Ill. 45. Detail of open tunnel construction: Cast iron pillar with reinforced concrete core.

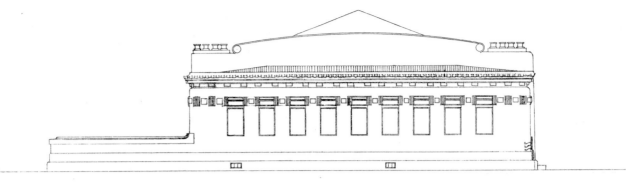

Ill. 47. Rossauerlände station on the Donaukanallinie (built 1900): View from the road.

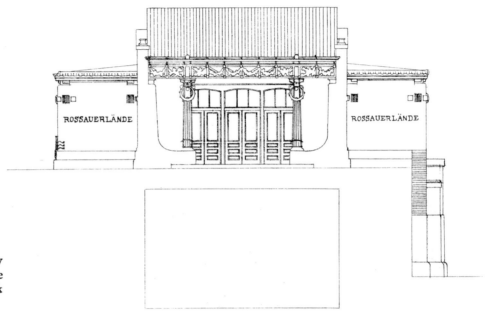

Ill. 48. Rossauerlände station: Front view showing the towpath level (right) and the maximum dimensions for the rolling stock (bottom centre).

Ill. 49. Rossauerlände station: View shows section of the promenade above the track.

Ill. 46. Friedensbrücke (formerly Brigittabrücke) station on the Donaukanallinie (built 1900-1): Capital of one of the pillars in the ticket section.

Ill. 50. Rossauerlände station with the Danube Canal in the foreground.

Ill. 51. Schottenring station on the Donaukanallinie (built 1900-1): View of the station looking towards the Danube Canal (top) and ground-plan (bottom).

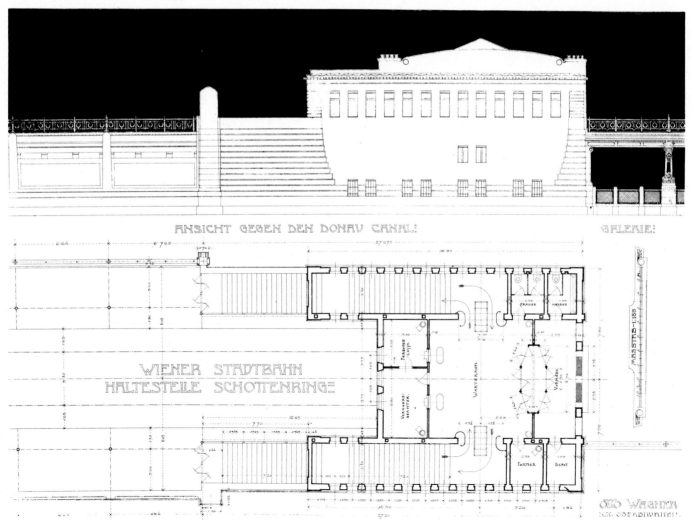

ANSICHT GEGEN DEN DONAU CANAL.   GALERIE.

WIENER STADTBAHN
HALTESTELLE SCHOTTENRING.

OTTO WAGNER

Ill. 52. Rossauerlände station and stairs leading to the towpath.

METROPOLITAN

From *Illuminations*

From the indigo straits to Ossian's seas, on pink and orange sands washed by the vinous sky, crystal boulevards have just risen and crossed, immediately occupied by poor young families who get their food at the greengrocers'. Nothing rich.—The city!

From the bituminous desert, in headlong flight with the sheets of fog spread in frightful bands across the sky, that bends, recedes, descends, formed by the most sinister black smoke that Ocean in mourning can produce, flee helmets, wheels, boats, rumps.—The battle!

Raise your eyes: that arched wooden bridge; those last truck gardens of Samaria; those faces reddened by the lantern lashed by the cold night; silly Undine in her noisy dress, down by the river; those luminous skulls among the rows of peas,—and all the other phantasmagoria —the country.

Roads bordered by walls and iron fences that with difficulty hold back their groves, and frightful flowers probably called ,loves and doves, Damask damning languorously,—possessions of magic aristocracies ultra-Rhenish, Japanese, Guaranian, still qualified to receive ancestral music—and there are inns that now never open any more,— there are princesses, and if you are not too overwhelmed, the study of the stars —the sky.

The morning when with Her you struggled among the glitterings of snow, those green lips, those glaciers, black banners and blue beams, and the purple perfumes of the polar sun.—Your strength.

Arthur Rimbaud

Ill. 53. Bridge across the Zeile (Gürtellinie, not far from its junction with the Wientallinie; opened in 1898).

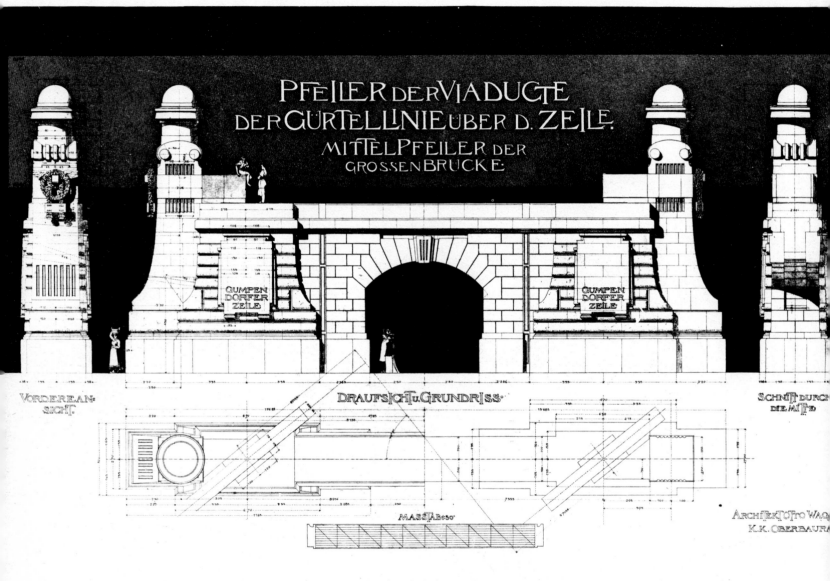

Ill. 54. Bridge across the Zeile. Drawing and ground-plan of the central arch.

Ill. 55. Bridge across the Zeile. Note the oblique position of the central arch.

Ill. 56. Bridge across the Döblinger Hauptstrasse (Gürtellinie).

Ill. 57. Scale drawing showing the positions for the bridge's 'decoration's.

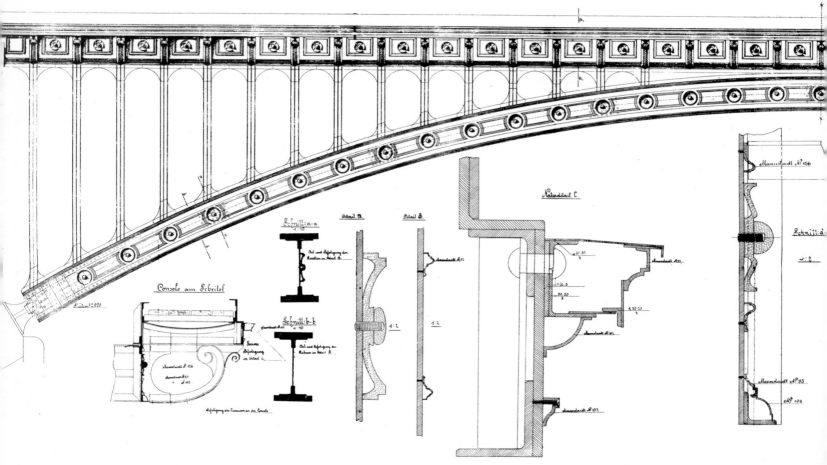

Ill. 58. Gumpendorfer Strasse station on the Gürtellinie (built 1896-7).

Ill. 59. Gumpendorfer Strasse station: Ground-plan (street level).

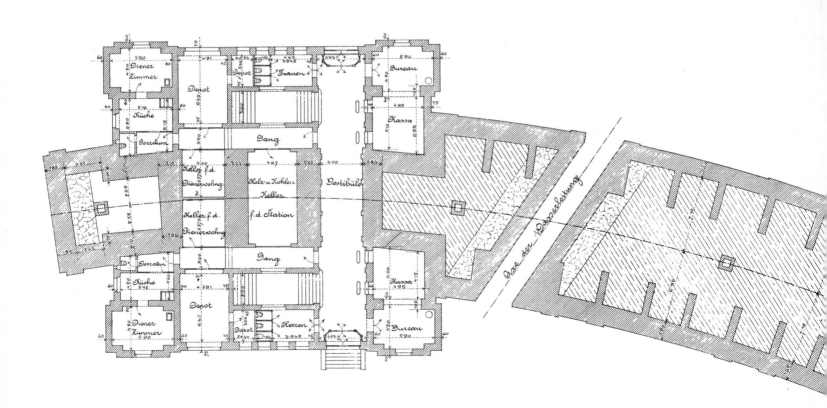

Ill. 60. Gumpendorfer Strasse station. View from the dome of the church of Maria vom Siege.

Ill. 61. Josefstädter Strasse station on the Gürtellinie (built 1896).

Ill. 62. Josefstädter Strasse station: Front view.

Ill. 63. Josefstädter Strasse station: View of platforms.

Ills. 64, 65. Alser Strasse station on the Gürtellinie (built 1896-7).

Ill. 66. Bridge across the Währinger Strasse on the Gürtellinie. The Währinger Strasse station is on the farther side of the bridge.

Ill. 67. Radetzkyplatz station on the line to the IInd district (built 1899, now demolished).

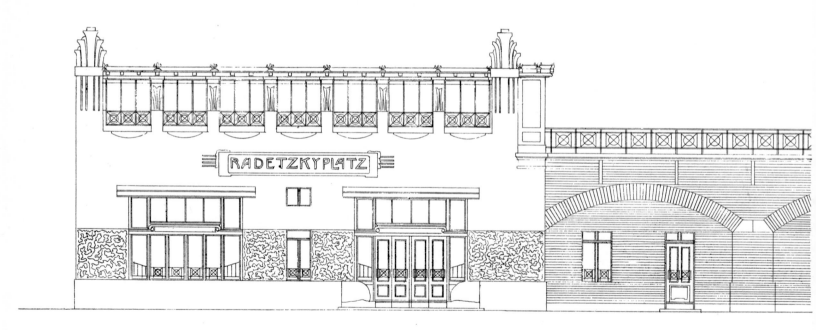

THE BUILDINGS ON THE DANUBE CANAL

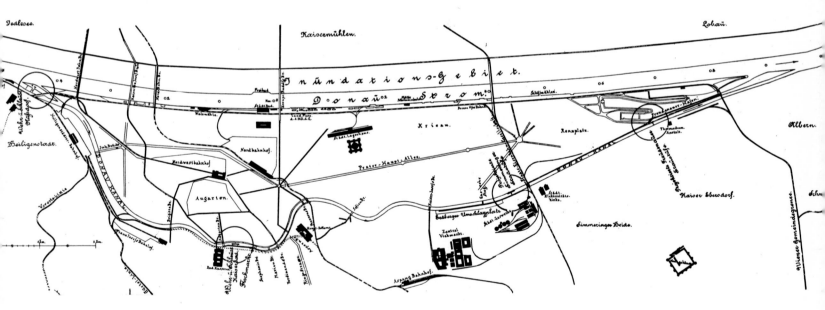

Ill. 68. General plan of the Danube Canal. The four circles mark (from left to right) the Nussdorf Dam and sluice-gate, the Kaiserbad Dam and the dams at Simmering and Freudenau. The Simmering and Freudenau schemes were abandoned but Wagner was responsible for both the Nussdorf and the Kaiserbad installations and also for the quayside installations between the Augartenbrücke (on the map, in the second circle from the left) and the rail bridge of the line to the IInd district. Those sections of the Stadtbahn which run alongside the Danube Canal are shown on the map by a dotted line.

The Viennese Transport Bill of 1892 stipulated that the construction of the Stadtbahn and the regulation of the river Wien and the Danube Canal were to be undertaken simultaneously. The canal was to be enlarged and made navigable for shipping irrespective of the state of the tide and was then to be used as a commercial harbour, especially in the winter months. Between 1894 and 1908 the commission responsible for the regulation of the Danube, to which Wagner had been appointed artistic adviser, built two of the four projected sluice-gate installations and also the quayside installations between the Augartenbrücke and the Verbindungsbahnbrücke (see *Ill. 68*). The architect was of course Wagner.

Work was first started in Nussdorf, which lies at the upper entrance to the Danube Canal. Originally it was intended that this monumental sluice-gate should simply complement the ship caisson constructed by von Engerth in the course of the earlier regulation of the Danube (1869-75). Very soon, however, von Engerth's installation proved quite unnecessary. Wagner's sluice-gate effectively protected the low-lying areas of the city, the principal municipal canals and, above all, the low-level sections of the Stadtbahn which ran at the same height as the new quays, from flooding; it also kept the canal free from drift ice. In 1898, after the works in Nussdorf had been completed, the quayside installations were erected in the more central parts of the town. Wagner built new quays on the banks of the canal, which were separated from the town

(either by retaining walls or by the open tunnels of the Stadtbahn with the promenades above them) and were used as open-air markets. It was not until 1901 that this section of the Stadtbahn was brought into commission. The loyal address presented to the emperor by the Academy in 1898 contained a drawing of the proposed quayside installations and the replanned Stubenviertel behind it *(Ill. 89)*.

None of the bridges which Wagner designed for the Danube Canal was ever commissioned. He made his first design for the Ferdinandsbrücke, which he had hoped to build in conjunction with the quayside installations, in 1896. In 1905 he made a second design *(Ills. 91, 92)* and, when the municipality decided that the weight-bearing members of this bridge, which rose up above the road surface in a suspended-deck construction, were unsightly, he made a third design before the year was out. In 1904 Wagner had also designed the Vindobonabrücke *(Ill. 90)* and in 1917, shortly before his death, he planned the conversion of the Brigittabrücke.

The Kaiserbad Dam *(Ills. 93-109)*, which was built next to the Schottenring station, was the last of the new installations on the canal. The most interesting part of this dam from an architectural point of view, the control building, was built in 1906-7. The sluice at Kaiserbad has been dismantled and it is to be feared that the control building, which has been allowed to fall into a very bad state of repair, may suffer a similar fate when the Danube Canal express route is built.

Ill. 69. Nussdorf Dam and administration block: Preliminary design (1894). View is downstream with the Danube in the background.

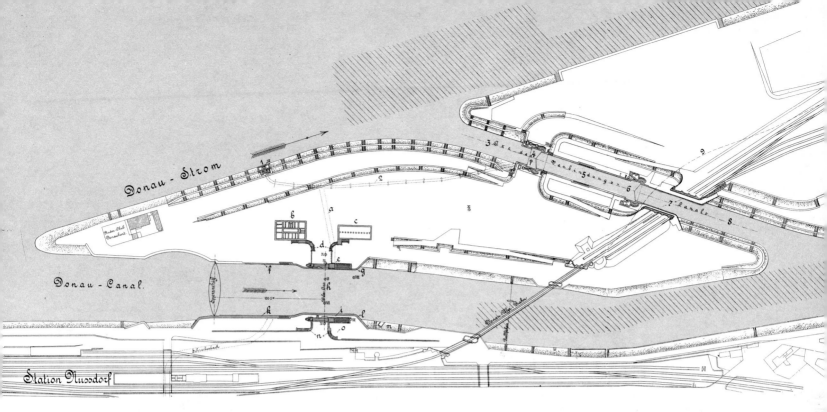

Ill. 70. Ground-plan of the Nussdorf Dam and sluice installation (built 1894-8). Key: b = foundations of the administration block, c = foundations of the chain storehouse, d and n = steps leading from street and bridge level to quay level, e and i = abutments for the dam, f-g and k-l = quay retaining walls, h = dam, 5 = sluice, 4 and 6 = upper and lower ends of sluice, 7 = railway bridge across the link canal.

Ill. 71. Nussdorf Dam and administration block.

The Nussdorf installation also incorporates an administration block and a chain storehouse. These were built on the island *(Ill. 70)*, which is linked with the Nussdorf bank by the bridge surmounting the dam *(Ill. 69)*. Both buildings stand at quayside level, which is one storey below the level of the bridge. Two flights of steps give access to the bridge from the island quay. On the opposite side of the canal the deck of the bridge is level with the approach road. The ground floor of the chain storehouse was fitted out as a repair shop and smithy. The administration block was finished in white stucco while the storehouse was faced with white clinkers. The ground floor walls of the two buildings, the walls of the dam, the sluice and the adjoining quays were made of granite blocks, 40,000 in all. 'The roofing, which was being used for the first time and which *(mutatis mutandis)* promised to "last for ever"', Wagner said, 'consisted of a mixture of iron, monnier, asphalt, gravel and hardcore'. The administration block is surmounted by an observation post. The dam is supported by three main vertical trusses, the approach road lying between two of these. Between them the foundations and abutments have to resist the pressure exerted by a head of water 40 metres wide and anything up to 10 metres high. The abutments, are surmounted by pylons. They are 20 metres wide and rest on foundations sunk by the compressed-air process. The two bronze lions were executed by Rudolf Weyr. The moving parts of the dam consist of iron uprights suspended from the underside of the bridge, which can be rotated on powerful steel axles and are raised and lowered by means of chains. When the dam is open they are accommodated immediately beneath the transverse girder. When it is closed they are lowered into their

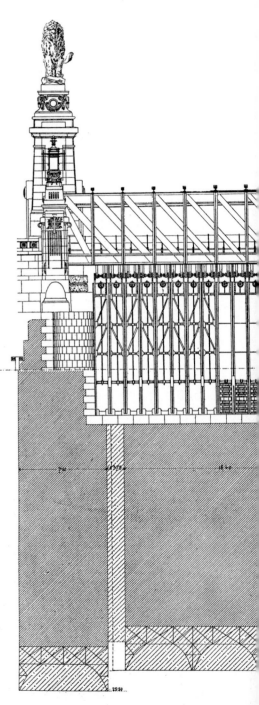

Ill. 72. Nussdorf administration block with the Danube Canal in the foreground.

Ill. 73. Drawing of the Nussdorf Dam and transverse section of the Danube Canal above the dam showing the foundations for the abutments and for the dam.

vertical position, where they serve as guides for the metal plates which actually control the flow of water. These plates are operated by a portable crane, the water level in the canal being governed both by the number of plates in use and their height in the water. The mechanism is accurate to within centimetres.

Wagner's Nussdorf installation was one of the architectural sensations of its day. The work on the foundations, which involved a number of entirely new techniques and was executed with astonishing precision, engaged the attention of bridge builders from far and wide. This is hardly surprising, for the foundations were sunk to a depth of 25 metres. (A detailed study of caisson disease was a by-product of the work.) The construction site was very large: 4.3 kilometres of wide gauge railway track were built on it.

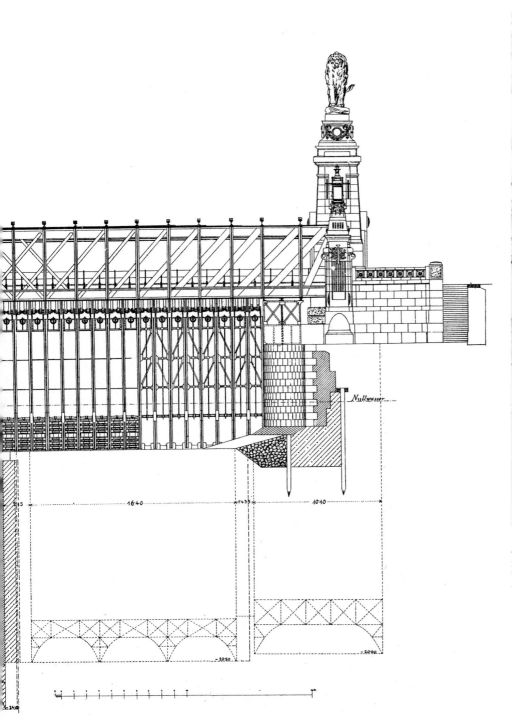

Ill. 74. Nussdorf Dam. The chains for raising the dam can be seen beneath the bridge. The bronze lion is one of a pair executed by Rudolf Weyr.

VIRIBUS
UNITIS.

Ill. 75. Nussdorf Dam: Sectional drawing showing one of the abutments.

Ill. 76. Nussdorf Dam: Administration block and chain storehouse.

Ill. 77. Photograph of the southern abutment which was sunk by the compressed-air process in the winter of 1895. The stone blocks set in the stonework of the caisson formed the joint with the dam's foundations.

Ill. 78. Nussdorf Dam: View of the construction site in the autumn of 1896. The southern caisson is being sunk to the bed of the canal. Photograph taken looking upstream.

Ills. 79, 80. Nussdorf Dam, open and closed. The administration block is on the right of the picture. The timber casing and glass roof were introduced at a later stage to protect the portable crane. Photograph taken looking upstream.

Ill. 81. Nussdorf Dam: Underside of bridge and abutment.

Ill. 82. Nussdorf Dam: Platform on the abutment with bridge girder bolted to it.

Ill. 83. Nussdorf administration block (back centre) with steps leading from the bridge to quayside level (front) and chain storehouse (right).

Ill. 84. Nussdorf Dam: Steps leading down from the bridge to quayside level.

Ill. 85. Chain storehouse and administration block with abutment in the foreground.

Ill. 86. Nussdorf administration block, with the pylons of the dam in the background, seen from across the Danube.

Ill. 87. Nussdorf Dam: Ground-plan of the granite foundations.

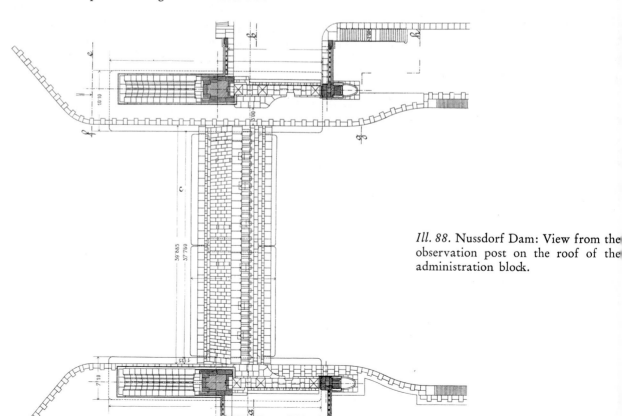

Ill. 88. Nussdorf Dam: View from the observation post on the roof of the administration block.

Ill. 89. Drawing (1897) showing the quayside installations, the Stubenviertel and the new canal bridges. This drawing was appended to the loyal address presented to Emperor Francis Joseph by the Academy on the occasion of his jubilee. The Aspernbrücke, which was planned as an extension of the Ringstrasse, is in the foreground, the Ferdinandsbrücke is in the background.

Ill. 90. Vindobonabrücke (1904). The bridge was planned as an extension of the Rotenturmstrasse.

Ill. 91. Ferdinandsbrücke (1905) with suspended-deck type of arch. The building on the left of the picture is the newly designed Stadtbahn station.

Ill. 92. Ferdinandsbrücke with suspended-deck type of arch. Reinforced concrete pylons faced with white and gold glazed tiles; balustrades and figures in tombac.

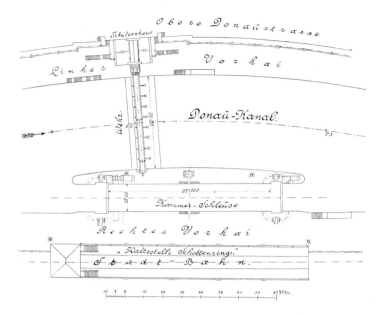

Ill. 93. Ground-plan of the Kaiserbad Dam (built 1904-8).

The Kaiserbad Dam was built just opposite the Schotten-ring Stadtbahn station which is on the border of the 1st district. Its sluice, which is identical with that at Nussdorf, is separated from the Danube Canal by an island faced on all sides with granite. This island housed the automatic switching gear which operated the sluice-gates. The Kaiserbad Dam produced an adequate depth of water even at the upper end of the canal at Nussdorf.

The control building on the north bank is a strictly functional structure (*Ills. 94-103, 106*). The central part of the upper floor and the whole of the attic, which had a section projecting beyond the general line of the building at two points, were occupied by a fixed crane fitted with a winch (*Ills. 104, 105*). This crane was used to raise and lower the two independent frame constructions (*Ills. 106-9*) which together formed the dam and which could be dropped into a cavity in the bed of the canal, the upright members of the frames being pivoted at the bottom and flexibly mounted on narrow bridges at the top. When the dam was raised these bridges joined up in the middle and, with the help of two short link pieces at either end, connected the control building with the island. This bridge was fitted with rails to receive the special car for transporting the sluice-plates and the portable sluice-crane, which were both housed on the ground floor of the control building. This floor also contained the storeroom and a tool shop. The cabin for the driver of the fixed crane was situated at the front of the attic, which was made almost entirely of glass (*Ills. 102, 103*).

Ill. 94. Control building at the Kaiserbad Dam (built 1906-7): View from the road.

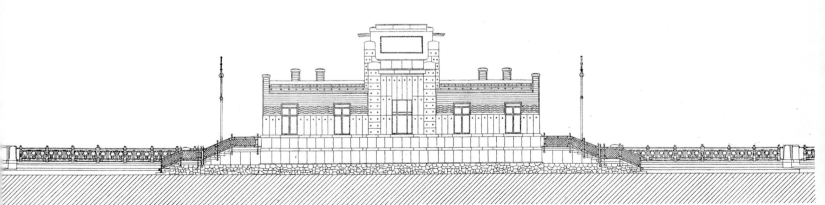

Ill. 95. Control building: View of the underside of the crane driver's cabin (top) and the balcony (bottom). The floor of the balcony incorporated the final section of the supporting girders for the fixed crane.

Ill. 96. Kaiserbad Dam: Transverse section of the Danube Canal above the installation showing the control building, the dam and the island. One of the platforms of Schottenring Stadtbahn station appears on the right of the drawing.

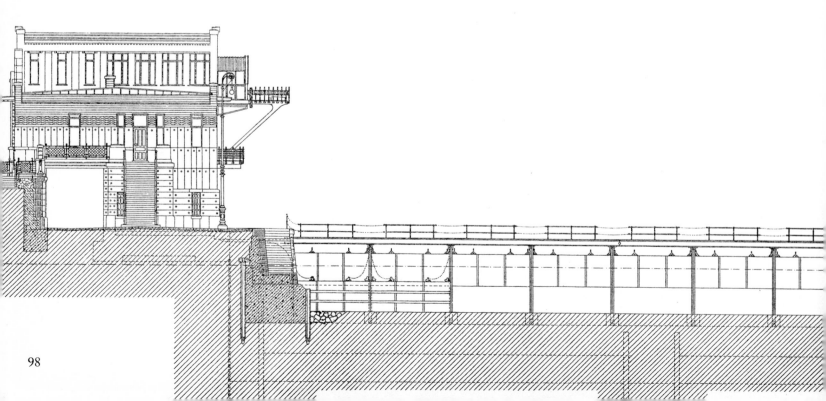

Ill. 97. Control building: View downstream.

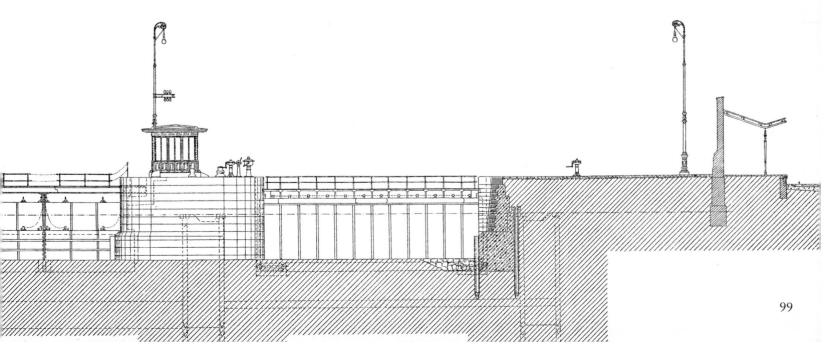

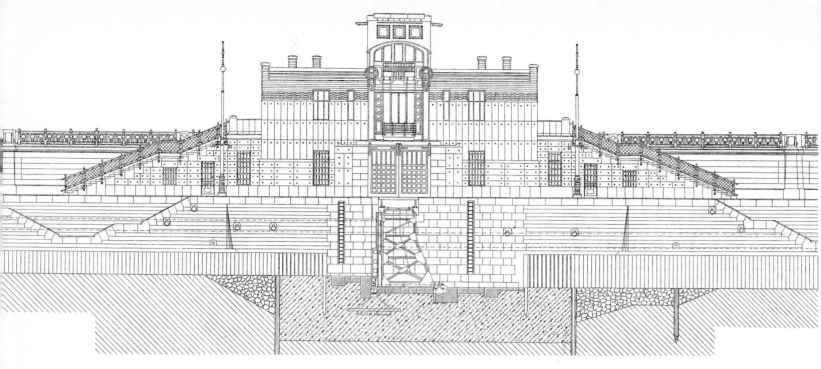

Ill. 98. Kaiserbad Dam: Transverse section of the sluicegate with view of the control building as seen from the canal.

Ill. 99. Ground-plan of control building (street level).

Ill. 100. Ground-plan of control building (quayside level).

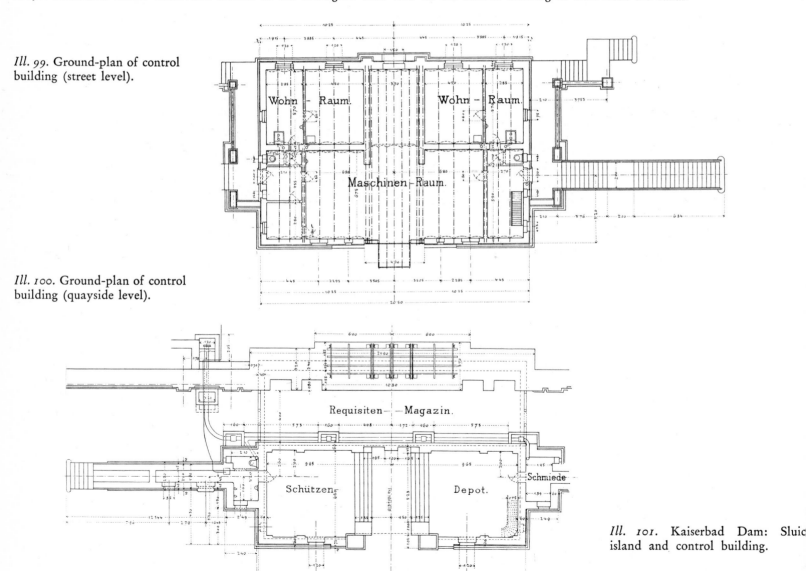

Ill. 101. Kaiserbad Dam: Sluic[e] island and control building.

Ill. 102. Control building: Granite quay-side wall and plinth
surmounted by sheets of white
marble bolted to the wall with
a band of tiles (cobalt blue offset by white wavy line) immediately beneath the eaves. The
bars on the window are slightly
convex.

Ill. 103. Detail of control building: Projecting cabin for crane driver
with corrugated copper roof.

Ill. 104. Construction drawing of the fixed crane.

Ill. 105. Assembly of the fixed crane. Photograph taken on the
construction site.

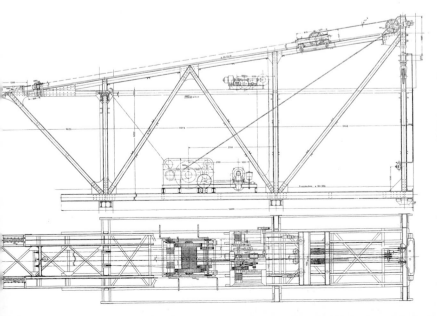

Ill. 106. Control building. Note the sluice-crane in the open door of the storeroom.

Ills. 107, 108. Raising the dam into position.

Ill. 109. Kaiserbad Dam: A full head of water. Note the position of the sluice-crane.

RESIDENTIAL
AND BUSINESS HOUSES

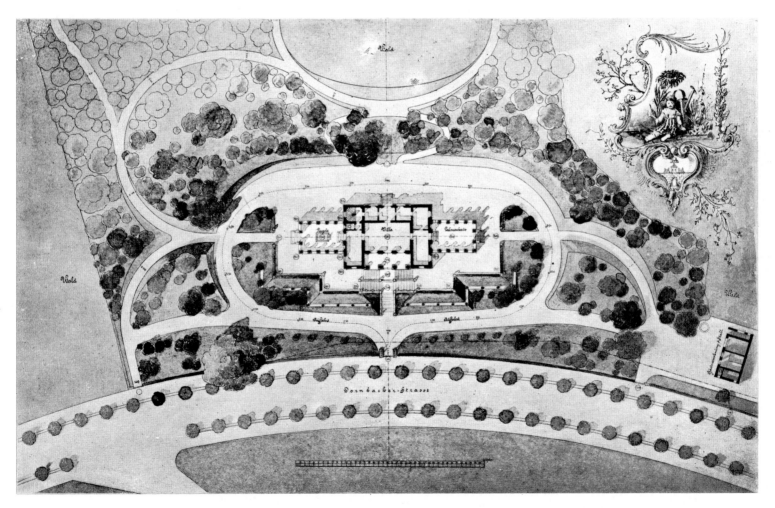

Ill. 110. The first Villa Wagner, Hüttelbergstrasse 26 (built 1886-8): General plan and ground-plan. The pergola on the left was converted into a studio in 1900; the pergola on the right, which was originally a conservatory, was converted into a living room in 1895.

Ill. 111. The first Villa Wagner.

Wagner always asked his first-year students at the Academy to design 'an apartment house of the most ordinary kind'. He regarded municipal dwellings as 'concentrations of cells, whose smooth façades—disrupted as they were by a multiplicity of matching windows'—needed the 'fortunate disruption' afforded by 'artistic' buildings with specialised functions, just as these needed a uniform environment. In point of fact, however, if we disregard the (numerous) early works, Wagner's apartment buildings—which, according to his theory, needed to be 'disrupted'—actually helped to disrupt the monotony and confusion of the municipal environment. Following the apartment house at Universitätsstrasse 12 (*Ill. 118*), he built in groups of two or three houses; he always complied with the town planning regulations and he was himself both builder and architect. In 1890-1 he put up a group of three houses on Rennweg and the central house in this group (No. 3, or Palais Hoyos) became his own town residence (*Ills. 119-22*). Unfortunately the façade of another of these (No. 1) has since been altered beyond recognition. In 1898-9 Wagner built a further group of three apartment houses on the corner of the Wienzeile and the Köstlergasse (*Ills. 128-38*), for which he used different façades, in different price brackets, and also introduced an experimental layout and street corner design. Although Wagner was able to employ weatherproof finishes on quite a few of his buildings he was able to use the 'polychrome façade' (whose durable qualities he had long and loudly proclaimed) on only one occasion: the Majolica House, Wienzeile 40, (*Ills. 128-31*), which he built on his own account. Finally, between 1909 and 1912, he built the two adjoining houses on the corner of the Neustiftgasse and the Döbler-gasse (*Ills. 139-42*), whose façades provide the best illustration of the smooth surfaces on which he was always insisting.

Perhaps there is no such thing as a revolutionary design for an apartment house. At all events, Wagner did not produce one. It is misleading when critics try to compensate for the traditionalism of his early apartment houses by crediting him with special achievements in this sphere. The houses which he designed for his own personal needs are far more interesting. These were the Palais Hoyos, already mentioned, and the two villas on the Hüttelbergerstrasse, (which were not in his possession at the same time). The first of the villas, No. 26, built in 1886-88 (*Ills. 110-17*), was a spacious and dignified residence which, despite all the rumours to the contrary, was never intended for Crown Prince Rudolph. The second, No. 28 (*Ills. 144-51*), built in 1912-13, was a relatively modest but by no means ungenerous building.

In 1895 Wagner built two business buildings each with wall glass curtain projecting beyond the line of the building from street level to the top of the first floor. Of these the Ankerhaus on Graben (*Ills. 124-7*) is still well preserved, apart from the ground floor. But the Neumann department store on the Kärntnerstrasse (*Ill. 123*) no longer exists. Originally the front façade of the store consisted of a series of display windows surmounted by a white marble rendering decorated with gilded porcelain while the inner courtyard was covered by a glass shell suspended on cables. The department store which Wagner designed for the Karlsplatz in 1904 (see *Ill. 217*), was never built. In his article "Vienna After the War" he also proposed a chain of co-operative stores to meet the needs of the various districts. His plans for these stores have been lost.

Ill. 112. First Villa Wagner: Entrance portal. The pillars of the balustrade were surmounted by coloured porcelain.

Ill. 113. First Villa Wagner: Lateral section of the building. The garden gate is on the extreme left.

Ill. 114. (overleaf) First Villa Wagner before the conversion of the pergolas.

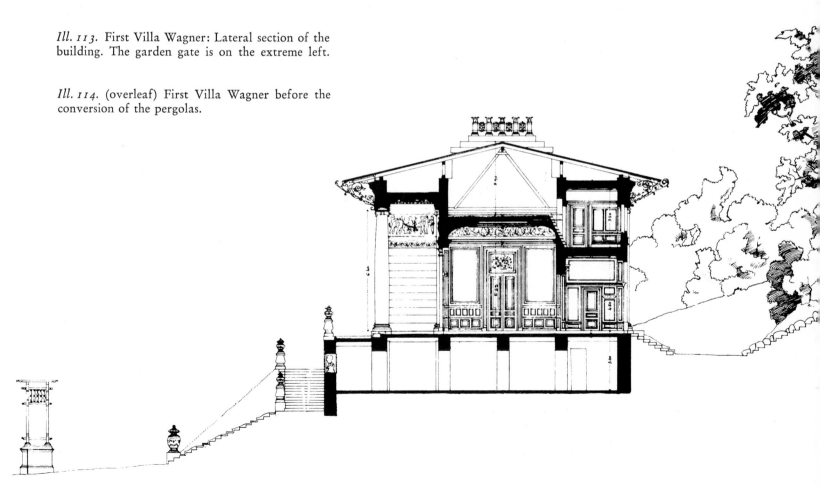

Ill. 115. First Villa Wagner: Exterior of the pergola which was converted into a studio in 1900.

Ill. 116. First Villa Wagner: Interior of the studio. The window, "Autumn Landscape in the Wienerwald", was by Adolf Böhm.

Ill. 117. First Villa Wagner: Water trough on the outer wall of the studio wing.

Ill. 118. Apartment house, Universitätsstrasse 12 (built 1888).

114

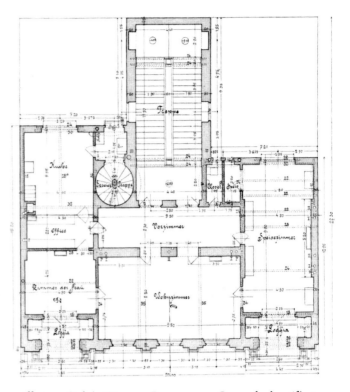

Ill. 119. Palais Wagner, Rennweg 3 (later renamed Palais Hoyos; built 1890-1). Front view.

Ill. 120. Palais Wagner, Rennweg 3. Perspective of section of façade.

Ill. 121. Palais Wagner, Rennweg 3. Ground-plan (first floor level).

Ill. 122. Palais Wagner, Rennweg 3. Ground-plan of street level.

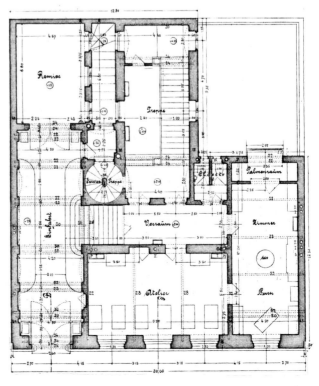

Ill. 123. Neumann department store, Kärntner Strasse (built 1895, now demolished): View of façade and ground-plan (street level).

Ill. 124. The Anker building on Graben (built 1895): View of the photographic studio.

Ill. 125. The Anker building: Ground-plan (street level).

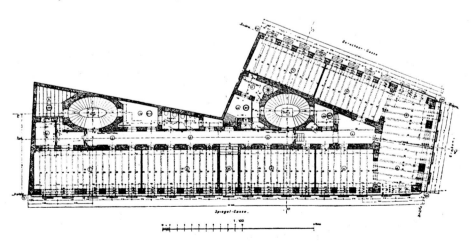

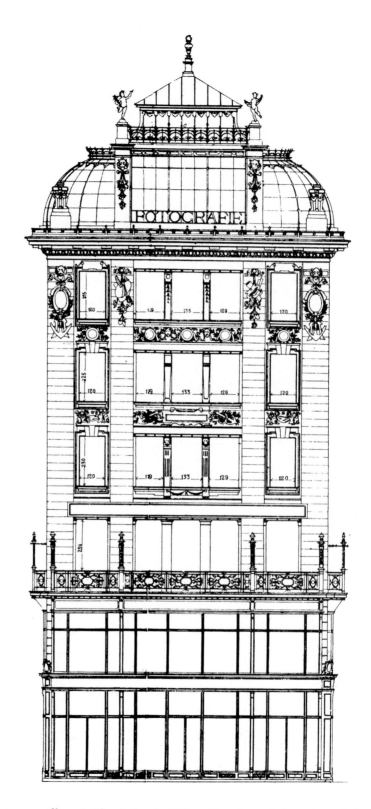

Ill. 126. The Anker building: Drawing of the principal façade.

Ill. 127. The Anker building: Photograph of the principal façade. The house on the right is a town residence built by Johann Lukas von Hilde-brandt.

Ill. 128. Apartment house, Linke Wienzeile 40 (Majolica house, built 1898-9). The house on the right is No. 38. The bronze half-length figure above the gutter is one of four by Othmar Schimkowitz. Originally the figures were gilded.

Ill. 129. Apartment house, Linke Wienzeile 38 (built 1898-9). On the left the Majolica house, on the right the apartment house, Köstlergasse 3.

Ill. 130. Apartment house, Linke Wienzeile 40 and 38.

Ill. 131. Apartment house, Linke Wienzeile 40: Detail of façade.

Ill. 132. Apartment house, Linke Wienzeile 38. The walls were finished in gilded stucco, the gilded medallions were by Kolo Moser.

Ill. 133. Apartment houses, Linke Wienzeile 38: Street corner design.

Ill. 134. Apartment house, Linke Wienzeile 38: Banister and guard rails for the lift shaft.

Ills. 135, 136. Apartment house, Linke Wienzeile 40: Staircase and lift gates.

Ill. 137. Apartment house, Linke Wienzeile 38: Entrance at Köstlergasse 1.

Ill. 138. Apartment house, Linke Wienzeile 38: Cellar hatch.

Ills. 139, 140. Apartment house, Neustiftgasse 40 (built 1909-10). Rendered façade decorated with strips of black glazed tiles.

Ill. 141. Apartment house, Döblergasse 4 (built 1912 next to Neustiftgasse 40): Staircase.

Ill. 142. Apartment house, Döblergasse 4: Entrance. Wooden doors partially faced with aluminium.

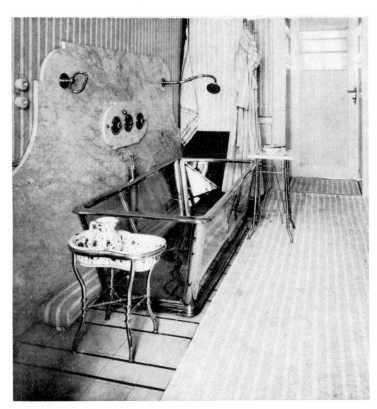

Ill. 143. Wagner's bathroom. The glass bath was shown at the jubilee exhibition in Vienna in 1898 and later installed in Köstlergasse 3.

Ill. 144. Second Villa Wagner, Hüttelbergstraße 28. (Preliminary design, 1905).

Ill. 145. Second Villa Wagner (built 1912-3).

Ill. 146. Second Villa Wagner: Ground-plan (mezzanine level) and general plan.

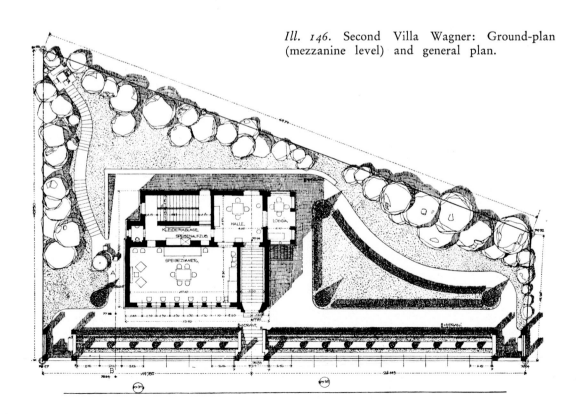

Ill. 147. Second Villa Wagner.

Ill. 148. Second Villa Wagner drawing showing vertical section through the entrance door and detail of the underside of the eaves for the house and the loggia.

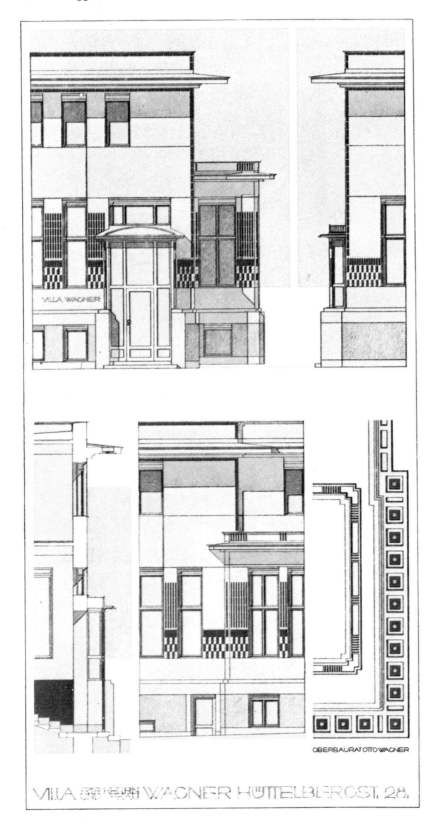

Ill. 149. Second Villa Wagner: Detail of façade showing the entrance door.

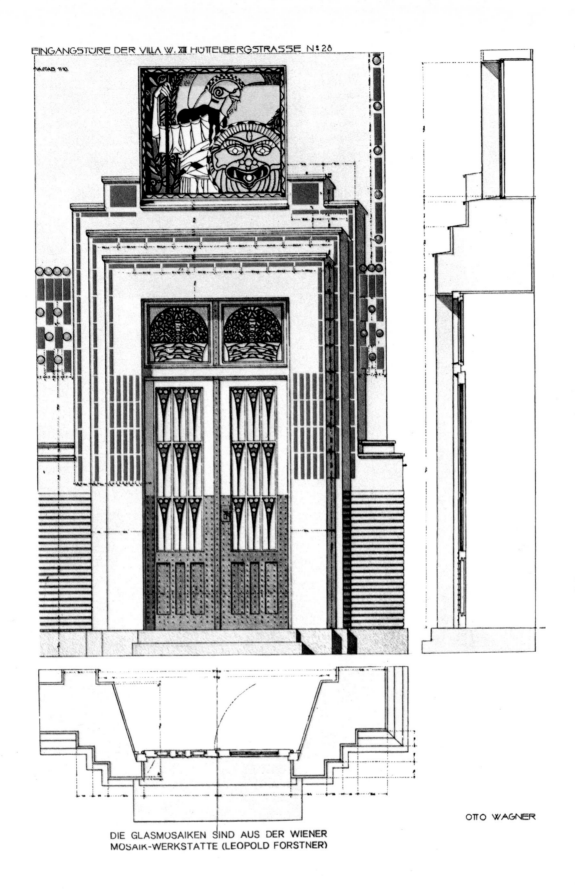

EINGANGSTÜRE DER VILLA W. XIII HÜTELBERGSTRASSE N° 28

DIE GLASMOSAIKEN SIND AUS DER WIENER
MOSAIK-WERKSTÄTTE (LEOPOLD FORSTNER)

OTTO WAGNER

Ill. 150. Second Villa Wagner: Front view, perpendicular and horizontal sections of the entrance. Wooden doors faced with aluminium. The window above the doors was by Kolo Moser.

Ill. 151. (overleaf) Second Villa Wagner: Detail of the loggia. Façade faced with glazed tiles, which were fixed to the wall with aluminium bolts. The mosaics in the loggia were by Kolo Moser.

SANATORIA
AND HOTELS

Ill. 152. Lupus sanatorium (built 1910-13): Entrance wing.

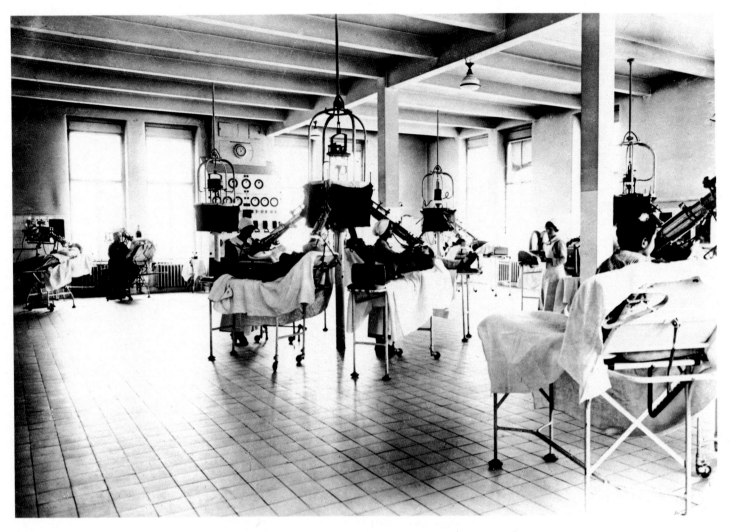

Ill. 153. Lupus sanatorium: Ray treatment section.

In the explanatory report which he appended to his plan for the general regulation of Vienna (1893) Wagner called for 'the even distribution of the municipal sanatoria—apart from those for epidemic diseases—throughout the entire city'. In the same report he also proposed that a mental hospital should be erected on the site Am Steinhof. The various pavilions for this installation were subsequently built there under the auspices of the Lower Austrian State Building Department between 1905 and 1907 and Wagner's general plan for the site (*Ill. 256*), which he had submitted with his competition design for the Church Am Steinhof, was consulted by the authorities. The Lupus sanatorium (*Ills. 152-7*), whose 'design specifications—particularly in matters of detail—naturally call for a number of different specialists', was built between 1910 and 1913 and is therefore one of Wagner's latest works. The external surfaces of the building were rendered and decorated with a blue edging consisting of glazed tiles set flush with the wall. As in the Post Office Savings Bank the ceilings were

beam and slab structures. A central feature was the arrangement of the beds, which stood in single rows along one side of the wards. In his article, "Vienna After the War", Wagner recommended that this arrangement be used in all new sanatoria.

In his design, made in 1914, for a heliotherapeutic mountain sanatorium near Brixen (*Ill. 162*) Wagner succeeded in creating an even tighter layout than that employed in the Lupus sanatorium, which was already extremely well defined. The new installation was entirely symmetrical. The various sections, which all faced south to facilitate the open-air and sunbath treatment prescribed for the patients, were incorporated into a single elongated building. The staircases, which projected at right angles from the northern side of the building, gave access to the wards, which also had single rows of beds. Within the limits imposed by the structural system Wagner's use of space was extremely flexible, the size of the individual units being determined by the size of the beds and the amount of

Ill. 154. Lupus sanatorium: Entrance section. The glazed blue tiles are set flush with the wall surfaces.

space required for the beds to be wheeled to the sun-balconies on the southern side. The design allowed for an optional extension of the wards by the distance between five windows measured from centre to centre. During the First World War Wagner produced a design for 'a bungalow installation for convalescent soldiers which could later be used as a tuberculosis sanatorium'. In "Vienna After the War" he urged that tuberculosis sanatoria should be built near the major cities and suggested that these could subsequently be adapted for other types of hospital patient. In this way he hoped to deal with the various social evils one by one. Shortly before his death he designed a 'Haus des Kindes' (House for Children), which incorporated a day nursery for infants, a home for children in need of temporary care and a public kindergarten.

Wagner's hotel rooms, his Passagierzimmer (transit rooms), had much in common with the wards in a sanatorium: 'what is required of hotel accommodation in nearly all cases is a quiet, clean, hygienic room, where the guest is able to sleep undisturbed and attend to his physical needs'. And so, in place of 'the "princely apartments" which are usually requested', Wagner proposed carefully furnished single and double rooms of minimum size, which could be quickly and easily connected for all necessary purposes. In his view a good Viennese hotel, like those which he himself designed for the Ringstrasse (Hotel Wien, 1910, *Ills. 158-60*) and the Karlsplatz (1910-1, *Ill. 161*), should have 'not less than 400 and not more than 800 beds'. He considered that the 'genuine objects' provided in his rooms 'would give far greater comfort and create a stronger artistic impression and would certainly be an improvement on the frippery in current use'.

Ill. 155. Lupus sanatorium: Detail showing the staircase section which linked the front of the building with the side wing.

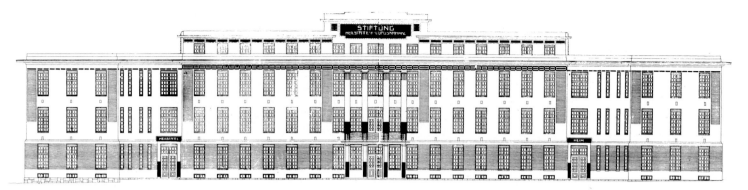

Ill. 156. Lupus sanatorium: Front view.

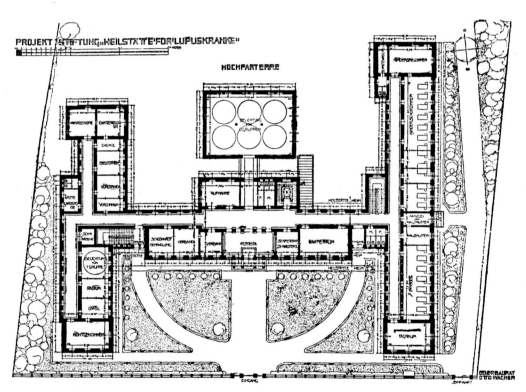

Ill. 157. Lupus sanatorium: Ground-plan (mezzanine level).

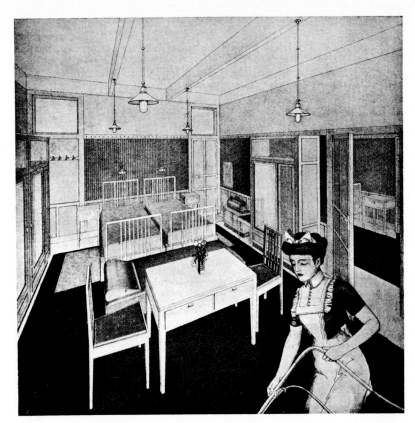

Ill. 158. Hotel Wien on the Ringstrasse (1910): Double room. The communicating door on the right gives access to a single room.

Ill. 159. Hotel Wien: Ground-plan of single and double room with inventory and perspective of the whole apartment.

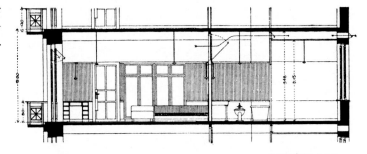

INVENTORY

1. CLOAKROOM
2. CURTAIN
3. CHEST WITH COPPER LID FOR SHOES AND CASES
4. BED
5. TAPESTRY
6. WASHABLE MAT
7. COUCH
8. CLUB ARMCHAIR
9. TABLE
10. WRITING DESK
11. DRESSING TABLE
12. EASY CHAIR
13. CHAIRS
14. MOVABLE WARDROBE WITH DRAWERS, HANGING SECTION, MIRROR AND HAT COMPARTMENT
15. SIMILAR WARDROBE BUT WITHOUT DRAWERS
16. BEDSIDE CUPBOARD WITH DRAWER
17. BATH
18. BIDET
19. TOILET
20. WASH TABLE
21. EASY CHAIR
22. GLASS SHELF
a) BORDERS OF CARPET
b) BORDERS OF MATS AND DUST-CLOTHS
c) ELECTRIC LAMPS.
ON THE WALL ABOVE THE WRITING DESK ARE A MAP OF VIENNA, A COPY OF THE TRAIN TIMETABLE, A LIST OF THE MOST IMPORTANT RAIL CONNECTIONS AND AN ELECTRIC CLOCK. ON THE WALL BY THE DOOR IS A LIST OF ROOM PRICES AND CHARGES FOR BREAKAGES.
I SCREENS
o HEATING

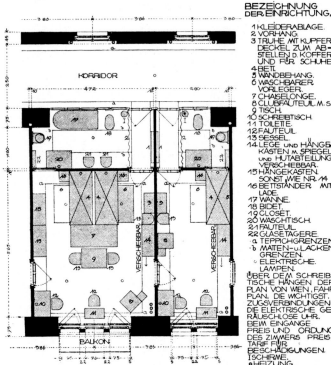

BEZEICHNUNG DER EINRICHTUNG.

1 KLEIDERABLAGE.
2 VORHANG.
3 TRUHE MIT KUPFER DECKEL ZUM AB-STELLEN D. KOFFER UND FÜR SCHUHE.
4 BETT.
5 WANDBEHANG.
6 WASCHBARER VORLEGER.
7 CHAISELONGE.
8 CLUBFAUTEUIL. M. S.
9 TISCH.
10 SCHREIBTISCH.
11 TOILETTE.
12 FAUTEUIL.
13 SESSEL.
14 LEGE UND HÄNGE-KASTEN M. SPIEGEL UND HUTABTEILUNG. VERSCHIEBBAR.
15 HÄNGEKASTEN. SONST WIE NR. 14.
16 BETTSTÄNDER MIT LADE.
17 WANNE.
18 BIDET.
19 CLOSET.
20 WASCHTISCH.
21 FAUTEUIL.
22 GLASETAGERE.
a TEPPICHGRENZEN.
b MATTEN- u. LACKEN-GRENZEN.
c ELEKTRISCHE LAMPEN.
ÜBER DEM SCHREIB-TISCHE HÄNGEN DER PLAN VON WIEN, FAHR-PLAN, DIE WICHTIGST. ZUGSVERBINDUNGEN DIE ELEKTRISCHE GE-RÄUSCHLOSE UHR. BEIM EINGANGE PREIS UND ORDUNG DES ZIMMERS PREIS TARIF FÜR BESCHÄDIGUNGEN.
I SCHIRME.
o HEIZUNG.

Ill. 160. Hotel Wien with the Ringstrasse in the foreground.

Ill. 161. Hotel on the Karlsplatz (1910-11): Preliminary sketch.

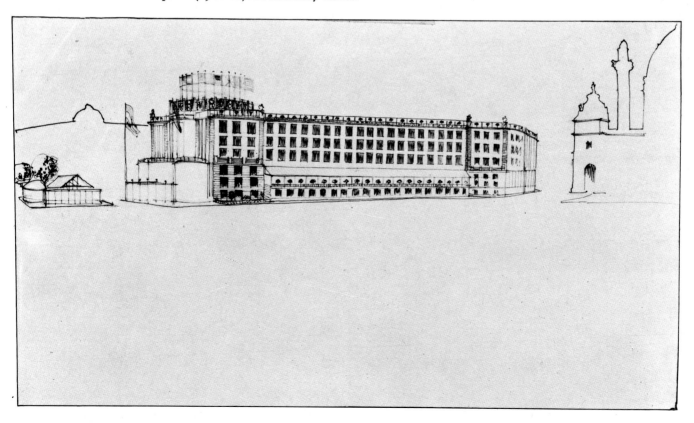

Ill. 162. Heliotherapeutic mountain sanatorium ("Palmschloss") near Brixen (1914). The consulting and treatment rooms are in the central section; the two sections on either side are occupied by wards with single rows of beds and sun balconies. The wards can be extended if required.

BANKS AND FINANCIAL INSTITUTIONS

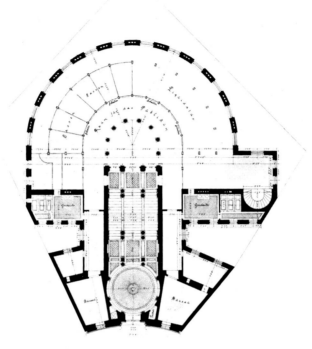

Ill. 163. Central offices of the Viennese Giro- und Kassenverein (Deposit and Current Account Banking Association). Wagner's competition design, 1880: Ground-plan.

Ill. 164. Central offices of the Viennese Giro- und Kassenverein. Winning competition design by Emil von Förster, 1880: Ground-plan.

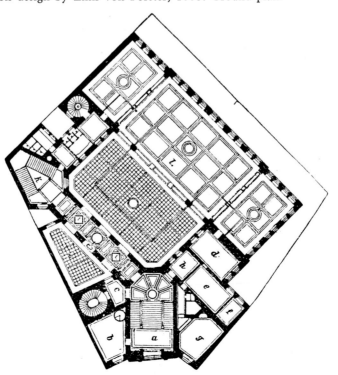

Ill. 165. Länderbank (Provincial Bank), built 1883-4: Light-well above the counter section.

Ill. 166. Länderbank: Second floor corridor. The windows on the left overlook the light-well.

Ill. 167. Länderbank: Counter section with glass roof.

Illustrations 163 and *164* show the contrast between the ground-plan of Wagner's competition design for the Viennese Giro- und Kassenverein building, which was placed third, and the wasteful ground-plan of the design by Emil von Förster, which was actually commissioned. The competition (1880) posed considerable problems, for the building site, which lay on the bend in the Rockhgasse, had an extremely short frontage. Wagner overcame these problems by planning his building around a semicircular counter section. The customers would have approached this counter from the inside of the semi-circle while the tellers would have had direct access to all of the front offices, which were to be set out adjacent to one another and parallel to the street and would therefore also be accessible from the rear.

This system was extremely flexible and Wagner subsequently adapted it for the Länderbank on the Hohenstaufengasse (*Ills. 165-8*) which was built in 1883-84. Wagner's admirers were particularly impressed by the way in which he resolved the difficulty posed by the sudden change in the axis of the Länderbank site. Like the circular foyer itself (which, incidentally, was integrated with considerable skill) the sections immediately above it formed the principal junctions of their particular floors. As these were ringed by offices they posed a light problem which Wagner solved by putting either a dome or a circular opening in the middle of each junction. The glass ceiling of the counter section, which was suspended from visible lattice-web beams, was also surmounted by a glass-roofed light-well. This well, which was two storeys high, lit the office corridors, which encircled it, by means of the wide and in some cases curved windows set in their outer walls. The partition walls in the offices were light and flexible. Part of the floor in the counter section was glazed and so served as a source of light for the rooms on the floor below. A similar system was used for the counter section of the Post Office Savings Bank, where the floor incorporated glazed panels.

In 1884 Wagner took part in the competition for the new offices for the Austrian Bodenkreditanstalt (Land Credit Association), but the commission again went to von Förster. If the trapezoid ground-plan of Wagner's design (*Ill. 169*) is imagined as a rectangle it will be seen to correspond very much to the entrance hall and central part of the first section of the Post Office Savings Bank (*Ill. 179*). In the competition for the Exchange building in Amsterdam (*Ills. 170, 171*), the 'competitor *par excellence*' as Wagner was called at the time, was again unsuccessful. Amsterdam's new Exchange was based on Berlage's design; it was described by Lux as a 'brutal brick warehouse'.

The Imperial and Royal Post Office Savings Bank, which was built in two stages, 1904-06 and 1910-12, (*Ills. 14-6, 172-200*), is rightly regarded as one of the showpieces of early modern architecture. It was the exterior which caused the greatest stir. Although he was always advocating the process, there were only three buildings on which Wagner was able to face all the external surfaces with thin sheets of white Sterzing marble. The Post Office was one of these. Wagner took immense pains over the detail of this building. For example, the marble sheet on the projecting faces were curved outwards so as to produce a plastic structuring of the horizontal plane. The foundation walls were faced with slabs of granite and the bolts holding them in position were countersunk. The result was to give them even greater prominence. The heads of all the bolts, the pillars of the entrance porch, the acroteria (by Othmar Schimkowitz) and the wreaths were made of aluminium.

The outer sections of all four sides of the Post Office Savings Bank were given over to single rows of offices, which opened inwards on to a continuous corridor 2.8 metres in width. The triple-naved counter section for the clearance of cheques was situated towards the front of the inner part of the building, where it was flanked by two parallel rows of pay offices, while the large pay office, which handled securities and bonds, occupied the area immediately behind it. Access to the large pay office, which was installed during the second stage of the construction programme, was from the rear of the building. In his original competition design of 1903, which defeated a field of thirty-six entrants (one of whom incidentally, had proposed a Viennese Belvedere Post Office building),

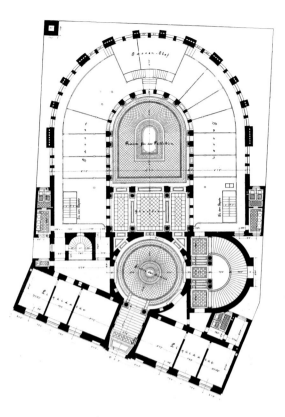

Ill. 168. Länderbank: Ground-plan.

Ill. 169. Bodenkreditanstalt (Land Credit Association), competition design, 1884: Ground-plan.

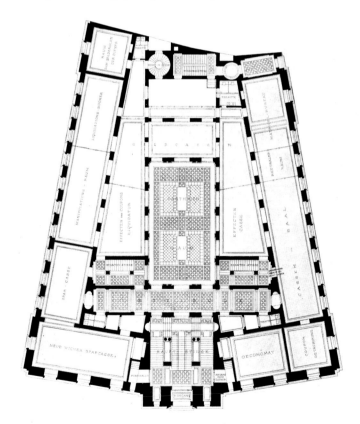

Ill. 170. The Exchange building in Amsterdam (Competition design, 1884): General view.

Ill. 171. The Exchange building in Amsterdam: Ground-plan.

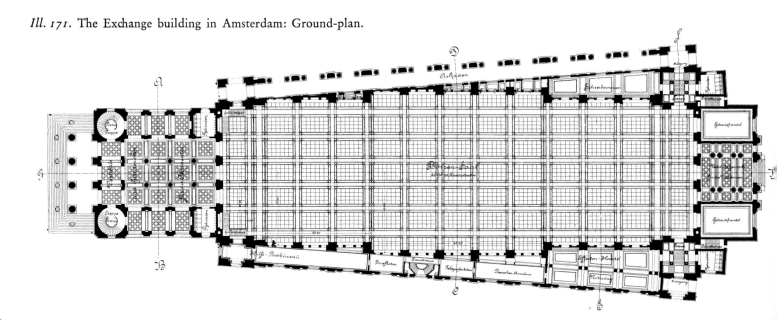

Ill. 172. Post Office Savings Bank (built 1904-6): Attic section above the main projecting face. The acroteria by Othmar Schimkowitz and the wreaths are in aluminium.

Wagner had incorporated a glass-roofed light-well after the style of the Länderbank and had suspended the three-part glass ceiling above the counter section from wire cables. In the final design both the light-well and the suspended ceiling were scrapped. The glass roof was then placed immediately above the glass ceiling and both were supported by fixed beams, which lay between the two surfaces. The heating system for the counter section (hot-air pipes with the famous aluminium 'blowers') was supplemented by special under-roof heating, which kept the roof free from snow. The walls of the courtyard were faced with ceramic tiles. Apart from the glass ceiling in the counter section all the ceilings in the building were made of reinforced concrete. The floors and the sawdust and cement mixture for the roof were laid on top of these without screeds. Most of the staircases were made of concrete or iron and were fitted with marble treads 3 centimetres thick. The walls of all rooms, corridors and staircases used by the general public were faced with marble or glass. The partition walls in the offices were moveable. The special furniture used throughout virtually the whole building was designed to a standard specification, although the materials, *i. e.*, timber, covers, metal fittings, etc., varied from one section to another. The Post Office Savings Bank is still in an excellent state of repair and functions perfectly in present day conditions.

Ill. 173. Post Office Savings Bank (Competition design, 1903): View of the main entrance. This design still featured the light-well surmounted by a glass roof.

Ill. 174. Post Office Savings Bank: Part of the main projecting face in perspective.

Ills. 175, 176. Post Office Savings Bank: Two drawings of the front façade. Above: Variant of the competition design. Below: Final design.

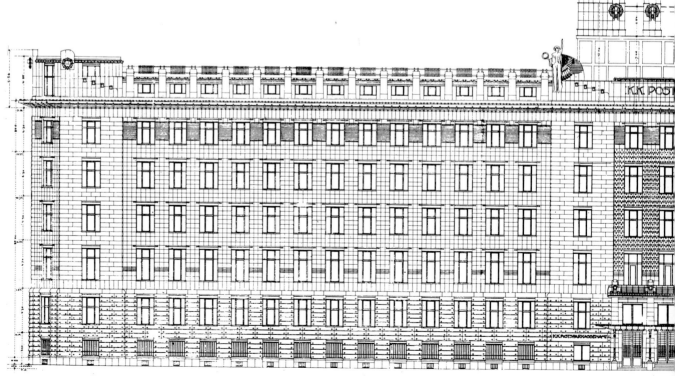

Ills. 177, 178. Post Office Savings Bank: Two views of the main entrance. The pillars supporting the porch are aluminium. The governor's rooms are situated behind the balcony.

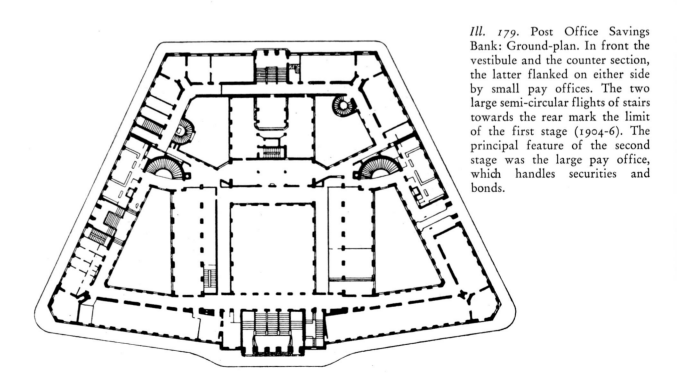

Ill. 179. Post Office Savings Bank: Ground-plan. In front the vestibule and the counter section, the latter flanked on either side by small pay offices. The two large semi-circular flights of stairs towards the rear mark the limit of the first stage (1904-6). The principal feature of the second stage was the large pay office, which handles securities and bonds.

180. Post Office Savings Bank: View from the War Ministry building.

CITIES II

From *Illuminations*

The official acropolis outdoes the most colossal conceptions of modern barbarity: impossible to describe the opaque light produced by the immutably gray sky, the imperial brightness of the buildings, and the eternal snow on the ground. With a singular taste for enormity, all the classical marvels of architecture have been reproduced, and I visit exhibitions of painting in premises twenty times as vast as Hampton Court. What painting! A Norwegian Nebuchadnezzar built the stairways of the government buildings; even the subordinates I saw were already prouder than ***, and I trembled at the aspect of the guardians of colossi and the building supervisors. By grouping the buildings around squares, courts and enclosed terraces, they have ousted the cabbies. The parks present primitive nature cultivated with superb art, there are parts of the upper town that are inexplicable: an arm of the sea, without boats, rolls its sleet-blue waters between quays covered with giant candelabra. A short bridge leads to a postern directly under the dome of the Sainte-Chapelle. This dome is an artistic structure of steel about fifteen thousand feet in diameter.

From certain points on the copper footbridges, on the platforms, on the stairways that wind around the markets and the pillars, I thought I might form an idea of the depth of the city! This is the prodigy I was unable to discover: what are the levels of the other districts below and above the acropolis? For the stranger of our day exploration is impossible. The business district is a circus in a uniform style with arcaded galleries. No shops are to be seen, but the snow of the roadway is trampled; a few nabobs, as rare as pedestrians on Sunday morning in London, are making their way toward a diamond diligence. A few red velvet divans: polar drinks are served of which the price varies from eight hundred to eight thousand rupees. At the thought of looking for theatres on this circus, I say to myself that the shops must contain dramas quite dismal enough. I suppose there is a police force; but the law must be so strange that I give up trying to imagine what adventurers can be like here.

The suburb, as elegant as a beautiful Paris street, is favoured with air like light. The democratic element counts a few hundred souls. There, too, the houses do not follow each other; the suburb loses itself queerly in the country, the "County", that fills the eternal west with forests and prodigious plantations where gentlemen savages hunt their news by the light they have invented.

Arthur Rimbaud

Ill. 181. Post Office Savings Bank: View of part of the front façade and the roof superstructure.

Ill. 182. Post Office Savings Bank: Detail of front façade illustrating the corner design. The roof railings are of aluminium. The attic facing consists of sheets of black glass.

Ill. 183. Post Office Savings Bank: Corner design. Note the pointed eaves and the curved marble plates on either edge, which mark the line of the projecting faces.

Ill. 184. Post Office Savings Bank: View of the inner courtyard showing the glass roof of the counter section and the superstructure on the roof. The walls of the courtyard were faced with white and black tiles.

Ill. 185. Post Office Savings Bank: View of the foundation walls, which were faced with granite slabs. The bolts had aluminium heads.

186, 187. Post Office Savings Bank: Two views of the staircase leading from the vestibule to the counter section. The
treads consist of slabs of marble 3 centimetres thick resting on indented concrete girders. Stair rails and ventilation ducts are
aluminium.

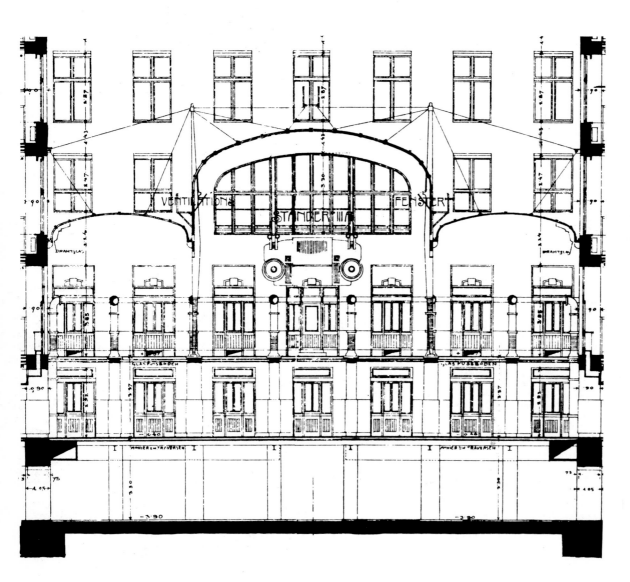

Ill. 188. Post Office Savings Bank: Sectional drawing of the counter section as designed for the competition. The ceiling was just a glass shell suspended from cables; in this design the whole of the inner courtyard was to have received a glass roof.

Ill. 189. Post Office Savings Bank: Counter section as seen from the vestibule of the governor's office. The glass span roof shown in *Ill. 184* is situated immediately above the glass ceiling. The rooms beneath the counter section were lit through the glazed panels in the floor.

Ill. 190. Post Office Savings Bank: Detail of the counter section.

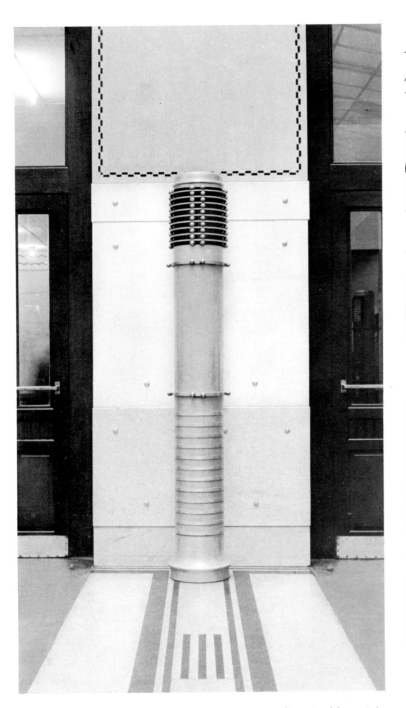

Ill. 191. Post Office Savings Bank: Aluminium hot-air 'blower' in the counter section.

Ill. 192. Post Office Savings Bank: Pillar in the counter section. The lower part is encased in aluminium.

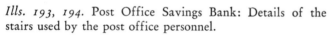

Ills. 193, 194. Post Office Savings Bank: Details of the stairs used by the post office personnel.

Ill. 195. Post Office Savings Bank: Corridor in one of the office sections. The stairs can be seen in the background.

Ill. 196. Post Office Savings Bank: Library.

Ill. 197. Post Office Savings
Bank: Vice-governor's room.

Ill. 198. Post Office Savings Bank: Detail of vice-governor's room.

Ill. 199. Post Office Savings Bank: Conference room. The portrait of Emperor Francis Joseph is by Wilhelm List.

Ill. 200. Post Office Savings Bank: Stairs leading to the large pay office for securities and bonds (second stage, built 1910-2).

MUSEUMS, SCHOOLS AND LIBRARIES

Ill. 201. " 'Artibus', an Ideal Design for a Museum enclave" (1880): General plan.

Ill. 202. " 'Artibus', an Ideal Design for a Museum enclave":
Bird's-eye view.

In 1876 Wagner produced a design for a private museum for
an anonymous client. Four years later he created his "Artibus".
This 'ideal design for a museum enclave' (*Ills. 201, 202*) was
based on an idea which he had first conceived as a young
man. The central feature was a 'pantheon of art', which stood
on the bank of an artificial lake and was surrounded by
colonnades with triumphal arches, an elaborate museum wing
and a library wing. A series of waterfalls were laid out on
the rising ground directly behind the pantheon. In his later
museum designs Wagner concentrated more on the immediate
environment, *i. e.*, the exhibition rooms, which he insisted must
always be subordinated to the actual exhibits. Although the
design for a Museum of Plaster Casts, (1896) on the site later

used for Olbrich's Secession, was not as well integrated as the designs for the Muncipal Museum (see ground-plans, *Ills. 214, 221*), it already incorporated an open-plan staircase.

In 1898, with the backing of his fellow professors, Wagner produced his first design for a new Academy of Fine Arts (*Ills. 203-5*). His second, which was prompted by the resiting of this project on the Schmelz, dates from 1910 (*Ills. 206-7*). In both designs the proposed installation consisted of one principal building (containing an *aula*, lecture rooms, administration offices and museums for paintings and plaster casts) and a large number of studio pavilions spread out in a regular pattern over landscaped grounds. When he was preparing his first design Wagner explicitly rejected the idea of a site with natural clusters of trees and an undulating terrain, because then his building 'would have had to fit in' with the landscape.

As an active member of the Kunstrat (Art Council) Wagner in 1900 designed the Moderne Galerie (*Ills. 208-10*). The main hall of this building and the first floor rooms which surrounded it were all lit from above and had no side windows. The external wall surfaces at this level were to be used for a mural. The first section of this, a majolica low relief covering the whole of the front façade, was designed by himself. The remaining sections of the mural (like the interior of the museum, which was also left unfinished, were to have been executed by later artists in the course of the coming century. Wagner subsequently tried to revive public interest

Ill. 203. Academy of Fine Arts (1898): Bird's-eye view from a height of 100 metres. The ceremonial entrance hall and *aula* were flanked by museums for pictures and plaster casts, which were flanked in turn by class and lecture rooms and offices for the administrative staff. The grounds to the rear, which housed the studio pavilions, were cut off from the main buildings by a beech hedge 10 metres high.

in this project by suggesting that it should be built as an 'annex' to his Municipal Museum. In "Vienna After the War", the article which he published in 1917, he was still pressing its claims.

None of Wagner's designs in this category was ever commissioned with the exception of his two exhibits for the International Exhibition in Paris in 1900. These were the exhibit for the directors of the Imperial and Royal Hofgarten (*Ill. 228*), which was, Ludwig Hevesi wrote, 'by common consent the principal attraction in the *palais d'horticulture*', and his 'Group VI. Engineering'.

In 1900 Wagner produced his first design for the Emperor Francis Joseph Municipal Museum on the Karlsplatz and brought pressure to bear on the competent authorities to approve the scheme. In this he met with some success, for within the year it was decided to erect a museum on the east side of the square. An open preliminary competition was then held in 1901 and of the thirty-five designs submitted Wagner's (*Ill. 212*)

received one of the eight prizes. But in the closed competition of 1902, although the case for his design (*Ill. 226*) was pleaded in a 'minority report', the reactionaries who drafted the 'majority report' opted for Friedrich Schachner. A further competition was then held, in which models were exhibited, and Wagner again opposed what Hevesi called Schachner's 'belated Renaissance'. But still the issue remained undecided.

In Wagner's first design for the Karlsplatz the east side of the square was occupied by two buildings—the museum and a detached apartment house—while in his three competition designs it accommodated three separate buildings—the museum, the Moderne Galerie and a reception building—which were linked by two pairs of bridges.

But in 1903 he produced a new, composite design for the Karlsplatz (*Ill. 215*), in which the east side was closed to form a single unit. In this design Wagner retained the reception building (for the emperor) but he did away with the road, which had cut the main building in two, and also trans-

Ill. 204. The Academy of Fine Arts: Ceremonial entrance hall in front of the *aula*. The hall itself was to have been built partly from granite blocks, partly from bricks faced with granite, the free-standing pillars were to have been carved from granite while the crown surmounting the dome was to have been constructed from iron and gilded bronze. The snakes and rings on the pillars also appeared on the Olbrich Secession but in a different arrangement. The pergolas to the right and left of the hall lead to the museums.

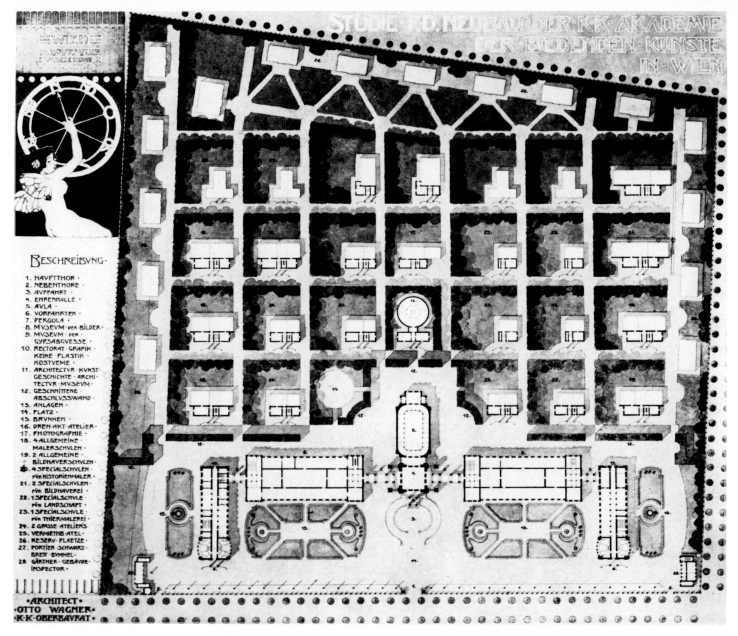

BESCHREIBVNG·

1. HAVPTTHOR·
2. NEBENTHORE·
3. AVFFAHRT·
4. EHRENHALLE·
5. AVLA·
6. VORFAHRTEN·
7. PERGOLA·
8. MVSEVM·DER·BILDER·
9. MVSEVM·DER·
   GYPSABGVESSE·
10. RECTORAT·GRAFIK·
    KEINE·PLASTIK·
    KOSTVEME·
11. ARCHITECTVR·KVNST·
    GESCHICHTE·ARCHI·
    TECTVR·MVSEVM·
12. GESCHNITTENE·
    ABSCHLVSSWAND·
13. ANLAGEN·
14. PLATZ·
15. BRVNNEN·
16. DREH·AKT·ATELIER·
17. PHOTOGRAPHIE·
18. 4 ALLGEMEINE·
    MALERSCHVLEN·
19. 2 ALLGEMEINE·
    BILDHAVERSCHVLEN·
20. 4 SPECIALSCHVLEN·
    FVR·HISTORIENMALER·
21. 2 SPECIALSCHVLEN·
    FVR·BILDHAVEREI·
22. 1 SPECIALSCHVLE·
    FVR·LANDSCHAFT·
23. 1 SPECIALSCHVLE·
    FVR·THIERMALEREI·
24. 2 GROSE·ATELIERS·
25. VERMIETHB·ATEL·
26. RESERV·PLAETZE·
27. PORTIER·SCHWARZ·
    BRETT·BVMMEL·
28. GÄRTNER·GEBÄVDE·
    INSPECTOR·

·ARCHITECT·
·OTTO WAGNER·
·K·K·OBERBAVRAT·

Ill. 205. The Academy of Fine Arts: General plan.

Original is in the possession of the Historisches Museum der Stadt Wien.

ferred the main museum entrance from the front of the building to the side. This realignment created an extremely compact ground-plan which, however, was modified in three subsequent designs; from the last two of these in 1907 and 1909 (Ills. 216-21) Wagner removed the reception building. Then, in 1910, he built a canvas mock-up of the museum, which aroused little public enthusiasm and so sealed the fate of his Karlsplatz project. His two designs for a Municipal Museum on the Schmelz (1910, Ills. 222, 223 and 1912, Ills. 224, 225, 227) were equally unsuccessful.

While the Municipal Museum project was still undecided Wagner produced a number of designs for other exhibition buildings. There was the design for an Arts and Crafts Museum of 1903, there was the Zedlitzhalle of 1907, the House of Glory of 1908 (Ills. 229-30) and finally the competition design for the Technical Museum for Industry and Crafts of 1909, which, like the design submitted by Loos, was unjustifiably rejected by the adjudicators.

In 1905, when he evolved his scheme for the library section of the Palace of Peace in The Hague (Ills. 239-42) Wagner created the system of cells which he subsequently adapted for the university library. In the first of his library designs (1910, Ills. 231-3) the two wings containing the cells ran parallel to one another and were linked by a central section, which housed the staircases, the toilets, the service lifts for the books and the paternoster for the library slips. The whole of the ground floor—which had an extremely flexible layout thanks to the skeleton construction—was given over to the readers. The reinforced concrete cells, which were only 2.22 metres high to allow easy access to the books, were fitted with automatic doors and were both air and fireproof. The second design for the university library (1914) was shaped like a foreshortened V (Ill. 234). The book cells occupied the two converging wings, which were linked at the narrow end by the top section of a low T-shaped building. Although this made for a less compact design the general layout of the reading rooms was clearer. In 1913 Wagner again designed a building for twentieth-century art. This building was the Zedlitzhalle, which had already featured in his 1907 design (see above) and which he now planned to convert into an exhibition hall for craft products (Ill. 235). Finally, in 1916, he designed a forest school in the Wienerwald.

Ill. 206. The Academy of Fine Arts on the Schmelz (1910): Bird's-eye view. The four wings of the principal building, which were grouped around the *aula,* contained classrooms and a library on the ground floor and collections of paintings and a Museum for Plaster Casts on the first floor. The two buildings in the inner courtyards were annexes of the Museum for Plaster Casts and were intended to house oversize objects.

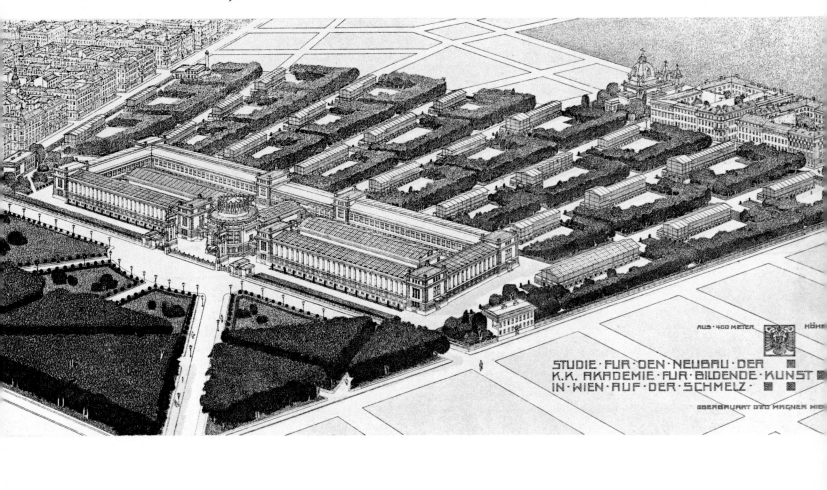

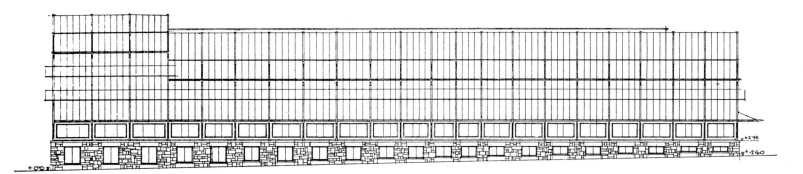

Ill. 207. The Academy of Fine Arts on the Schmelz: View of the northern face of a sculptor's studio.

Ill. 208. Moderne Galerie (1900): Entrance portal. The cornice and projecting roof were to have been lined with chased copper.

s. 209, 210. Moderne Galerie: Front view and perspective. Title of the majolica low relief ('since', Wagner said, 'a title is fortunately always asked for'): "The arts raise the veil which was spread over mankind".

Original in the possession of the Historisches Museum der Stadt Wien.

Ill. 211. Emperor Francis Jo
seph Municipal Museum on th
Karlsplatz (1903 design): R
ception building with ar
over the ceremonial court an
a dome surmounting the burg
master's hall. Proposed mat
rials: granite, white marble, al
minium and gilded bronze.

Ill. 212. Emperor Francis Jo
seph Municipal Museum on th
Karlsplatz (design for the ope
competition of 1901): Exhib
tion hall for sculptures (for
ground) and main buildin
(background).

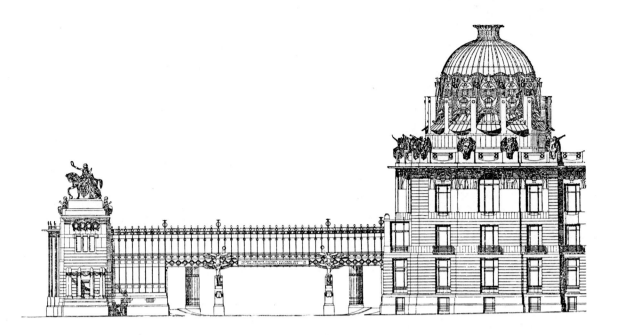

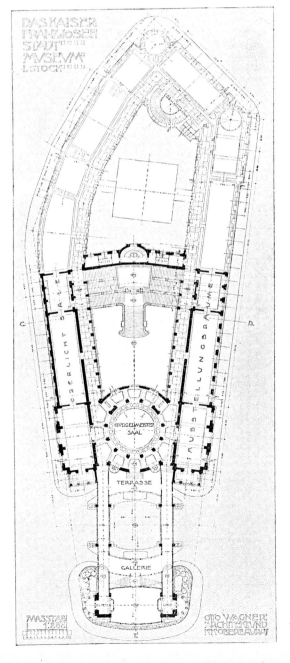

Ills. 213, 214. Emperor Francis Joseph Municipal Museum on the Karlsplatz (1903 design): View of the entrance section from the Karlsplatz and ground-plan (first floor level). The sections enclosed by heavy black lines were to have been built in the first stage.

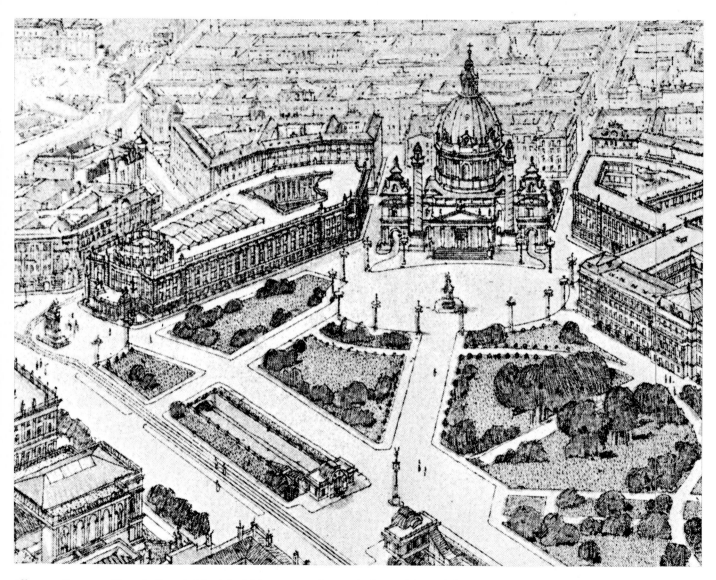

Ill. 215. Emperor Francis Joseph Municipal Museum on the Karlsplatz with Karlskirche. *1903 design.*

Ill. 216. 1909 design for Municipal Museum (detail of *Ill. 217)* featuring the statue of "Culture".

l. 217. Bird's-eye view of the Karlsplatz (1909 design): The buildings on the far side of the square are (from left to right): Emperor Francis Joseph Municipal Museum, Karlskirche, Technical College, Hansen's Evangelical School and Wagner's department store (designed 1904). The Wienzeile, which Wagner had proposed as the site of the new 'Naschmarkt', joins the square on the far right. Olbrich's Secession is in the near right hand corner. On the near side of the square, directly opposite Wagner's department store, is the monumental fountain designed in 1905 (*Ill. 293*).

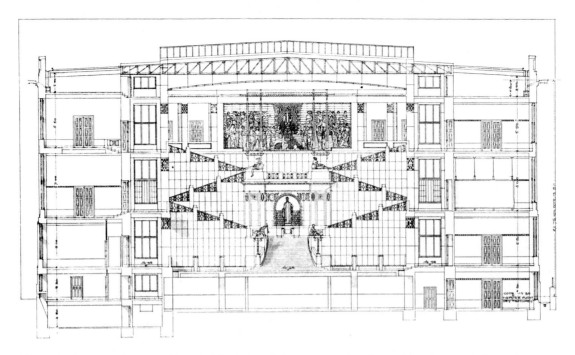

Ill. 218. Emperor Francis Joseph Municipal Museum on the Karlsplatz (1909 design): Interior cross-section showing the roof above the inner courtyard and the position of the main staircase.

Ill. 219. Emperor Francis Joseph Municipal Museum on the Karlsplatz (1909 design) with Karls-kirche on the right and the "Culture" statue in the foreground.

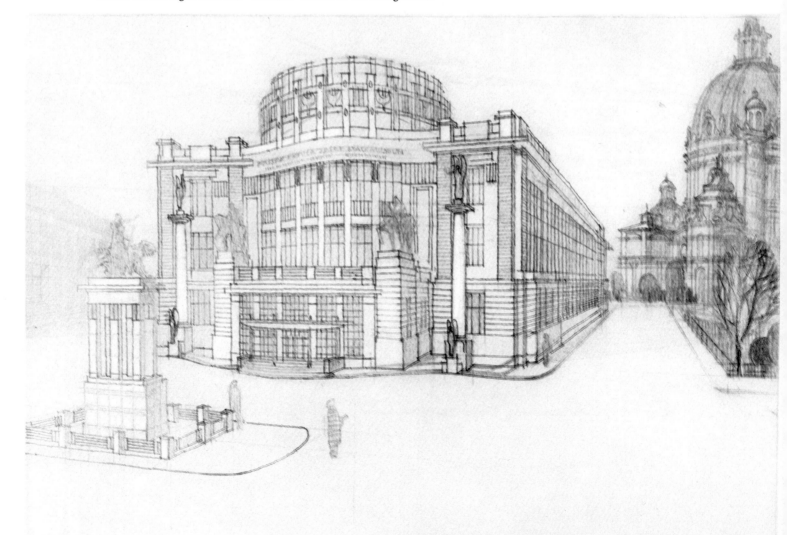

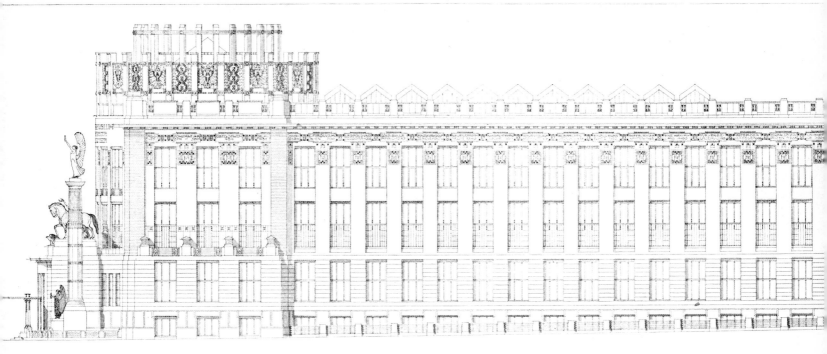

Ills. 220, 221. Emperor Francis Joseph Municipal Museum on the Karlsplatz (1909 design). Above: Detail of entrance section. Below: Ground-plan (mezzanine level).

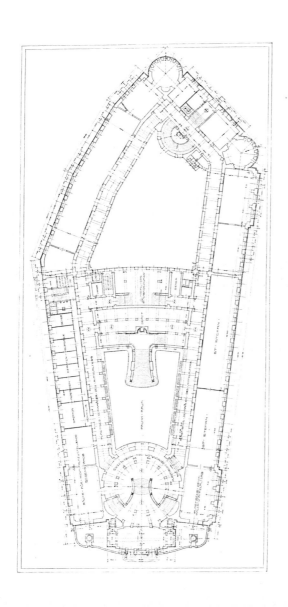

Ill. 222. The Academy of Fine Arts on the Schmelz and the Emperor Francis Joseph Municipal Museum (1910). The *aula* is immediately behind the museum.

Ill. 223. Emperor Francis Joseph Municipal Museum on the Schmelz and the Vindobona monument (1910). The Academy is behind the museum.

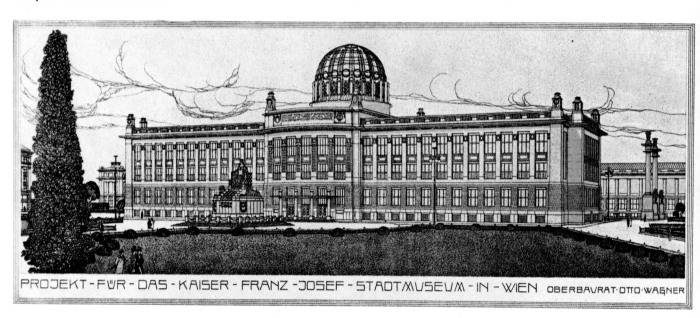

PROJEKT · FÜR · DAS · KAISER · FRANZ · JOSEF · STADTMUSEUM · IN · WIEN OBERBAURAT · OTTO · WAGNER

224, 225. The Emperor Francis Joseph Municipal Museum on the Schmelz. ('Opus IV', the 1912 competition design.) Ground-plan (mezzanine level) with the proposed first stage shaded in.

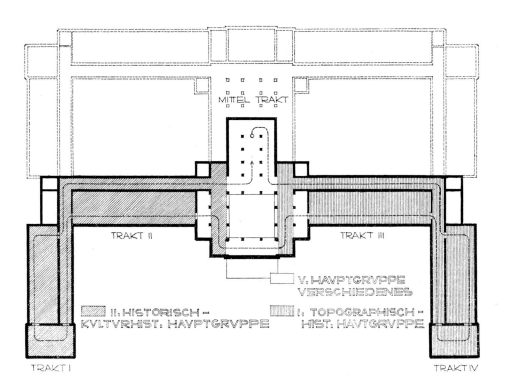

Ill. 226. Emperor Francis Joseph Municipal Museum on the Karlsplatz (1902 closed competition design): Central hall as seen from the gallery.

Ill. 227. Emperor Francis Joseph Municipal Museum on the Schmelz (Opus IV): Interior of vestibule showing group of figures for Raphael Donner's "Providentia" fountain.

228. Exhibit for the directors of the Hofgarten as shown at the International Exhibition in Paris in 1900.

Ills. 229, 230. House of Glory (1908) with **two** ground-plans (street and first floor level).

HOUSE OF GLORY.

PERFORMANCE: BRICK' STONE ARMYBETON' GRANITÉ' MARBLE IRON' BRONCE' ALUMINIUM' GLASS

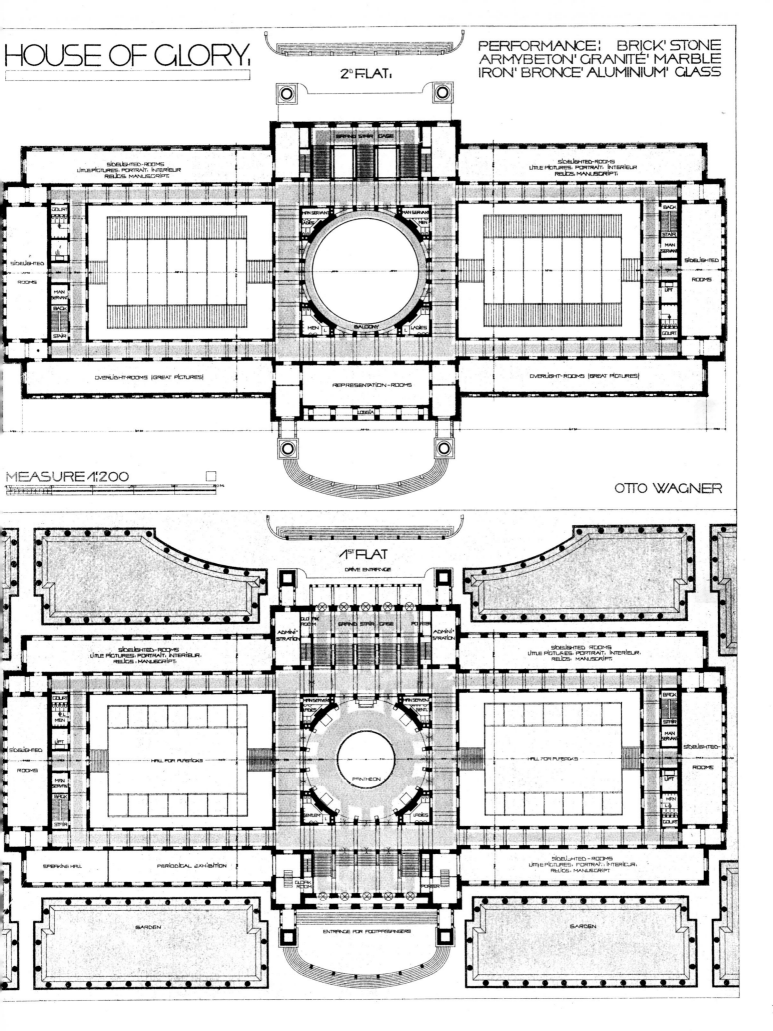

2ᴰ FLAT.

MEASURE 1:200

OTTO WAGNER

1ˢᵀ FLAT

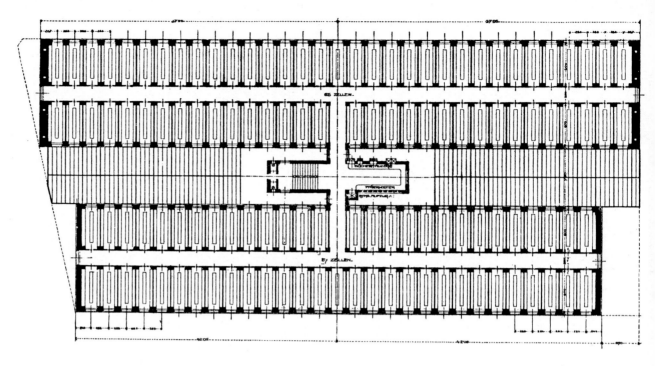

Ills. 231, 232. University library (first design, 1910). Below: Ground-plan at mezzanine level. Above: Ground-plan of one of the upper floors. The service lifts for the books and the paternoster for the library slips were housed in the central section.

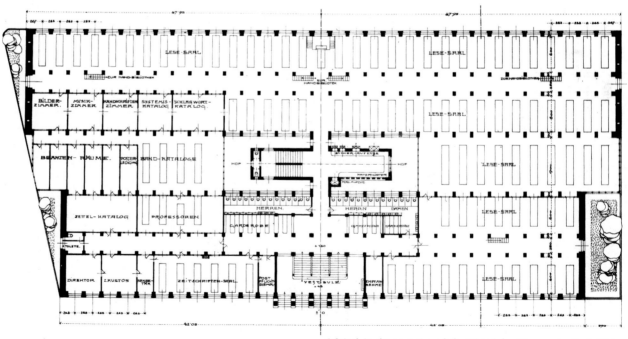

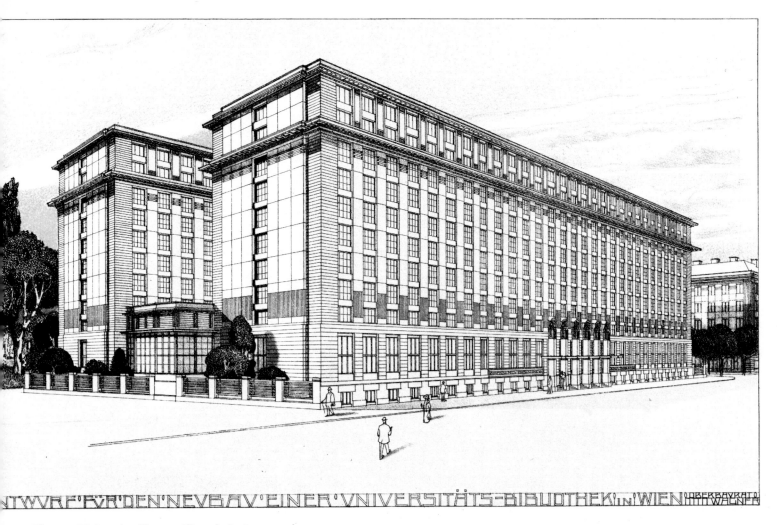

NTWVRF'FVR'DEN'NEVBAV'EINER'VNIVERSITÄTS-BIBLIOTHEK'in'WIEN OBERBAVRAT OTTO WAGNER

Ill. 233. University library (first design).

Ill. 234. University library (second design, 1914).

Original in the possession of the Historisches Museum der Stadt Wien.

ARCH. HOFRAT OTTO WAGNER

Ill. 235. Zedlitzhalle (second design, 1913, for an arts and crafts exhibition hall: View one of two identical entrance sections.

OTHER PUBLIC BUILDINGS

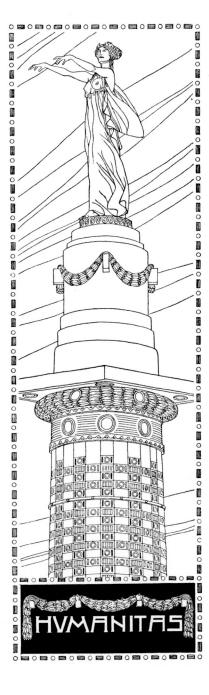

Ill. 236. Palace of Peace in The Hague (competition design, 1905): Monument to Peace. Aluminium and porcelain figure on concrete column faced with coloured glass and bronze (See *Ills. 239-42* for the Palace of Peace).

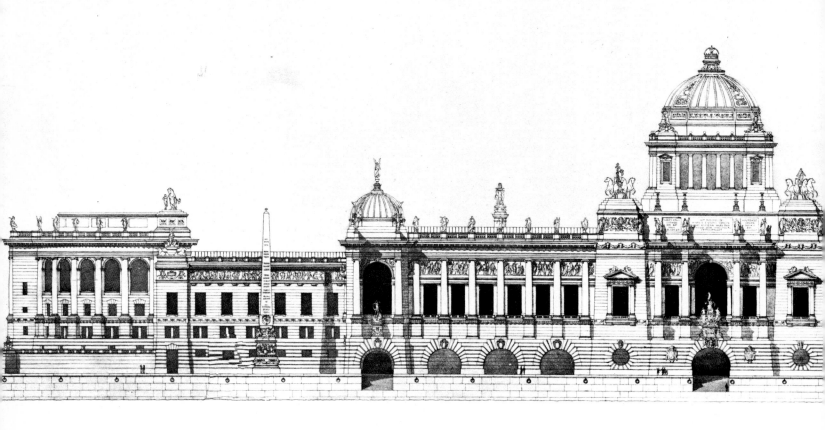

Wagner was never asked to design genuinely prestigious buildings. The 'establishment' had cast him in the role of the technical architect and the most it was prepared to grant him was an occasional bank, a sanatorium or a church for the grounds of a public institution. But he never gave up. Time and again he set his sights on commissions for the Ringstrasse scheme: in 1874 he entered the competition for the Palace of Justice; in 1899 he submitted proposals for the conversion of the Hofburg; in 1906 he designed his "Palace for Viennese Society" (Ills. 243, 244) with guest accommodation, shops, galleries, large multi-purpose halls and a theatre wing based on his 1902 design for a 'little theatre' and which he replaced before the year was out by a concert hall (Ills. 245, 246), in response to numerous representations. But, as was only to be expected, these endeavours came to nothing and in 1907-08, when he failed to win the competition for the War Ministry building (Ill. 247) after refusing to accept the conditions of entry, Wagner lost his last possible chance of influencing the development of the Ringstrasse. Although he was promised that the conditions would be revised, this was never done. Wagner also produced two designs for the Ministry of Trade building in Vienna, the first when he was working on his general plan for the regulation of the city, the second in conjunction with his War Ministry design.

He also produced a whole series of competition designs for important projects outside Vienna. Some of them won prizes, some were even commissioned, but not one was executed. These designs were for: the Landtag building in Lemberg (1875), the Rathaus in Hamburg (1876), the Reichstag in Berlin (1882, Ill. 238), the parliament building in Budapest, in which the debating chambers were located in the two additions at either end of the building (1882, Ill. 237), and the Palace of Peace sponsored by the Carnegie Foundation in The Hague (1905, Ills. 236, 239-42). Wagner modified this last design in the following year when he brightened up the façade out of deference to his critics, who thought it too 'simple'.

Ill. 237. Parliament building in Budapest (competition design, 1882). View from the quay.

Ill. 238. Reichstag in Berlin (competition design, 1882).

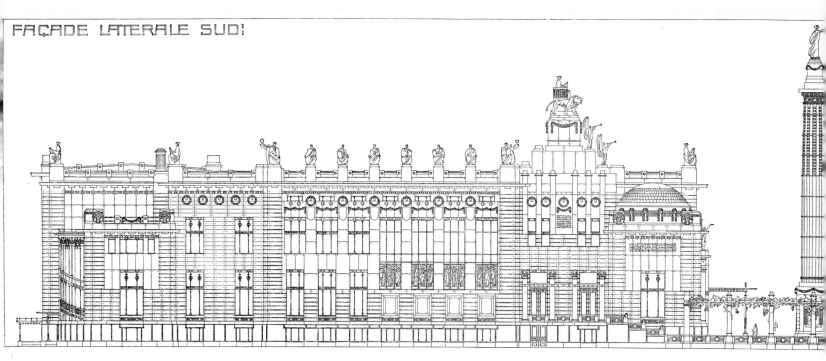

Ill. 239. Palace of Peace in The Hague (competition design, 1905): Side view. The high windows in the middle belong to the smaller of the two courtrooms. The projecting circular structure on the far left is the stair-well for the library and was made entirely of glass.

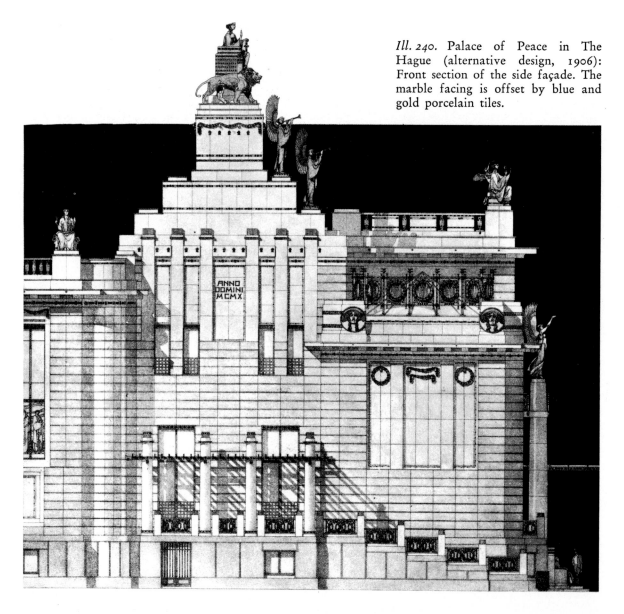

Ill. 240. Palace of Peace in The Hague (alternative design, 1906): Front section of the side façade. The marble facing is offset by blue and gold porcelain tiles.

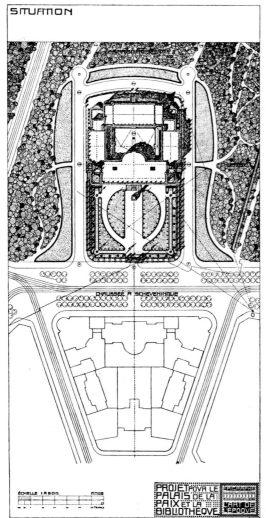

Ill. 241. Palace of Peace in The Hague (competition design): View of front and northern façades. Proposed materials: granite, white marble and tombac with tombac-faced iron windows.

Ill. 242. Palace of Peace in The Hague (competition design): General plan. The arbitration court is in the front of the building and opens on to the semi-circular staircase which projects into the inner courtyard; the two lateral sections house council chambers in the front and courtrooms in the rear. The library occupies the transverse section at the rear.

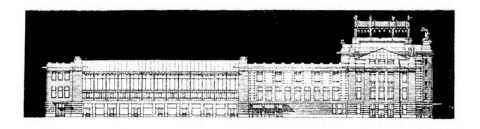

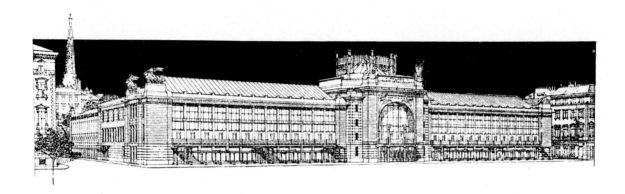

Ills. 243, 244. "Palace for Viennese Society" (first design, with theatre, 1906): Side view, perspective and ground-plan at street level.

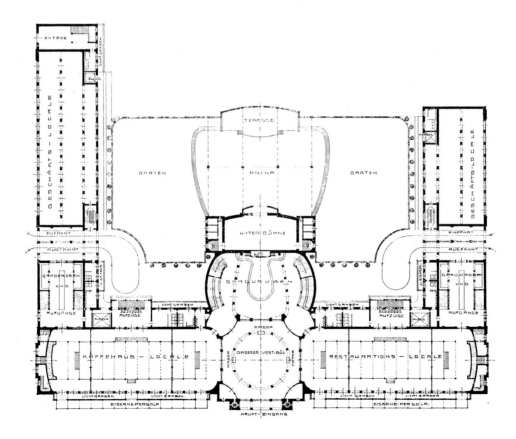

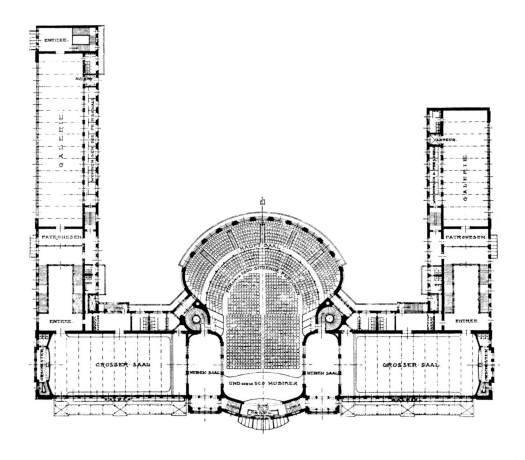

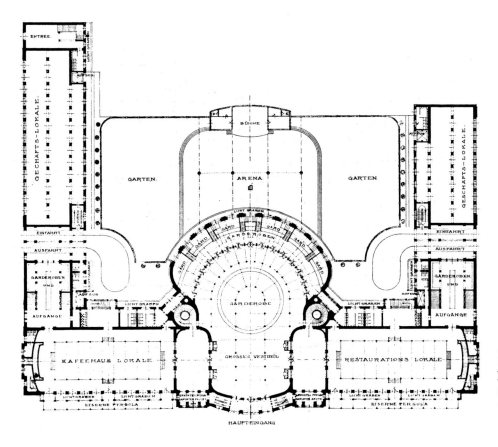

Ills. 245, 246. "Palace for Viennese Society" (second design, with concert hall, 1906). Above: Ground-plan (first floor level). Below: Ground-plan (street level).

Ill. 247. War Ministry (competition design, 1907-8): Entrance section and Radetzky monument.

RELIGIOUS BUILDINGS AND MONUMENTS

Ill. 248. Synagogue in Budapest (built 1871): Drawn in perspective section.

Ill. 249. Study for the Berliner Dom project (1891). The Requiem and Funeral Church on the left, which gives access to the Imperial Crypt, is matched by the small church on the right. The 'Preaching' Church is in the centre.

Commenting in 1900 on the first sacred building which Wagner was asked to erect—the Moorish-style synagogue in Budapest (*Ill. 248*)—Ludwig Hevesi wrote: 'He himself has almost forgotten this enterprise.' Between the synagogue of 1871 and the Johanneskapelle (*Ill. 250*) of 1895, which was executed in conjunction with the Stadtbahn project and looks strangely out of place amidst the viaducts of the railway system, Wagner worked on three other religious buildings.

In 1879 he made a design for the church in Soborsin, in which he still employed a 'dome ring'. This was followed in 1890 by a design for the parish church in Esseg, whose exterior gives no hint of the iron pillars and framework trusses on either side of the nave, which helped support the ornamental ceiling and whose lower members Wagner purposely left unfaced. And in 1891 he made a study for the Berliner Dom project, which provided for a preaching church with 2,060 seats, a pulpit directly in front of the altar and partitions, between the central church and the two smaller churches on either sides. Pulpit and seats could be lowered out of sight.

Then, in 1898, he produced a design for the parish church in Währing (*Ill. 252*), a single-span building to accommodate a congregation of 2,900. Wagner used this design to demonstrate the theories which had developed in "Modern Movements in Church Architecture". By then he was fifty-seven, and since he had abandoned his belief in 'an unknown God' some two years before, his principal object was to ensure that the members of the congregation should at least be able to see and hear

their priest; nor did he consider it superfluous to provide heating and ventilation, sanitary installations and a first-aid room 'for the living'; he even provided a special confessional for those who were hard of hearing. By exhibiting his Währing project in the Secession in the autumn of 1899 Wagner hoped to dispel 'the traditional and—one is tempted to add—thoughtless impression of the church' which was still prevalent 'and to persuade even the layman that in its external appearance a building such as this corresponded exactly to the needs of modern man'. In both versions of the study for the conversion of the Capuchin church with its monastery and imperial crypt, which Wagner made in 1898 (*Ills. 253-5*), the religious site was integrated into the surrounding townscape, thus rendering a 'gasometer' (*i. e.* circular) ground-plan unnecessary. But the Church Am Steinhof, which stood in open country, was not built in the round either, a fact which can scarcely be explained simply in terms of size (it was a far smaller building and held only 800 people), since Wagner also eschewed the tholos construction for the great Friedenskirche, or Armistice Church, the last and, in his opinion, the most important of his works.

The Catholic church of St Leopold Am Steinhof was built for the Lower Austrian Heil- und Pflegeanstalt (State Sanatorium and Institution), which subsequently came under the jurisdiction of the city of Vienna. This was one of the works which contributed, quite as much as his theoretical writings, to Wagner's international reputation. The church and the asy-

Ill. 250. Johanneskapelle in Währing (built 1895).

lum were built simultaneously between 1905 and 1907. The planning authorities no doubt drew on Wagner's plan for the general site but he was not asked to build the individual pavilions. This design, like the design for the Greek Orthodox church at Patras in the Peloponnese, was submitted in 1902.

Although the Church Am Steinhof *(Ills. 256-91)* was intended for 'quiet' patients, the nurses could remove any inmate in case of need, since each pew seated only four persons. The male and female patients entered the church separately through the side entrances (the main entrance being reserved for festive occasions) while the staff and their relatives were able to hear mass from the gallery. A crypt had been planned but was not built. Provision had also been made for a first-aid room and toilets in the basement.

This single-span church complied extremely well with Wagner's insistence on space. The pillars at the intersection of the nave and the transept, which support the dome, are relatively narrow; they are made of plain brickwork and are entirely free from thrust. The main body of the church receives a great deal of light from Kolo Moser's stained-glass windows but the presbytery is lit only from the side to preclude the possibility of glare. Wagner, who hated canvasses and 'the unreliable fresco technique which created so many difficulties' ensured that the picture above the high altar (by Remigius Geyling) and the two pictures above the side altars (by Rudolf Jettmar) were executed in a new and special kind of mosaic consisting of pottery, marbles with different surface consisten-

cies, vitrified enamel and glass. The pictures were not completed until 1913. To improve the congregation's view of the altar—which was already raised—the floor of the church was given an imperceptible slope, which ran from the vestibule down to the communion rail. Wagner indulged his aversion to 'abnormal height factors' and also sought to ensure good acoustics by building a vaulted ornamental ceiling inside the dome, which considerably reduced its internal volume. This ceiling consists of Rabitz panels inserted into a framework of unfaced T-irons, whose visible lower faces were gilded. The space above the ornamental ceiling was divided into two separate sections by a concrete floor which provided a working surface, from which to operate the winches for the chandeliers and the cradle used for cleaning the ceiling. The outside brickwork was protected by sheets of marble 2 centimetres thick, which were held in position by stout marble bands and fixed to the walls with bolts fitted with screw-on copper caps. In fact, all the exposed metal parts were made of copper; even the iron windows were coated with copper. The lapped copper tiles on the roof of the dome were originally gilded and the projecting lip at the top of each tile was meant to act as a screen against hailstones. The various flat roofs on the church were asphalted and covered with gravel.

In 1905, the year in which work began on the Church Am Steinhof, Wagner produced his design for the Interimskirche *(Ill. 292).* The pairs of parabolic girders—which taper as they approach the apex—form a series of arches supporting

Ill. 251. National Monument (1897): Sketch.

a framework of T-irons fitted out with Rabitz panels at the top and projecting beyond the line of the walls towards the bottom. But just as these roof girders pierce the line of the walls, so too the walls pierce the line of the roof to form two rows of dormer windows. The Friedenskirche (Armistice Church), which Wagner designed in 1917 (*Ill. 294*), was to have been lit from above by means of a very large octagonal lantern. This church must surely be the same as the Victory Church which Wagner referred to in his article "Vienna After the War".

Almost without exception the monuments designed by Wagner were based on stereotyped ideas and conceptions. This stricture applies to his Goethe statue of 1881, his monuments to the emperor and the nation of 1897 (*Ill. 251*) and even

his "Culture" statue of 1909 (*Ill. 6*). He tended to favour imperial monuments for the simple reason that these were more likely to be commissioned. In 1895 he considered the 'question of monuments' with a view to the execution of a statue on the square in front of the Burgtheater and succeeded in designing a tolerable equestrian monument; in 1903 he designed a monumental fountain for the Karlsplatz (*Ill. 293*) and, following the emperor's death, he planned a further equestrian statue. As far as his ideological works in this sphere were concerned—*e. g.*, the fountain, the statue of humanity for the Palace of Peace in The Hague (1905, *Ill. 236*), the "Culture" statue, and the Vindobona statue for the Municipal Museum on the Schmelz (1910, *Ill. 223*)—Wagner could never be accused of having conceived these for the sake of the idea

Ill. 252. Paris Church in Währing (1898): View of lateral façade showing the side entrance to the church and the crypt. The bridge gave access to the dome above ceiling level.

which they were intended to embody. On the other hand, he rightly insisted on the physical durability, and the maintenance of his statues and, for that matter, of all his works. He wanted to produce 'a monument which could be cleaned properly and cheaply (with hoses) so that it would always retain the colourful appearance with had been originally intended'. With his system of coloured glazed tile with bevelled edges and dovetail joints he would doubtless have achieved this objective if he had received a commission. As it was, the only monument he ever erected was the family vault in the Hietzing cemetery, a stone and wrought-iron structure which was probably completed in 1894.

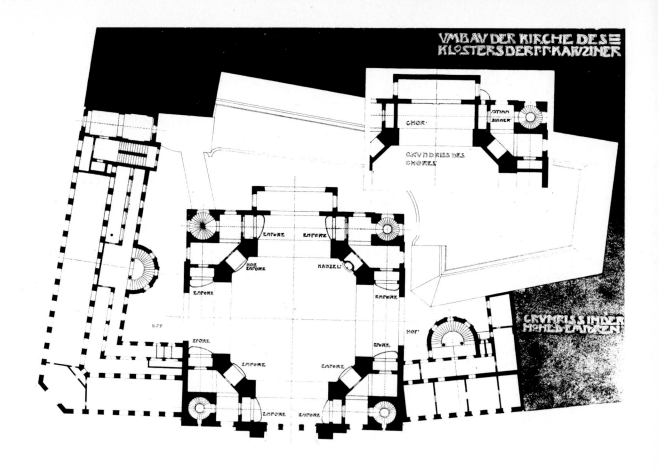

Ills. 253, 254. Capuchin church and monastery (design for conversion, 1898). Above: ground-plan (gallery level). Below: ground-plan (street level).

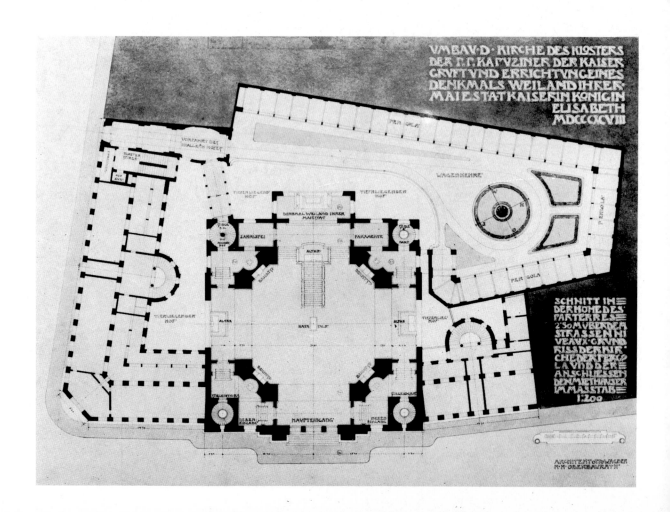

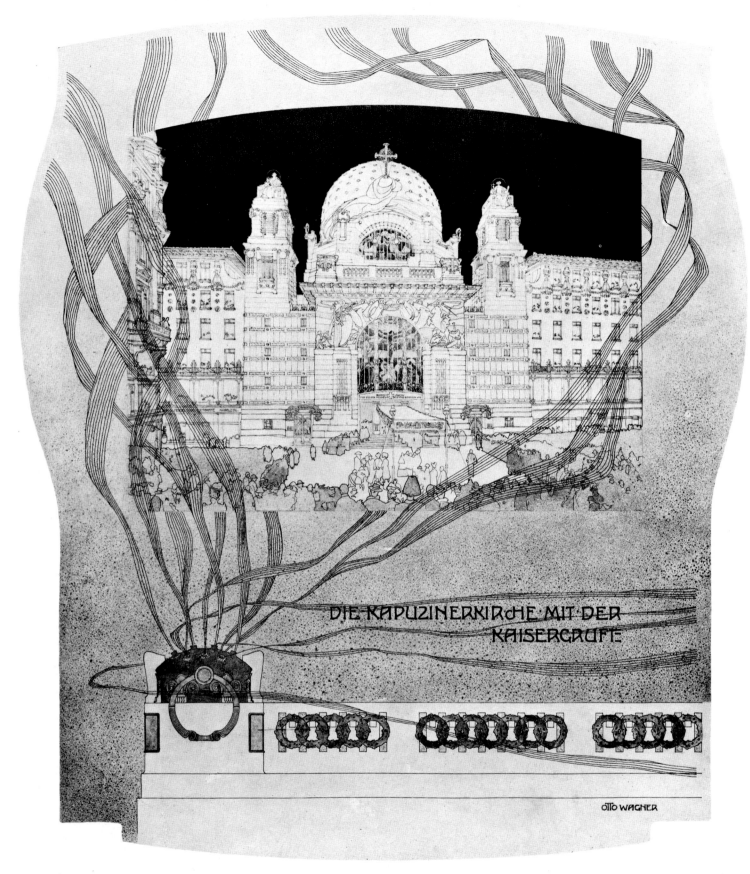

Ill. 255. Capuchin church (design for conversion). Proposed materials: Granite blocks and sheets. The cross was to be supported by the clouds, 'which surround the church like a headband'.

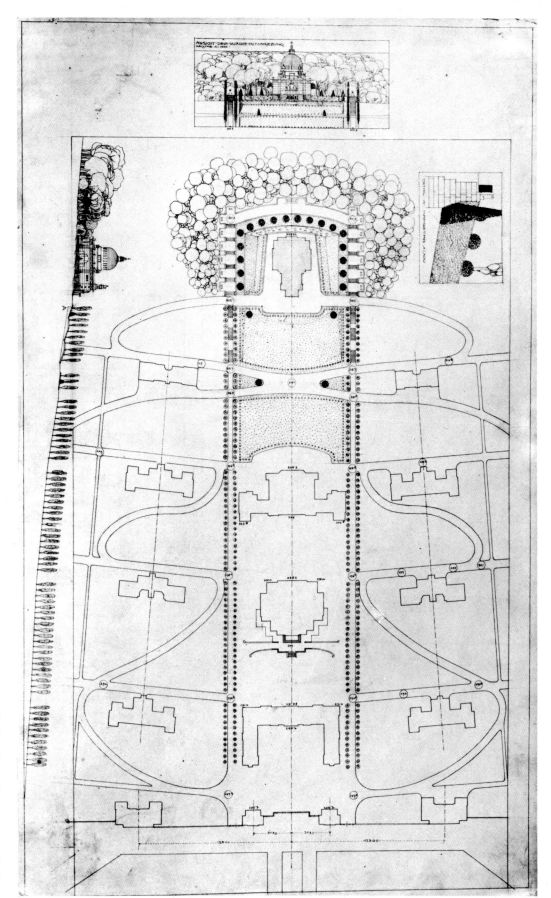

Ill. 256. Lower Austrian State
Sanatorium and Institution Am
Steinhof (built 1905-7): Plan
for the central section of the
installation. Although Wagner
was only commissioned to build
the church his general plan for
the whole installation was consulted by the authorities.

Ill. 257. (opposite) Church Am
Steinhof (St Leopold's; built
1905-7).

Original in the possession of the Historisches Museum der Stadt Wien.

212

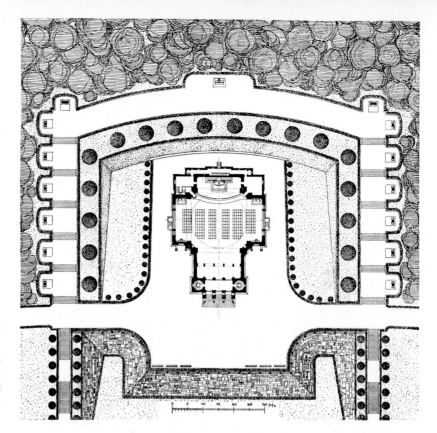

Ill. 258. Church Am Steinhof: General plan and ground-plan. There were separate entrances, one on either side, for the male and female patients. The main entrance was used only on festive occasions.

Ill. 259. Church Am Steinhof: Photograph of the site seven months after the start of work.

Ill. 260. (opposite) Church Am Steinhof. The figures on top of the towers were effigies of local saints executed by Richard Luksch.

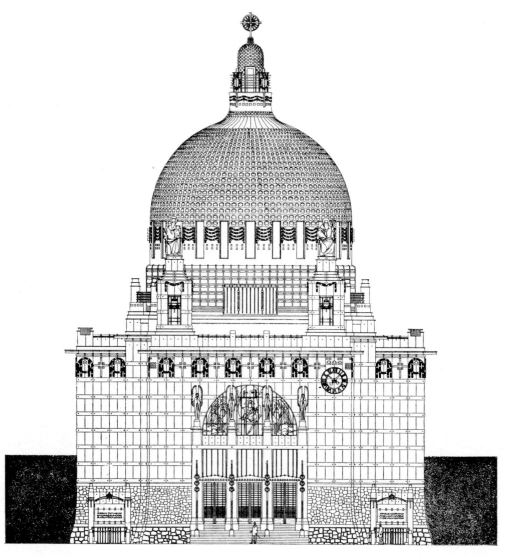

Ill. 261. Church Am Steinhof: Front view. The entrances to the crypt (extreme right and left) were removed from the final design.

Ill. 262. Church Am Steinhof: Main entrance.

Ill. 263. Church Am Steinhof: Side view of main entrance. The porch pillars were made of bronze.

Ill. 264. Church Am Steinhof: Angels above the main entrance, executed by Othmar Schimkowitz in gilded copper. The walls were faced with sheets of white marble. The bolts have screw-on copper caps.

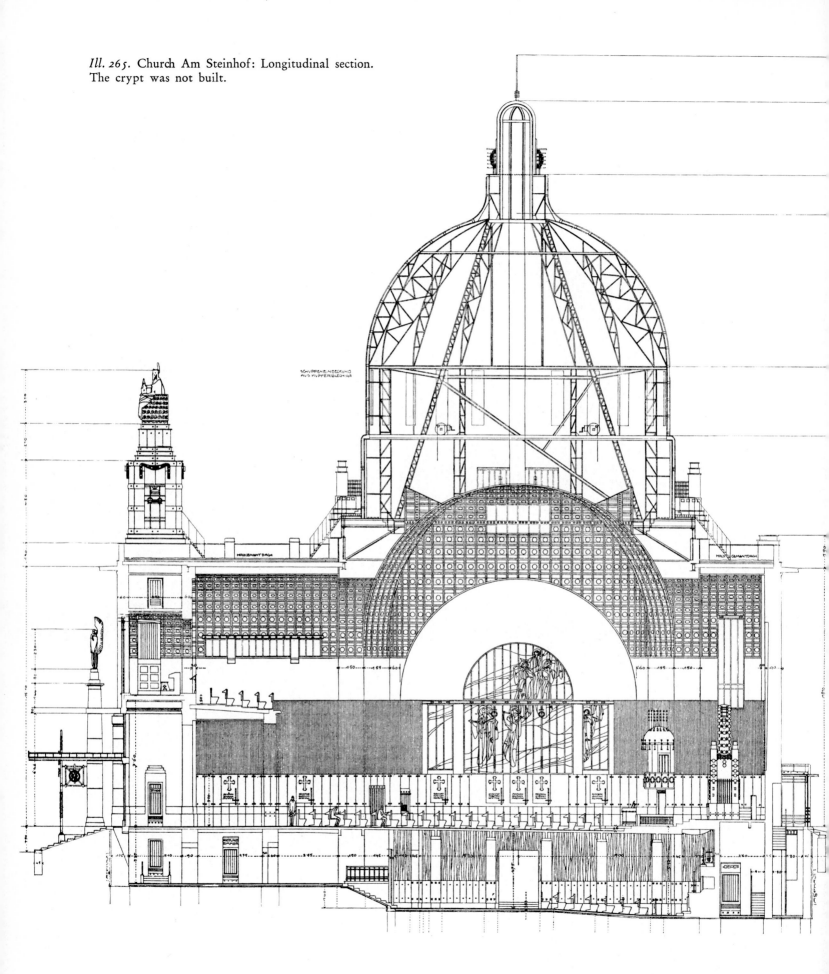

Ill. 265. Church Am Steinhof: Longitudinal section.
The crypt was not built.

Ill. 266. Church Am Steinhof: View of the towers from the roof of the transept. The figures on the towers, the crosses and the wreaths were made of copper. The iron windows were coated with copper.

Ill. 267. Church Am Steinhof: View of the dome and towers from the lantern gallery.

Ill. 268. Church Am Steinhof: View of the dome showing the copper tiles connected by lap joints, which were originally gilded.

Ill. 269. Church Am Steinhof: Tambour and windows of the upper section of the dome.

Ill. 270. Church Am Steinhof: Lantern gallery with copper guard rails and crosses.

Ills. 271, 272. Church Am Steinhof: View (left) and construction drawing (right) of the lantern.

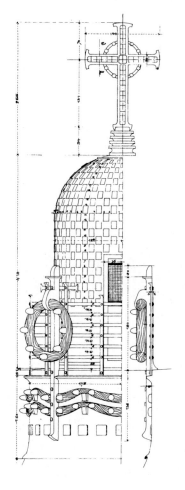

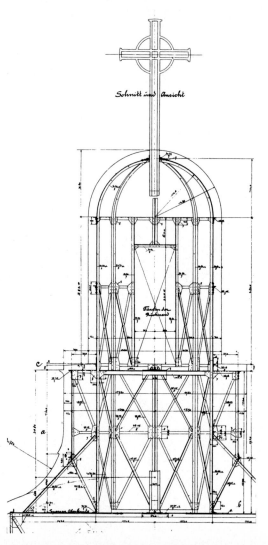

Ill. 273. Church am Steinhof: Interior of upper section of dome.

Ill.274. Church Am Steinhof: Interior of lower section of dome showing the reverse side of the ceiling (Rabitz panels set in a framework of *T*-irons) and the low windows set in the brickwork surmounting the intersection of the nave and transept.

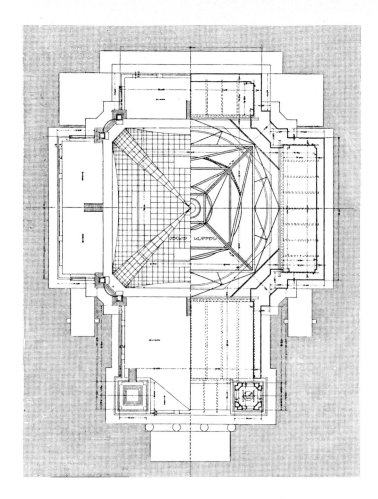

Ill. 275. Church Am Steinhof: Working drawing of dome and lower side of ornamental ceiling above the intersection.

Ill. 276. Church Am Steinhof: Ornamental ceiling above the intersection. Gilded *T*-irons. The dark lines in the diagonals are the cable of the chandeliers. The windows were by Kolo Moser.

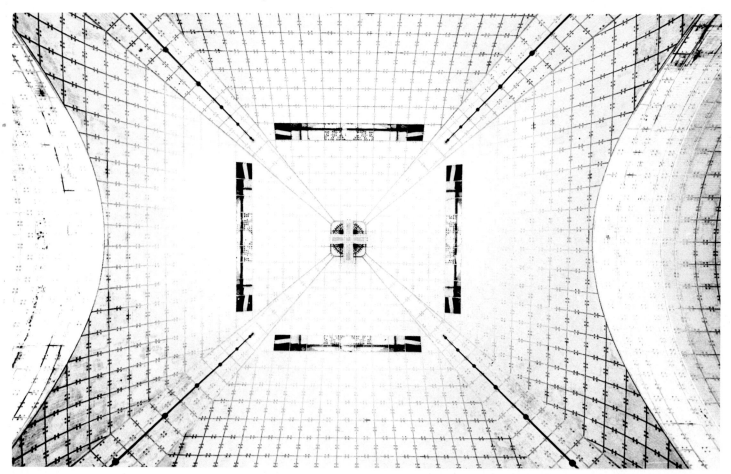

Ill. 277. Church Am Steinhof: View of presbytery from the choir gallery. The mosaic, which was executed by Remigius Geyling in pottery, marble, enamel and glass, was not completed until 1913.

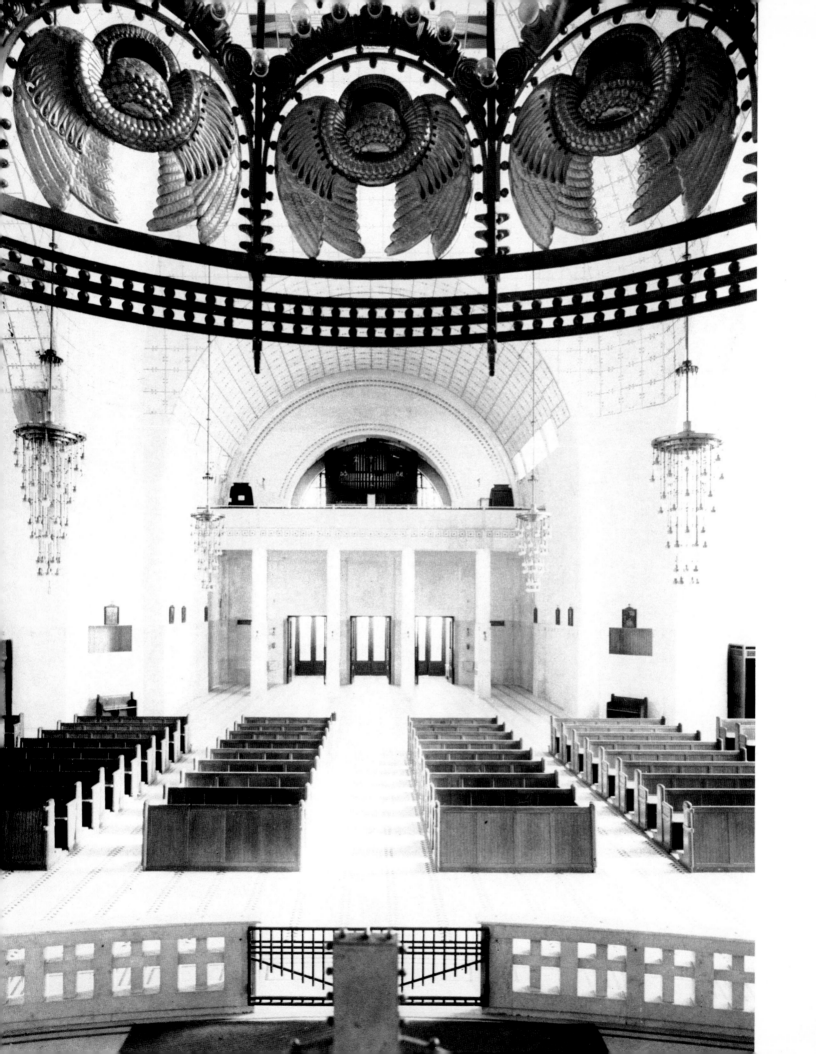

Ill. 279. Church Am Steinhof: Underside of chancel ceiling.

Ill. 280. Church Am Steinhof: Confessional and pews.

Ill. 278. Church Am Steinhof: View of the interior from the altar steps. Note the hot-air grills in the pillars on either side of the nave.

Ill. 281. Church Am Steinhof: Interior of side window showing framework. The stained-glass window is by Kolo Moser.

Ill. 282. Church Am Steinhof: Chandeliers. The winch was housed in the upper section of the dome.

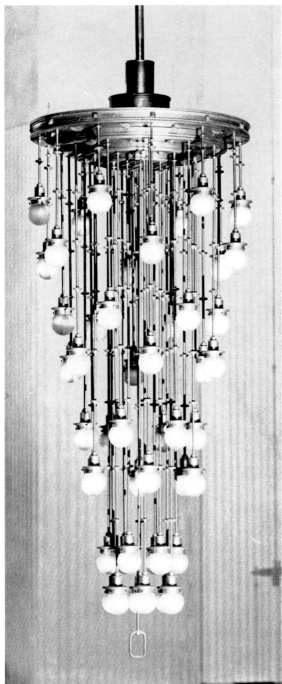

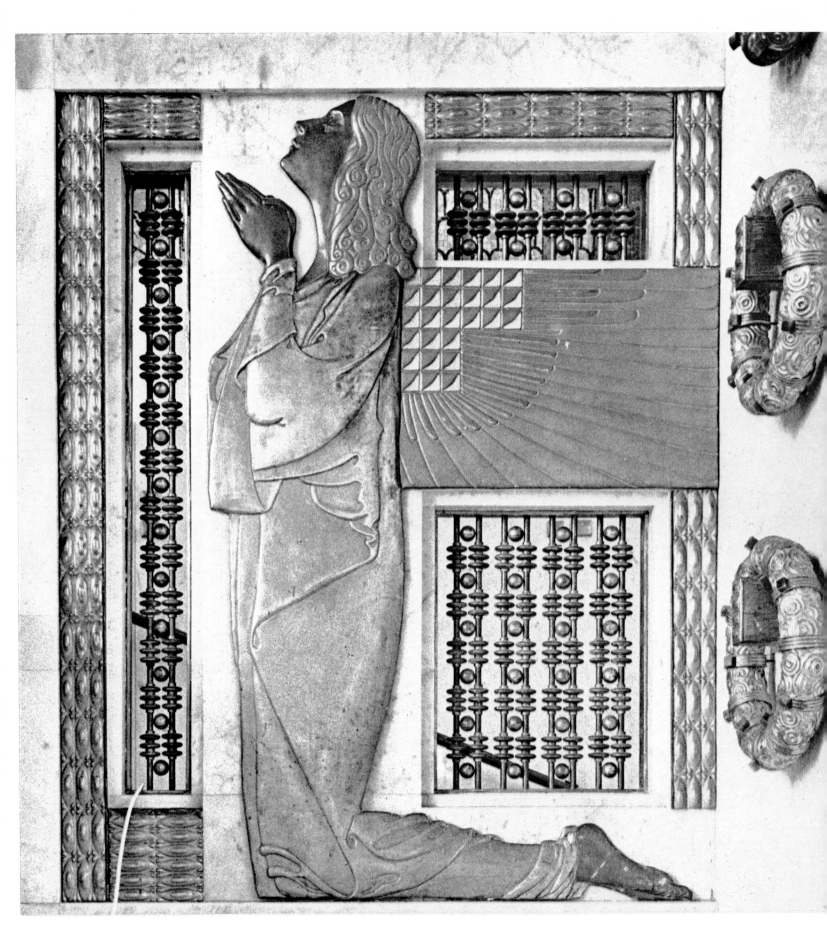

Ill. 283. Church Am Steinhof: Angel on the high altar chased in copper and gilded; by Othmar Schimkowitz.

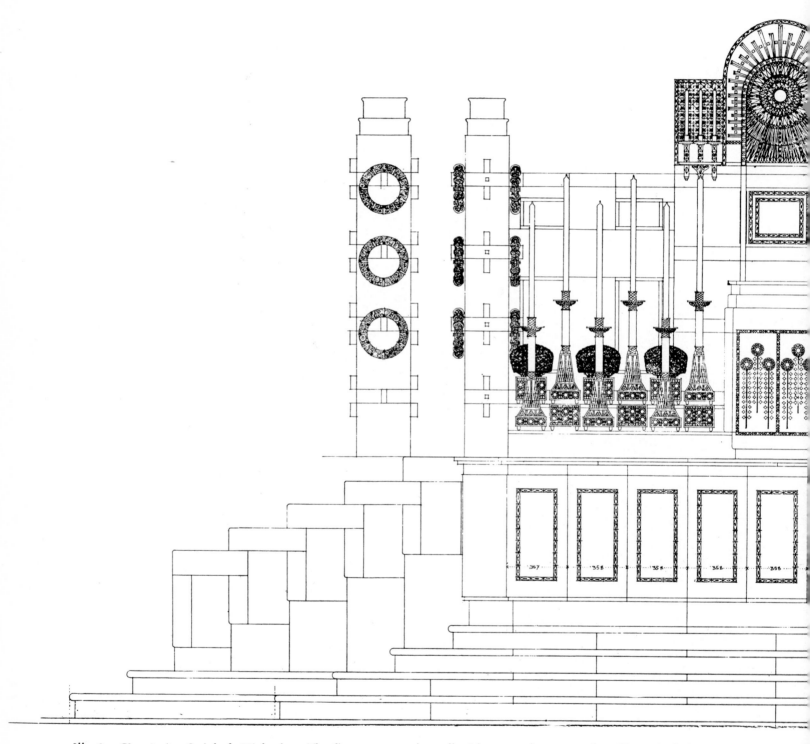

Ill. 284. Church Am Steinhof: High altar. The flower pots and candlesticks were also executed to Wagner's design.

Ill. 285. (overleaf) Church Am Steinhof: Presbytery. Access to the chancel is from the sacristy.

From "The Second Song"
Maldoror

Having spoken thus Maldoror does not leave the cathedral but stands staring at the lamp in that holy place. He thinks he sees some kind of provocation in the attitude of that lamp that irritates him to the highest degree by its untimely presence. He tells himself that if there is any soul concealed within that lamp it is cowardly not to reply sincerely to a straightforward attack. He beats the air with his sinewy arms and wishes that the lamp could be transformed into a man; he promises himself that he would put him through a bad quarter-hour. But the means by which a lamp changes into a man are unnatural. He does not resign himself to this but goes seeking on the floor of that wretched pagoda a flat stone with sharp edges. This he flings violently through the air . . . the chain is cut through the middle like grass before the scythe and the religious instrument falls to the ground spreading its oil upon the flagstones. He seizes the lamp to carry it outside but it resists and begins to increase in size. He seems to see wings sprouting from its sides and its upper part takes on the form of an angel's bust. It tries to take flight but he restrains it with a firm hand. One does not often see a lamp and an angel united in the same body. He recognises the shape of the lamp; he recognises the form of the angel; but he cannot distinguish them in his mind. Indeed, in reality they are joined together and form together one free and independent body. But he feels that some cloud has veiled his eyes and caused him to lose slightly the excellence of his eyesight. Nevertheless he prepares himself bravely for the struggle, for his adversary has no fear.

There are naive persons who assert that the sacred door closed of its own accord, swinging on its battered hinges, in order that none should witness that impious struggle the vicissitudes of which were about to develop within the precincts of that violated sanctuary.

The cloaked man, while undergoing cruel punishment from an invisible sword, strove to draw the angel's face to his mouth. He thought only of that and all his struggles were to that end. The lamp-angel weakens and seems to feel a presentiment of its destiny. Its struggles become feebler and the moment is imminent when its adversary will be able to embrace it at his ease, if that is what he intends to do.

Now the moment is come. Exerting his muscles he compresses the throat of the angel, who can no longer breathe, and crushes him against his loathsome breast. For a moment he feels pity for the fate awaiting this heavenly being, of whom he would have willingly made a friend. But he reminds himself that it is an envoy of the Lord and he can no longer restrain his wrath. It is irrevocable: something horrible is about to enter the cage of time! He bends down and applies his salivated tongue to that angelic cheek despite the imploring glances of his victim. For several moments he passes his tongue over that cheek. Oh! Look! Look there! The pink and white cheek has turned black, black as coal! It exhales a miasma of putrefaction. This is gangrene, no further room for doubt. The gnawing disease extends over the whole face and from there continues its ravages until soon the whole body is reduced to a great loathsome wound. Maldoror himself appalled (for he did not realise his tongue contained so virulent a poison) snatches up the lamp and flees from the church. Once outside he perceives in the air a blackish shape that bears itself wearily on singed wings up towards the regions of heaven. They look upon one another while the angel ascends towards the serene heights of virtue and Maldoror, on the contrary, descends into the vertiginous abyss of evil. What a look passes between them! All that humanity has thought in sixty centuries and much more that it will think could easily have been contained therein, so much do they say to one another in that supreme farewell! But one is aware that these are thoughts more elevated than those which spring from human intelligence; in the first place because of the persons involved and then because of the circumstances. That look binds them together in an eternal friendship.

Maldoror is astonished that the Creator can have missionaries with such noble souls. For an instant he believes himself mistaken and asks himself whether he should have followed the ways of evil as he has done. But the shadow passes and he remains firm in his resolution. And it would be glorious, according to him, sooner or later to conquer the All-in-All and to reign in his place over the entire universe and over legions of angels as beautiful as that one.

The ascending angel gives Maldoror to understand that he will resume his original form as he mounts toward Heaven; lets fall a tear to refresh the brow of *that one* who afflicted him with gangrene; and disappears little by little like a vulture amid the clouds.

Comte de Lautréamont

Ill. 286. Church Am Steinhof: Baldachin above the high altar. Made of copper and partly gilded.

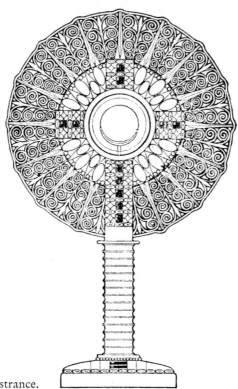

Ill. 287. Church Am Steinhof: The monstrance.

Ill. 288. Church Am Steinhof: Side view of the high altar and baldachin.

Ill. 289. Church Am Steinhof: False door at the side of the transept. The pillars were for the projected porch for the entrance to the crypt.

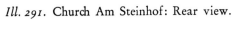
Ill. 290. Church Am Steinhof.

Ill. 291. Church Am Steinhof: Rear view.

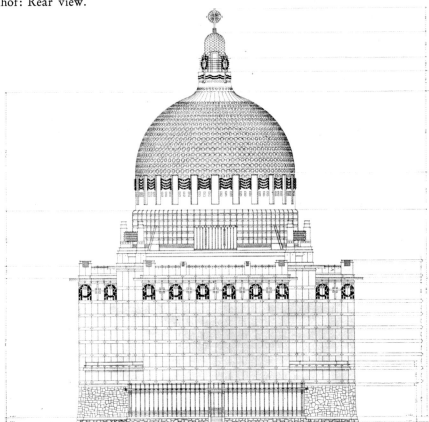

Ill. 292. Interimskirche ('Temporary Church', 1905): Ceiling construction: Rabitz panels in a framework of T-irons.

Ill. 293. Monumental fountain on the Karlsplatz (second design, 1905). Concrete pillars and super-structure faced with monnier and decorated with glazed tiles in white, black, blue and gold. Figures in porcelain, aluminium and copper. (For site of the fountain see *Ill. 217*).

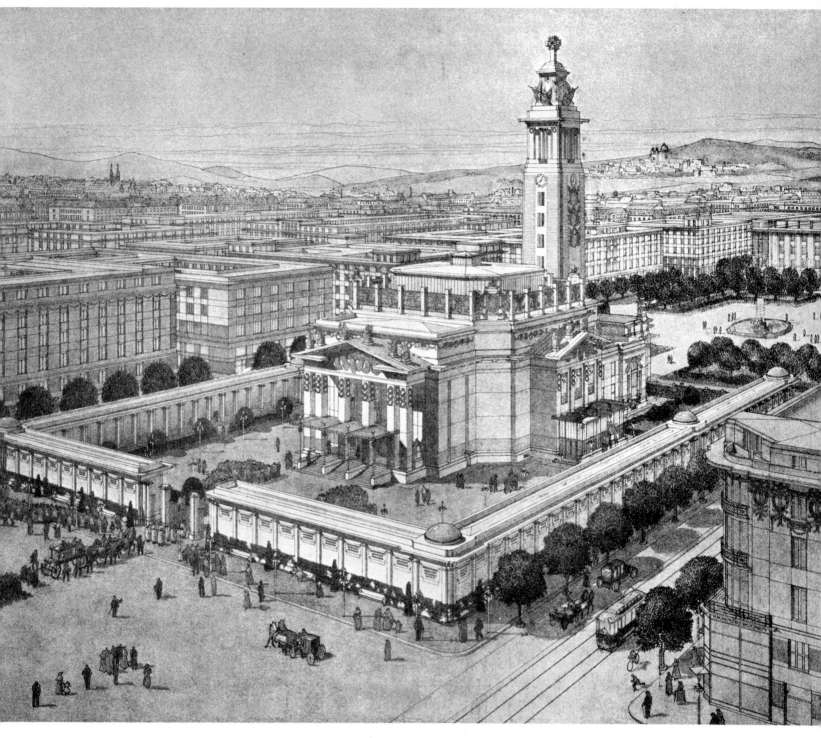

Ill. 294. Friedenskirche (or Siegeskirche 1917, Armistice, or Victory church). The silhouette of the Church Am Steinhof can be seen in the background.

STREET-PLAN SHOWING
WAGNER'S BUILDINGS
IN VIENNA

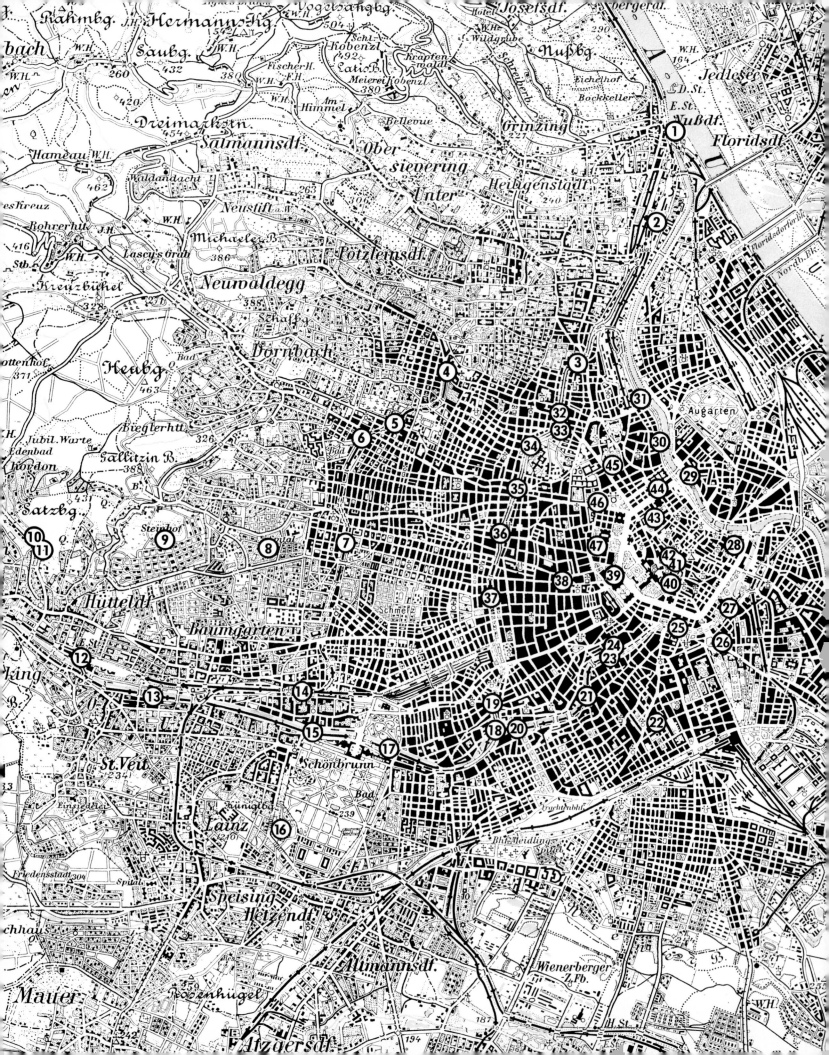

The following lists, in alphabetical order, all Wagner buildings extant in Vienna in 1965. Apart from two particularly important bridges the only Stadtbahn buildings listed are the stations. The Roman numerals denote city districts; the figures in brackets refer to the relevant illustrations; the italicised figures refer to the numbers on the streetplan.

Reproduced by kind permission of the Bundesamt für Eich- und Vermessungswesen (Landesaufnahme) in Wien, Zl. L 61 545/64. (Federal Office for Weights and Measures and Surveys [Land Records]).

CHRONOLOGICAL TABLE

The chronological table is arranged in four columns—two on the verso, two on the recto. Capitals have been used for the names of all buildings and important projects (columns 2 and 4), for the titles of books and important newspaper articles by Wagner and for publications by members of the 'Wagner school' (column 3). Simultaneous or closely related designs and buildings have been linked with brackets.

WAGNER'S DESIGNS		WAGNER'S COMPLETED BUILDINGS
Villas, hunting lodge (?) (Sketchbook)	1859	
Hunting lodge.	1860	
Casino in the Stadtpark, competition design.	1863	
	1864	—65 THEATRE IN THE WASAGASSE.
	1869	APARTMENT HOUSE, Bellariastrasse 4.
	1871	SYNAGOGUE IN BUDAPEST.
	1873	—74 GRABENHOF (with O. Thienemann).
Palace of Justice, competition design.	1874	
Landtag building in Lemberg, competition design.	1875	
Rathaus in Hamburg, competition design.	1876	
House for Herr K.		
Private museum for . . .		
	1877	APARTMENT HOUSE, Schottenring 23.
	1878	DIANABAD (conversion).
Church in Soborsin.	1879	DECORATIONS FOR THE MAKART
Apartment house on the Stadiongasse.		PROCESSION.
Apartment house on the Freisingergasse for the Assicurazione Generali, competition design.		
'Artibus', an Ideal Design for a Museum Enclave.	1880	—81 APARTMENT HOUSE, Rathausstrasse 3.
Offices of the Giro- und Kassenverein, competition design.		
Goethe monument.	1881	DECORATIONS FOR THE RECEPTION OF PRINCESS STEPHANIE.

BIOGRAPHICAL EVENTS

1841		Born July 13, in Penzing, near Vienna.
1846		Death of father.
1850	—52	Attended Viennese Akademisches Gymnasium.
1852	—57	Pupil at the Kremsmünster Boarding School.
1857	—59	Attended Viennese Polytechnic.
1860	—61	Attended the Königliche Bauakademie in Berlin.
1861	—63	Studied under Siccardsburg and van der Nüll at the Academy of Fine Arts in Vienna.
1863		Married Josefine Domhart.
1864		Birth of son Otto.
1865		Birth of son Robert.
1867		Birth of daughter Susanne.
1879		Made a citizen of Vienna.
1880		Death of mother. Divorced from Josefine Domhart.
1881		Married Louise Stiffel.

EVENTS IN VIENNA

1843		A. von Siccardsburg became professor at the Academy of Fine Arts.
1844		E. van der Nüll became professor at the Academy of Fine Arts.
1846		T. von Hansen settled in Vienna.
1848		Revolution, flight of Metternich. Emperor Francis Joseph's accession. Foundation of the Association of Austrian Engineers and Architects.
1849	—56	ARSENAL (A. von Siccardsburg, E. van der Nüll, L. von Förster, T. von Hansen, K. Rösner).
1856	—79	VOTIVE CHURCH (H. von Ferstel).
1857		Emperor decided to raze the bastions and enlarge the inner city.
1860	—61	EVANGELICAL SCHOOL on the Karlsplatz (T. von Hansen).
1861	—63	HEINRICHSHOF (T. von Hansen).
	—69	OPERA HOUSE (A. von Siccardsburg, E. van der Nüll).
1863		Death of L. von Förster, the Ringstrasse designer.
1864	—68	HOCH- UND DEUTSCHMEISTER-PALAIS (T. von Hansen).
1865	—85	RINGSTRASSE development.
1868		Suicide of A. von Siccardsburg and E. van der Nüll.
	—69	BUILDING FOR THE MUSICAL ASSOCIATION (T. von Hansen).
1869	—73	FIRST MOUNTAIN CONDUIT.
	—75	REGULATION OF THE DANUBE.
	—84	T. von Hansen became professor at the Academy of Fine Arts.
1871	—76	G. Semper in Vienna.
1872	—76	ACADEMY OF FINE ARTS on the Schillerplatz (T. von Hansen).
	—81	HOFMUSEEN [Imperial Museums] (G. Semper, K. von Hasenauer).
	—83	RATHAUS (F. von Schmidt).
1873		International Exhibition in Vienna. ROTUNDA (Scott-Russel, K. von Hasenauer and others).
	—84	UNIVERSITY (H. von Ferstel).
1874	—77	EXCHANGE (T. von Hansen).
	—83	PARLIAMENT BUILDING (T. von Hansen).
1879		H. Makart became professor at the Academy of Fine Arts.
1880	—86	BURGTHEATER (G. Semper, K. von Hasenauer).
1881	—1913	NEUE HOFBURG (G. Semper, K. von Hasenauer and others).

WAGNER'S DESIGNS		WAGNER' COMPLETED BUILDINGS
Reichstag building in Berlin, competition design. Parliament building in Budapest, competition design. Länderbank, competition design.	1882	—83 APARTMENT HOUSE, Stadiongasse 6-8.
Exchange Building in Amsterdam, Competition design. Land Credit Association, competition design.	1883 1884	—84 LÄNDERBANK. APARTMENT HOUSE, Lobkowitzplatz 1.
	1885	—86 VILLA HAHN IN BADEN (near Vienna), Weilburgstrasse 81.
Russian embassy.	1886 1888	—88 FIRST VILLA WAGNER, Hüttelbergstrasse 26. APARTMENT HOUSE, Universitätsstrasse 12.
Parish church in Esseg.	1890 —91	⌐ PALAIS WAGNER, Rennweg 3. APARTMENT HOUSE, Rennweg 1. ⌊ APARTMENT HOUSE, Auenbrugger-gasse 2.
Berliner Dom project.	1891	
⌐ Regulation of the Stubenviertel, competition 1892— design. General plan for the regulation of Vienna, ⌊ competition design. Ministry of Trade. Barracks for an infantry regiment. Monumental building in Innsbruck.	1893 1893	
	1894 (c.) —98 —98 —99	WAGNER'S TOMB. NUSSDORF DAM. ⌐ VORORTELINIE OF THE STADT-BAHN. GÜRTELLINIE OF THE STADTBAHN. UPPER WIENTALLINIE OF THE ⌊ STADTBAHN. LOWER WIENTALLINIE OF THE STADT-BAHN.
Equestrian statue for Emperor Francis Joseph.	1895	NEUMANN DEPARTMENT STORE, Kärnt-nerstrasse. ANKER BUILDING on Graben. JOHANNESKAPELLE.
Ferdinandsbrücke. Museum of Plaster Casts.	1896	
National Monument. Pavilion for the Jubilee Exhibition of 1898.	1897	
Academy of Fine Arts. Parish Church in Währing Capuchin church and cloisters Hofburg (Ausbau)	1898 —99 —1900 —1901 —1904	⌐ APARTMENT HOUSE, Linke Wien-zeile 38. APARTMENT HOUSE, Linke Wien-zeile 40. ⌊ APARTMENT HOUSE, Köstlergasse 3. ⌐ STADTBAHN LINIE TO THE IInd DISTRICT. DONAUKANALLINIE OF THE STADT-⌊ BAHN. QUAYSIDE INSTALLATIONS ON THE DANUBE CANAL.

BIOGRAPHICAL EVENTS		EVENTS IN VIENNA	
		1882	CONSERVATORY in Schönbrunn (F. Segenschmid)
		1883	Death of H. von Ferstel.
1884	Birth of son Stefan.	1884	Death of H. Makart.
1885	Birth of daughter Louise.		
1886	Collective exhibition in the Künstlerhaus.		
1889	Birth of daughter Christine.	1889	C. Sitte: *Municipal Building based on Artistic Principles.*
1890	'EINIGE SKIZZEN, PROJEKTE UND AUSGEFÜHRTE BAUWERKE, Vol. I.	1890	Incorporation of the suburbs on the south bank of the Danube into Greater Vienna.
		1891	Death of T. von Hansen.
			Death of F. von Schmidt.
		1892	Transportation Bill.
1893	EXPLANATORY REPORT, APPENDIX TO THE PLAN FOR THE REGULATION OF VIENNA, 1st edn.	1894	Death of K. von Hasenauer.
1894	2nd ed.		G. Klimt denied professorial post at the Academy of Fine Arts.
	Appointed full professor and head of a special School of Architecture at the Academy of Fine Arts in Vienna.		
	Appointed *Oberbaurat.*	—1907	REGULATION OF THE RIVER WIEN.
	Appointed artistic adviser to the Viennese Transport Commission and the Commission for the Regulation of the Danube Canal.	—1908	REGULATION OF THE DANUBE CANAL
1895	MODERNE ARCHITEKTUR, 1st ed.	1895	—99 L. Boltzmann: "Lectures on the kinetic theory of gases".
	Appointed to the permanent art commission and the Art Council in the Ministry of Culture and Education.		—1901 E. Mach appointed professor of philosophy in Vienna.
1896	Co-author of the Academy's "Loyal Address" to the emperor.	1896	Archduke Francis Ferdinand declared heir to the throne.
			A. Loos returned from the *U.S.A.*
			HERZMANSKY DEPARTMENT STORE, Stiftgasse (M. Katscher).
			—97 RIESENRAD (W. Basset).
			Founding of the Viennese Secession.
1897	EINIGE SKIZZEN, PROJEKTE UND AUSGEFÜHRTE BAUWERKE, Vol. II.		—98 SECESSION BUILDING (J. M. Olbrich).
	AUS DER WAGNERSCHULE (Publications by the 'Wagner school') 1897.		—1900 A. Loos: *Ins Leere gesprochen* [Talking to the Wind].
	Academy representative at the International Congress of Architects in Brussels.		—1910 K. Lueger became burgomaster.
1898	AUS DER WAGNERSCHULE 1898.	1898	Emperor Francis Joseph's official Jubilee.
	Contributed to the Jubilee Exhibition (especially bedroom and bathroom).		Jubilee exhibition.
	Appointed to the governing body of the Austrian Museum for Art and Industry.		J. Kotera (Wagner student) appointed to the staff of the School of Arts and Crafts in Prague.
	Awarded the Order of the Iron Crown (IIIrd Class).		
1899	MODERNE ARCHITEKTUR, 2nd ed.	1899	J. M. Olbrich invited to join the artists' colony in Darmstadt.
	AUS DER WAGNERSCHULE 1899.		J. Hoffmann (Wagner student) and K. Moser appointed professors at the School of Arts and Crafts.
	Juror at the competition for the buildings at the Viennese Central Cemetery.		K. Kraus founded *Die Fackel.*
	Joined the Viennese Secession.		CAFE MUSEUM (A. Loos).
			—1900 PORTOIS & FIX BUILDING, Ungargasse (M. Fabiani).

WAGNER'S DESIGNS		WAGNER'S COMPLETED BUILDINGS
Moderne Galerie. Emperor Francis Joseph Municipal Museum on the Karlsplatz, preliminary design.	1900	GROUP VI ENGINEERING and EXHIBIT FOR THE DIRECTORS OF THE HOF-GARTEN at the International Exhibition in Paris.
Emperor Francis Joseph Municipal Museum on the Karlsplatz, open competition design.	1901	
Emperor Francis Joseph Municipal Museum on the Karlsplatz, closed competition design. Church Am Steinhof, competition design. Cathedral of Patras, competition design. Little theatre.	1902	TELEGRAPH OFFICE OF *DIE ZEIT*.
Emperor Francis Joseph Municipal Museum on the Karlsplatz, Model competition.	1902 —1903	
⎡ Emperor Francis Joseph Municipal Museum on the Karls-platz. ⎢ Regulation of the Karlsplatz. ⎣ Monumental fountain on the Karlsplatz. Post Office Savings Bank, competition design. Exhibition building for the Museum of Arts and Crafts.	1903	
Department store for the Karlsplatz. Vindobonabrücke.	1904	—06 POST OFFICE SAVINGS BANK, First Stage. —08 KAISERBAD DAM.
Interimskirche. Palace of Peace in the Hague, competition design. ⎡ Emperor Francis Joseph Municipal Museum on the Karls-platz, (like 1903 design). ⎣ Monumental fountain on the Karlsplatz. Ferdinandsbrücke (two designs). Second Villa Wagner, preliminary sketch. Palace of Peace in the Hague (variant of 1905 design). Palace for Viennese Society (two designs). Colonnades in Karlsbad, competition design.	1905	—07 CHURCH AM STEINHOF.
	1906	
Emperor Francis Joseph Municipal Museum on the Karlsplatz (like 1909 design). Zedlitzhalle as art gallery.	1907	
War Ministry, competition design. Ministry of Trade. House of Glory. Lupus Sanatorium, Prel. Sketch.	1907 —1908 1908	
⎡ Emperor Francis Joseph Municipal Museum on the Karls-platz. ⎣ "Culture" statue. Technical Museum, competition design.	1909	—10 APARTMENT HOUSE, Neustiftgasse 40.

BIOGRAPHICAL EVENTS		EVENTS IN VIENNA	
1900	Juror at the International Exhibition in Paris.	1900	S. Freud: *Interpretation of Dreams.* A. Schnitzler: *Der Reigen.*
		—01	VILLA VOJCSIK, Linzer Strasse (O. Schönthal, Wagner student).
1901	AUS DER WAGNERSCHULE 1900. Made a member of the French *légion d'honneur.*	1901	—02 HAUS ARTARIA, Kohlmarkt (M. Fabiani).
		—02	APARTMENT HOUSE, Rechte Wienzeile 68 (J. Plečnik, Wagner student).
		—02	WORKERS' HOSTEL, Laxenburger Strasse (H. and F. Gessner, Wagner students).
		—03	VILLAS ON THE HOHE WARTE (J. Hoffmann, Wagner student).
1902	MODERNE ARCHITEKTUR, 3rd ed. WAGNERSCHULE 1901	1902	J. Kotéra (Wagner student): *The Works of Jan Kotéra and His Students 1898-1901.*
1903	WAGNERSCHULE 1902 Co-founder of the Association of Austrian Architects.	1903	Death of C. Sitte. Founding of the Wiener Werkstätte. O. Weininger: *Geschlecht und Charakter* [Sex and Character]. A. Loos: *Das Andere* [The Other].
		—05	ZACHERLHAUS, Brandstätte (J. Plečnik, Wagner student).
		—07	MOUTH OF THE RIVER WIEN in the Stadtpark (F. Ohmann, J. Hackhofer).
1904	—07 Contributed to the magazine, *Hohe Warte.*	1904	Incorporation of the suburbs on the north bank of the Danube into greater Vienna. GERNGROSS WAREHOUSE, Mariahilfer Strasse (F. Fellner, H. Helmer).
		—05	PURKERSDORF SANATORIUM (J. Hoffmann, Wagner student).
		—27	F. Ohmann professor at the Academy of Fine Arts.
1905	WAGNERSCHULE 1902-3 and 1903-4. Left the Secession with the Klimt group.	1905	Klimt group left the Secession.
		—10	J. Hoffmann (Wagner student) built the PALAIS STOCLET in Brussels.
1906	EINIGE SKIZZEN, PROJEKTE UND AUSGEFÜHRTE BAUWERKE, Vol. III. Took part in the International Congress of Architects in London.	1906	Founding of the mosaic shop of the Wiener Werkstätte. L. Hevesi: *Acht Jahre Sezession* [Eight Years Secession]. R. Musil: *Die Verwirrungen des Zöglings Törless.*
1907	Made a Commander of the Order of Emperor Francis Joseph.	1907	Death of F. Schachner. KÄRNTNERBAR (A. Loos).
		—08	LUITHLEN SANATORIUM, Auerspergstrasse (R. Oerley).
		—10	CHURCH AND PORTICOS at the Central Cemetery (M. Hegele). L. Trotsky in Vienna.
1908	President of the International Congress of Architects in Vienna. Awarded the *Jeton d'Or* by the Société centrale des architectes françaises.	1908	Death of J. M. Olbrich in Düsseldorf. A. Loos: *Ornament und Verbrechen.* HANDELSAKADEMIE, Hamerlingplatz (W. Deininger, Wagner student).
		—09	HAMMERBROT FACTORY (H. and F. Gessner, Wagner students). A. Hitler in Vienna.
1909	ZUR KUNSTFÖRDERUNG, EIN MAHNWORT. [On the Promotion of Art: A reminder].	1909	Death of E. von Förster.
		—10	URANIA (M. Fabiani).
		—13	WAR MINISTRY (L. Baumann).

WAGNER'S DESIGNS			WAGNER'S COMPLETED BUILDINGS
Academy of Fine Arts on the Schmelz.		1910	—12 POST OFFICE SAVINGS BANK, Second stage.
The Emperor Francis Joseph Municipal Museum on the Schmelz University library.			—13 LUPUS SANATORIUM.
Hotel on the Ringstrasse.			
Hotel on the Karlsplatz.	1910—	1911	
xxiind Viennese District.	1910—	1911	
Emperor Francis Joseph Municipal Museum on the Schmelz — Opus iv, competition design.		1912	APARTMENT HOUSE, Döblergasse 4.
			—13 SECOND VILLA WAGNER, Hüttelbergstrasse 28.
House of Art for the Twentieth Century.		1913	
The Zedlitzhalle as an exhibition hall for craft products.			
University library.		1914	
Palmschloss Sanatorium near Brixen.			
Bungalow installation for convalescent soldiers.	1914—	1915	
Equestrian monument of Emperor Francis Joseph.		1916	
Forest School in the Wienerwald.			
Brigittabrücke (design for a conversion).		1917	
Armistice Church.			
Haus des Kindes (House for Children).	1917—	1918	

BIOGRAPHICAL EVENTS		EVENTS IN VIENNA	
1910	WAGNERSCHULE 1905-6 and 1906-7. Invited to attend the International Congress of Municipal Art in New York. Academy representative on the executive committee of the Central Office for the promotion of Viennese fashion.	1910	HAUS GOLDMANN & SALATSCH, Michaelerplatz (A. Loos). HAUS STEINER, St. Veit-Gasse (A. Loos).
—11	Prorector of the Academy of Fine Arts.	—12	HEILIGGEISTKIRCHE, Herbststrasse (J. Plečnik, Wagner student).
1911	DIE GROSSSTADT [The Big City]. LAIENURTEILE IN DER KUNST [Lay Assessments in Art] (Neue Freie Presse).	1911	J. Plečnik (Wagner student) invited to teach at the School for Arts and Crafts in Prague. A. Schönberg: Harmonielehre [Doctrine of Harmony].
—12	'Year of Honour' at the Academy. Awarded the golden Salvator medaillon by the Viennese Municipal Council.	—12	STAND FOR THE VIENNESE TROTTING ASSOCIATION (O. Schönthal, E. Hoppe, M. Kammerer; all Wagner students).
1912	DAS EHRENJAHR OTTO WAGNERS [Otto Wagner's 'Year of Honour']. DIE QUALITÄT DES BAUKÜNSTLERS [The Quality of the Architect]. Vice president of the Permanent Commission of the Congress of Fine Arts in Paris. Appointed Hofrat. Permanent retirement.	1912	Founding of the Austrian Werkbund. HAUS SCHEU, La-Roche-Gasse (A. Loos). POLDIHÜTTE (J. Hoffmann, Wagner student).
1913 —15	Continued to teach the students with him at the time of his retirement; retained courtesy title of professor.	1913	S. Freud: Totem and Taboo. J. Stalin wrote Marxism and the National Problem in Vienna. KNIZE on Graben (A. Loos).
		—14	PALAIS LEMBERGER, Grinzinger Allee (J. Kotera, Wagner student).
		—14	KAASGRABEN VILLA COLONY (J. Hoffmann, Wagner student).
		—19	L. Bauer (Wagner student) appointed professor at the Academy of Fine Arts.
1914	DIE BAUKUNST UNSERER ZEIT [Architecture of our Time]. J. Lux published OTTO WAGNER.	1914	Assassination of Archduke Francis Ferdinand in Sarajevo. R. M. Schindler went to America.
1915	Illness and death of wife. Beginning of diary.		
1917	ÜBER ARCHITEKTENKAMMERN [On Architectural Committees] (Neue Freie Presse). VIENNA AFTER THE WAR (Neue Freie Presse). Preface to the diary. Awarded honorary doctorate (Engineering) by the Department for High Buildings at the Technical College in Dresden.	1916	Death of Emperor Francis Joseph.
		1917	G. Klimt made an honorary member of the Academy of Fine Arts.
1918	Died in Vienna on April 11.	1918	Death of G. Klimt. Death of K. Moser. Death of W. List. Death of E. Schiele.
		1919	A. Loos: Richtlinien für ein Kunstamt [Guidelines for a Ministry of Art] (With contributions by A. Schöneberg and others). Death of P. Altenberg.

BIOGRAPHICAL EVENTS		EVENTS IN VIENNA	
		1921	"Haus mit einer Mauer" [House with on Wall] (Patent by A. Loos). A. Berg: *Wozzek*.
1922	EINIGE SKIZZEN, PROJEKTE UND AUS-GEFÜHRTE BAUWERKE, Vol. IV. Hans Tietze published his *Otto Wagner*.	1922	K. Kraus: *Die letzten Tage der Menschheit* [The Last Days of Mankind]. HAUS RUFER, Schliessmanngasse (A. Loos).
		—36	P. Behrens professor at the Academy of Fine Arts.
		1923	Death of J. Kotera (Wagner student) in Prague.
		1924	Death of F. Kafka.

NOTES

LIFE

1. Hansen (1813-91) built the Heinrichshof, in which Wagner took up residence immediately upon completion, and the Academy on the Schillerplatz, in which Wagner later taught.
2. Luise Wick-Wagner: *Otto Wagner, wie ich ihn als Tochter sah* (A Profile of Otto Wagner by his Daughter), unpublished *ms.* p. 11.
3. Stummer von Traunfels (?-1890) had taught August von Siccardsburg, who subsequently taught Wagner.
4. Siccardsburg (1813-68) and van der Nüll (1812-68) committed suicide following the violent public and press reaction to the Opera House, which was then nearing completion.
5. In a preface written in 1917 for his diary, which covered the period from August 1915 to the end of March 1918. The full text of the preface has been lost but fragments are quoted in Luise Wick-Wagner (op. cit.) *Künstlerbriefe aus Oesterreich* (Letters by Austrian Artists), ed. by Max Eisler in: Oesterreich. Rundschau, 2. Jg., Vienna and Leipzig 1936, p. 300 ff.; *Otto Wagner* by Hans Ostwald, Diss E. T. H. Zürich, Baden 1948, pp. 16-7, 20-1, 24-5.
6. Letters to Louise Stiffel (Copies in the possession of Frau Lütgendorff-Gyllenstorm, mostly undated.)
7. Ibid.
8. See Wagner's *Die Baukunst unserer Zeit* (Architecture Today), Vienna 1914, p. 26, where Wagner states that no architect can be 'completely mature' before he is forty.
9. The dates refer to the construction period. Where no town is cited the building or project in question was intended for Vienna.
10. In a letter to Louise Stiffel (cf. note 6).
11. 'Otto Wagner was regarded as a newer and purer version of Piranesi. This was why he was honoured with a professorship at the Academy.' Joseph August Lux, *Otto Wagner*, Munich 1914, pp. 59-60.
12. Explanatory Report on the "Plan for the General Regulation of the Municipality of Vienna", Vienna 1893 and 1894.

13. The Academy also recommended that Wagner's friend Gustav Klimt be made a professor but this was turned down by the Ministry of Culture and Education.
14. *Baurat* and *Oberbaurat*: titles accorded to distinguished architects and engineers in Germany and Austria.
15. Wagner, *Moderne Architektur* (Modern Architecture), Vienna 1895, Preface.
16. Wagner, *Einige Skizzen, Projekte und ausgeführte Bauwerke* (Some Sketches, Designs and Buildings), Vol. III, Vienna 1906, Section 4, p. 11.
17. Ibid., Section 8, p. 5.
18. The Künstlerhaus, created in 1861, was an amalgamation of two professional societies. It became the sole authority on matters of artistic taste and was patronised by the court, the aristocracy and high society in general. In 1897 a group of its members (among them Klimt and Olbrich) formed an independent club and called themselves 'The Association of Austrian Artists—Secession'. Their aim was to elevate Austrian art to an international level and to integrate art with art forms generally. Olbrich built an exhibition hall for this group in 1898. Their views were aired in the magazine *Ver Sacrum*. Wagner became a member from 1899, but his advanced theories on architecture probably contributed to the establishment of the group in the first place. The Secession had close links with modern movements in other countries—notably the Impressionists in France, Henry van de Velde in Holland and Charles Rennie Mackintosh's Glasgow Group. Its members, in particularly Josef Hoffmann, Kolo Moser and Fritz Wärndorfer also formed the Wiener Werkstätte, a vast atelier which concerned itself with architectural designs, product design and various other commissions. However, in 1905, a further break-away group, centred on Gustav Klimt, was formed. It aimed at a greater integration of art and every aspect of contemporary life, as opposed to the remaining members of the Secession who were dedicated to art for its own sake and did not therefore wish to concern themselves with problems of product design, commercial art etc. The formation of this splinter group weakened the Secession very considerably.

19. Lux; op. cit., p. 69.
20. Wagner, op. cit., Section 21.
21. Ibid., Plates 26 and 27, p. 7. (See Hevesi's comment: 'Schachner's columns are 13.10 metres high [including the base] and 1.32 metres in diameter whilst those on the Karlskirche are only 9.85 metres high and 0.95 metres in diameter. The pediment on the church portal is 17.50 metres high, that on the museum portal 27.70 metres.' Ludwig Hevesi on Schachner's competition design in *Acht Jahre Sezession*, Vienna 1906, pp. 436-7.)
22. Ibid., p. 7.
23. Ibid., p. 12.
24. See Wagner, "Über Architektenkammern" (On Architectural Chambers) in *Neue Freie Presse*, Vienna, June 8, 1917. Architektenkammern (architectural chambers) are official institutions in Austria which are set up in all towns. Only the members of these chambers are allowed to practise as architects.
25. Lower Austria Provincial Council. Statement issued upon completion of the church, Vienna 1907.
26. Ludwig Hevesi, *Acht Jahre Sezession*, Vienna 1906, p. 138.
27. 'In 1912, while still a student, Schindler wrote a manifesto . . . in which he announced, "The old problems have been solved and the styles are dead . . . The architect has finally discovered the medium of his art: SPACE. A new architectural problem has been born." ' (Esther McCoy, "R. M. Schindler" in: *Five California Architects*, New York 1960, p. 152).
28. Hevesi, op. cit., p. 282.
29. See Adolf Loos, "Die Interieurs in der Rotunde" (Interior Design in the Rotunda) and "Das Sitzmöbel" (Chairs) in: *Ins Leere gesprochen* (Talking to the Wind), Innsbruck 1932, pp. 44 ff. and 48 ff.
30. *Illustrierte Zeitung*, Leipzig May 14, 1908, p. 941.
31. *Oesterreichs Illustrierte Zeitung*, Vienna, May 11, 1913, p. 782.
32. Luise Wick-Wagner, op. cit., p. 29.
33. A *Hofrat* was originally an Aulic councillor but by Wagner's day the title was a purely honorary one which was conferred on distinguished men in all walks of life.
34. Wagner's diary entry for October 26, 1915 (the day of his wife's death).
35. Diary entry for October 29, 1915.
36. Quoted in Lux, op. cit., pp. 143-4.
37. Wagner's diary entry for August 22, 1917
38. Diary entry for August 24, 1917.
39. Diary entry for September 13, 1917.
40. Diary entry for July 28, 1917.
41. Diary entry for May 27, 1917.
42. Diary entry for August 16, 1917.

THE EXPANDING CITY: THE BEGINNING OF MODERN ARCHITECTURE

1. Derived from the 'k. k.' of 'kaiserlich-königlich' (Imperial-Royal).
2. Robert Musil, *The Man Without Qualities*, London 1953. Translated from the German by Eithne Wilkins and Ernst Kaiser. Vol. I, pp. 33-5.
3. Wagner's preface to his diary.
4. Lux, op. cit., p. 38.
5. Wagner, *Einige Skizzen, Projekte und ausgeführte Bauwerke*, Vol. IV, Vienna 1922, p. 4 and Plate 33.
6. Le Corbusier, *The Modulor*. Translated from the French by P. de Francia and A. Bostock, London 1954, p. 60 ff.
7. Karl R. Holey, "Die Entwicklung der Architektur Wiens in den letzten fünfzig Jahren" (The Development of Viennese Architecture over the last Fifty Years) in: *Technischer Führer durch Wien* (Technical Guide through Vienna), 1910, p. 255.
8. Theophil von Hansen.
9. Built by Heinrich von Ferstel (1828-83).
10. Friedrich von Schmidt (1825-91). The Rathaus was completed in 1883.
11. Holey, op. cit., p. 248 ff.
12. Wagner, *Einige Skizzen, Projekte und ausgeführte Bauwerke*. Vol. IV did not appear until after Wagner's death.
13. Wagner, *Einige Skizzen . . .*, Vol. III, Section 17, p. 3.
14. Ibid., p. 3.
15. Ibid., Print 8, p. 10.

UNSYMPATHETIC AND ASSIMILATED TECHNOLOGY

1. Barlow (1812-1902), who also played a major part in the preliminary planning for the Firth of Forth bridge. See F. A. Talbot, *Railway Wonders of the World*, London 1913-14, Vol. 2.
2. C. L. F. Dutert (1845-1906) was the architect, cf. Nikolaus Pevsner, *Pioneers of Modern Design*, London 1960. (*Wegbereiter moderner Formgebung*, Hamburg 1957, p. 82) Contamin (1840-93) was the engineer. Cf. Pevsner op. cit.
3. Wagner, *Einige Skizzen . . .*, Vol. III, Section 8, p. 5.
4. H. Mathesius's publication, *Baukunst, nicht Stilarchitektur*, prompted Wagner to publis the 4th edition under the title, *Die Baukunst unserer Zeit*.
5. Wagner, *Die Grossstadt*, Vienna 1911, p. 17.
6. Wagner, *Die Baukunst unserer Zeit*, Vienna 1914, p. 47.
7. See Wagner, *Die Qualität des Baukünstlers* (The Quality of the Architect), Leipzig and Vienna 1912, p. 31.
8. Wagner, *Die Baukunst unserer Zeit*, Vienna 1914, p. 62.
9. Félix Candela, "Weg zu einer neuen Strukturauffassung" (The Way to a New Conception of Structure) in: *Baukunst und Werkform* (Architecture and Building Form) 1959, Issue No. 9, p. 470. Candela (born 1910) has shown that the over-refinement and oversimplification of the calculating methods derived from the theory of elasticity can lead to absurd results.
10. Wagner, *Die Baukunst unserer Zeit*, p. 62.
11. Ibid., p. 60.
12. Ibid., p. 61.
13. Ibid., p. 67.

THE DEMYSTIFICATION OF ART

1. Siegfried Giedion, *Space, Time and Architecture*, Cambridge 1956, p. 5.
2. Wagner, *Die Baukunst unserer Zeit*, p. 128.

3. Ibid., p. 41.
4. Ibid., pp. 45 and 46.
5. Ibid., p. 126.
6. Ibid., p. 135.
7. Albert Einstein, preface to *Wahrheit — relativ oder absolut?*, Zürich 1952, p. 5.
8. Wagner, op. cit., p. 39.
9. Ibid., p. 103.
10. Le Corbusier, "An Appeal to Students", published in the *Charte d'Athènes*, Hamburg 1962, p. 24.
11. Edgar Allen Poe, "The Philosophy of Composition" in: *The Centenary Poe*, London 1949, p. 492.
12. Wagner, op. cit., pp. 135-6.

THE AVOIDANCE OF SIMPLIFICATION IN ART

1. Otto Wagner, *Die Baukunst unserer Zeit*, 1914, p. 44.
2. Sergei Eisenstein, *Film Form,* New York 1957, p. 261.
3. Wagner, op. cit., p. 44.
4. *Ecclesiastes* I, 8, 9.
5. *Revelation* X, 6.
6. Wagner, preface to his diary.
7. Charles Darwin in: Sir Francis Darwin (ed.), *Autobiography of Charles Darwin*, London 1929, p. 144.
8. The fact that no temporal sequence can be established in a single moment, *i. e.,* in what modern psychology calls 'present time', had already been observed by John Locke (1632-1704): 'Whether these several ideas in a man's mind be made by certain motions, I will not here dispute; but this I am sure, that they include no idea of motion in their appearance...' (*Essay Concerning Human Understanding*, 2 Vols, London 1965, Vol. I, Chap. XIV, Para 16.)
9. Wagner, *Die Baukunst unserer Zeit*, p. 43.
10. Buddha, *Majhimanikaya*, Book XIII, 121.
11. Thomas Aquinas, *Quaestiones disputatae de veritate* I, 9.

THE EXPANDING CITY

1. The Congrès Internationaux d'Architecture Modern was founded in 1928 at La Sarraz.
2. Reyner Banham, *"CIAM"* in: *Knaurs Lexikon der modernen Architektur*, Munich and Zürich 1963, p. 64.
3. Produced by *CIAM* IV in 1933, which met to discuss the subject "The Functional City".
4. Le Corbusier, op. cit., pp. 94 and 124-5.
5. Wagner, *Die Grosstadt*, p. 21.
6. Ibid., p. 17.
7. The rings roads would also reduce the amount of through traffic in the inner city.
8. Wagner, op. cit., p. 10.
9. Georges Eugène Haussmann (1809-91) replanned the whole of Paris between 1853 and 1869 during the reign of Napoleon III, who took an active interest in the work.

10. Wagner, Explanatory Report appended to the "plan for the General Regulation of the Municipality", Vienna 1894, p. 22.
11. Georges Eugène Haussmann, *Mèmoires,* Paris 1890-93, Vol. III, p. 55.
12. Wagner, *Die Grosstadt*, p. 18 ff.
13. Ibid., p. 20.
14. For example, building apartment houses in such a way that they would yield the greatest return on capital.
15. Wagner, *Die Baukunst unserer Zeit*, p. 87.
16. The third and fourth belts, including the Ringstrasse.
17. Wagner, *Die Grosstadt*, p. 8.
18. Ibid., pp. 10-11.
19. Norbert Wiener, *Mensch und Menschmaschine*, West Berlin 1958, pp. 44-5.
20. Wagner. op. cit., p. 5.
21. Wagner, *Die Baukunst unserer Zeit*, p. 87.
22. Wagner, *Die Grosstadt*, p. 3; cf., *Die Baukunst unserer Zeit*, p. 77.
23. Wagner, *Die Baukunst unserer Zeit*, Vienna 1914, p. 87.
24. Wagner, *Die Grosstadt*, p. 3; cf., *Die Baukunst unserer Zeit*, p. 77.
25. Wagner, *Die Grosstadt*, p. 16.
26. James Joyce, *Ulysses*, London 1936, p. 90.
27. These 'centres' were intended to serve areas of a radius of 1 kilometre. They each contained a mortuary set in public gardens, depots for building materials and fuel and assembly points for the disposal of waste and snow.
28. Wagner, Explanatory Report appended to the "Plan for the General Regulation of the Municipality", Vienna 1894, pp. 66-7.
29. Wagner, *Die Grosstadt*, p. 17.
30. Ibid., p. 21.
31. Wagner, Explanatory Report appended to the "Plan for the General Regulation of the Municipality", 1894, pp. 21-2,

THE FUTURE

1. Wagner, *Die Grosstadt*, p. 22.
2. Konrad Wachsmann, *Wendepunkt im Bauen* (The Turning Point in Building), Wiesbaden 1959, p. 231.
3. Wagner, *Die Baukunst unserer Zeit*, p. 136.
4. Wachsmann, op. cit., p. 29.
5. Ibid., p. 232.
6. Figures based on a report by the American Academy of Science (Reuter report, April 18, 1963). Similar figures are given by Hans G. Schachtschabel in *Automation in Wirtschaft und Gesellschaft* (Automation in Economy and Society), Hamburg 1961, p. 106.
7. Stafford Beer, *Cybernetics and Management*, London 1959, p. 88.
8. Adolf Loos, *Trotzdem* (Nonetheless), Innsbruck 1931, p. 107.

LIST OF ILLUSTRATIONS

Where no sources have been given the illustrations have been supplied by Josef Dapra. *Einige Skizzen, Projekte und ausgeführte Bauwerke* has been abbreviated throughout to *Einige Skizzen*... Vols II, III and IV of this work by Otto Wagner were published by Anton Schroll & Co, Vienna.

BIBLIOGRAPHY

Otto Wagner: Einige Skizzen, Projekte und ausgeführte Bauwerke, Vol. I, Vienna 1890 [with a preface]; Vol. II, Vienna 1897 [with a preface], Vol. III, Vienna 1906 [with a preface and explanatory texts] Vol. IV, Vienna 1922. — Explanatory Report appended to the Plan for the General Regulation of the Municipality of Vienna [Motto: 'Artis sola domina necessitas'], 1st edition Vienna 1893, 2nd edition Vienna 1894. — Moderne Architektur [An Architectural Guide for Wagner's Students], 1st edition Vienna 1895; 2nd edition Vienna 1899; 3rd edition Vienna 1902. — Die Baukunst unserer Zeit. A Guide for Young Architects, Vienna 1914 [= 4th edition of Moderne Architektur]. — Die Kunst im Gewerbe *in:* Ver Sacrum, Jg. III, Vienna 1900, Issue No. 2, pp. 21-32. — Preservation, not Renovation of St. Stephan in Vienna *in:* Zeit, Vienna 1902, Issue No. 381. — The Karlsplatz and the Emperor Francis Joseph Municipal Museum. A contribution to the solution of these problems, Vienna 1903. — Explanatory Report appended to the Competition Design for the Imperial and Royal Post Office Savings Bank, Vienna 1903. — Explanatory Report appended to the Design for a Bridge over the Danube Canal linking the Rothenturmstrasse and the Lilienbrunngasse [Vindobonabrücke], Vienna 1904. — Explanatory Report appended to the Design for the Fontes Unitae, a project for linking the Mühlbrunn, Marktbrunn and Schlossbrunn Colonnades in Karlsbad, Vienna 1906. — Study for a Palace for Viennese Society on the Parkring, Vienna 1906. — Report on the Erection of Various Important State and Civic Buildings by Salaried Officials *in:* Transactions of the VIIth International Congress of Architects (London 1906), London 1908, pp. 109-11. — Obituary on Josef Olbrich *in:* Der Architekt, Jg. XIV, Vienna 1908, pp. 161-3. — On the Promotion of Art. A Reminder, Vienna 1909. — Explanatory Report appended to the Proposal submitted for the Competition for a Technical Museum for Industry and Craft, Vienna 1909. — Building a Hotel [Ringstrasse] *in:* Jahrbuch der Gesellschaft österr. Architekten [Annual of the Association of Austrian Architects] 1909-10, Vienna 1910, pp. 10-18. — Die Grossstadt [The Big City], A Study, Vienna 1911. — Lay Assessments in Art *in:* Neue Freie Presse, Vienna, Feb. 11, 1911. — On Architecture, Issue No. 7 [Special Wagner Issue], p. 300. — *Leitmotif in:* Otto Wagner's 'Year of Honour' at the Imp. and Roy. Academy of Fine Arts in Vienna (Ed. Schönthal, Otto), Vienna 1912. — The Quality of the Architect *in:* Der Architekt, Jg. XVIII, Vienna 1912. — Competition for a Military Monument *in:* Neue Freie Presse, Vienna Nov., 5, 1915. — Vienna After the War *in:* Neue Freie Presse, April 7, 1917. — On Architectural Committees *in:* Neue Freie Presse, June 8, 1917.

Abels, Ludwig, Introduction to Aus der Wagnerschule MDCCCIC published *in* Der Architekt, Supplementary Issue No. 5, Vienna 1899. — *Abels, Ludwig,* Modern Buildings and Interior Decoration in Vienna *in:* Dekorative Kunst, Jg. IV, Munich 1900, pp. 89-118. — *Achleitner, Friedrich,* Sins of Building. The Karlsplatz Stations *in:* Abendzeitung, Vienna, Feb. 28, 1961. — *Achleitner, Friedrich,* Sins of Building. The Renovation of the Stadtbahn *in:* Abendzeitung, Vienna April 25, 1961. See also Stadtrat Schwaiger's reply *in:* Abendzeitung, Vienna June 20, 1961. — *Achleitner, Friedrich,* Sins of Building. A City Makes its Bow (Lupus Sanatorium, Controls Building of the Kaiserbad Dam) *in:* Abendzeitung May 23, 1961. See also reply by Obersenatsrat Ernst *in:* Abendzeitung July 17, 1961. — *Achleitner, Friedrich,* Remember Otto Wagner *in:* Die

Presse, Vienna June 15, 1963. — *Achleitner, Friedrich,* Otto Wagner Returns *in:* Wort und Wahrheit, Jg. XVIII, Vienna 1963, Issue No. 8/9, pp. 565-7. — *Achleitner, Friedrich,* The Devil out of Beelzebub [Villa Wagner] *in:* Die Presse, Vienna Oct. 26, 1963. — *Achleitner, Friedrich,* The Austrian Contribution to Modern Architecture *in:* Christliche Kunstblätter, Linz 1963, Issue No. 4. — *Achleitner, Friedrich,* Defacement by Instalments [Stadtbahn] *in:* Die Presse, Vienna Feb. 8-9, 1964. — *Achleitner, Friedrich,* The Documentation of a Great Epoch *in:* Die Presse, Vienna May 23-4, 1964. — *Achleitner, Friedrich,* Viennese Architecture at the Turn of the Century *in:* der aufbau, Jg. XIX, Vienna 1964, Issue No. 4/5, pp. 144-52. — *Ahlers-Hestermann, Friedrich,* Stilwende. Aufbruch der Jugend um 1900. [Change of Style. Revolution of the Younger Generation at the Turn of the Century], Berlin 1941, pp. 75-8. — The Imp. and Roy. *Academy of Fine Arts* in Vienna between 1892 and 1917, Vienna 1917, pp. 60, 68-9, 300-02. — *Allgemeine Kunst-Chronik,* Monuments and Buildings in Vienna, Vienna 1880, Vol. V, Issue No. 3, p. 32: The Memorial Column. — *Amtsblatt der k. k. Reichshaupt- und Residenzstadt Wien,* Stenographer's Report of the Proceedings at the Public Meeting of the Municipal Council... [Municipal Museum on the Karlsplatz] *in:* Jg. XI, Vienna June 13, 1902, pp. 1112-17, Dec. 5, 1902, pp. 2187-97, Dec. 12, 1902, pp. 2235-51; Stenographer's Report... [Municipal Museum on the Schmelz] *in:* Jg. XXI, July 16, 1912, pp. 2012-16, Jg. XXII, June 24, 1913, pp. 1820-43; Jury's Assessment of the Designs for the Emperor Francis Joseph Municipal Museum [Schmelz] *in:* Jg. XXII, May 2, 1913, pp. 1312-13. — *Andics, Hellmut,* Wagner Changes Vienna *in:* Kurier, Vienna, Feb. 14, 1963. — *Ankwicz-Kleehoven, Hans,* Austria and 20th Century Architecture *in:* Austria-International, Jg. I, Vienna 1950, pp. 44-7. — *Ankwicz-Kleehoven, Hans,* The Early Days of the Viennese Secession *in:* Alte und Moderne Kunst [Ancient and Modern Art], Jg. V, Issue No. 6/7, p. 6ff. — *Ankwicz-Kleehoven, Hans,* Otto Wagner *in:* Grosse Österreicher, Vienna 1947. — *Arbeitsgruppe 4 (Holzbauer, Wilhelm; Kurrent, Friedrich; Spalt, Johannes),* New Church Architecture *in:* der aufbau, Jg. XVI, Vienna 1961, Issue No. 6, pp. 233-6. — *Arbeitsgruppe 4,* New Museum Architecture *in:* der aufbau, Jg. XVIII, Vienna 1963, Issue No. 2, pp. 48-58. — *Arbeitsgruppe 4,* Church Architecture at the Turn of the Century *in:* Der Aufbau, Jg. XIX, Vienna 1964, Issue No. 4/5, pp. 153-6. — *Arbeitsgruppe 4,* Residential Architecture at the Turn of the Century *in:* der aufbau, Jg. XIX, Vienna 1964, Issue No. 4/5, pp. 157-64. — Der *Architekt,* Jg. II, Vienna 1896, p. 32: The Anker Insurance Building; Jg. IV, 1898, p. 27: Architectonic Details of the Viennese Stadtbahn; Jg. VI, 1900, p. 1: The Buildings for the Viennese Stadtbahn and the Regulation of the Danube; Jg. VII, 1901, pp. 33-4: On the Reform of Artistic Competitions (Competition for the Municipal Museum in Vienna); Jg. VIII, 1902, p. 47: The Aluminium Entrance Door to the Telegraph Office; Jg. XIII, 1907, p. 1: The Competition for the Karlsbad Colonnades; Jg. XV, 1909, p. 73: Design for the Lupus Sanatorium; Jg. XIX, 1913, p. 53-9: Competition Requirements and Building Schedule for the Emperor Francis Joseph Municipal Museum [Schmelz]: Aus der Wagnerschule [See Wagnerschule]. — Der Aufbau, Jg. XIII, Vienna 1958, Issue No. 4, pp. 145-8: Profile of Otto Wagner.

Bahr, Hermann, Secession, Vienna 1900, pp. 64, 109-16 [Otto Wagner], 121, 155-60 [Church Am Steinhof], 177-8, 192, 200. — *Bahr, Hermann,* Otto Wagner *in:* Berliner Tageblatt, July 6, 1911. — *Bauer, Leopold,* The Old and the New Path in Architecture *in:* Jg. IV, Vienna 1898, p. 32. — *Bauer, Leopold,* Otto Wagner *in:* Der Architekt, Jg. XXII, Vienna 1919, pp. 9-23. — *Der Bautechniker,* Vienna 1911, p. 231: Study for new building for the Academy of Fine Arts. — Die *Bau-und Werkkunst,* Jg. IV, Vienna and Munich 1927-28, pp. 231-2: Article commemorating the 10th anniversary of Wagner's death. — *Beer, Stafford,* Cybernetics and Management, London 1959. — *Behne, Adolf,* Otto Wagner *in:* Deutsche Kunst und Dekoration, Vol. XXXV, Darmstadt 1914-15, pp. 382-90. — *Behne, Adolf,* Der moderne Zweckbau [Purpose-built Structure of Today], Munich 1926, pp. 11-7, 22, 58, 60, 70 and Berlin-Frankfurt/Main-Vienna 1964, pp. 14, 23, 55, 57, 66. — *Bennecke, L.,* The Conversion of the Danube Canal into a Commercial and Winter Harbour *in:* Centralblatt der Bauverwaltung, Berlin 1897, Issues No. 4, 5 and 7. — *Besset, Maurice,* Topics and Dissensions at the Turn of the Century *in:* magnum, Cologne 1961, Issue No. 34, p. 59. — Book Auction of Dec. 7, 1910 [including works *ex libris* of Otto Wagner] listed in the Mitteilungsblatt des k. k. Versatz-, Verwahrungs- u. Versteigerungsamtes 'Dorotheum'. — *Buddha,* Majhimanikaya, XIIIth Book, 121.

Caramel, Luciano and Longatti, Alberto, Antonio Sant'Elia, Como 1962, pp. 13-4, 18-9, 24-5, 33, 133-4. — *Castelliz, Alfred,* The Completion of the Karlsplatz in Vienna *in:* Der Architekt, Jg. XVI, Vienna 1910, pp. 51-6. — *Centralblatt der Bauverwaltung,* Jg. II, Berlin 1882, Issue No. 4, p. 35; Issue No. 5, pp. 37-9 [Competition Announcement], 43; Issue No. 7, p. 60: The New Reichstag Building. — Der *Cicerone,* Jg. X, Leipzig 1918, p. 141: Otto Wagner. — *Le Corbusier,* The Modulor, Vols. I and II, London 1954 and 1958, Translated from the French by P. de Francia and A. Bostock. — *Coudenhove-Kalergi, Barbara and Lehner, Peter,* What is left of Otto Wagner? *in:* Kurier Supplement, Vienna Aug. 24, 1963. — *Czech, Hermann,* We underestimate our Stadtbahn *in:* Die Furche, Vienna 1963, Issue No. 20. — *Czech Hermann,* The Unornamental Otto Wagner *in:* Die Furche, Vienna 1963, Issue No. 31. — *Czepelka, A.,* Municipal Railway Systems in Europe, America and Vienna *in:* Zeit, Vienna 1899, Issue No. 268.

Dahlen, Josef von, Review of Modern Architecture *in:* Österreichisch-Ungarische Revue, Vol. XXII, Vienna 1897, pp. 75-90. — *Dahlen, Josef von,* The Old and the New Path in Architecture *in:* Der Architekt, Jg. IV, Vienna 1898, p. 30. — *Charles Darwin in:* Sir Francis Darwin (Ed.), The Autobiography of Charles Darwin, London 1929. — *Degener, Hermann,* Wer ist's? [Who is it?], Leipzig, 7th ed. p. 1785, 8th ed. p. 1790. — *Deininger, Julius,* Stenographer's record of speech in which Deininger protested on behalf of the Artists' Association in the matter of the Municipal Museum designed by Otto Wagner for the Karlsplatz; speech delivered Jan 4, 1910 and printed in the Jahrbuch der Gesellschaft österr. Architekten 1909-10, Vienna 1910, pp. 43-55, and in Bildende Künstler, Vienna and Leipzig, Issue No. 7 [Special Issue on Otto Wagner], pp. 310-22. — *Deininger, Julius,* Obituary on Otto Wagner *in:* Zentralblatt der Bauverwaltung, Jg. XXXVIII, Berlin 1918, p. 175.

— *Deutsche Bauzeitung.* Competition for the Hamburg Rathaus *in:* Jg. x, Berlin 1876, Issue No. 85, p. 430; The Judges' Decision in the Competition for the Hamburg Rathaus *in:* Jg. x, 1876, Issue No 86, p. 431; The Competition for Designs for the Hamburg Rathaus *in:* Jg. x, 1876, Issue No. 93, pp. 463-4, Issue No. 99, pp. 495-7, Issue No. 101, pp. 503-5, Issue No. 103, pp. 513-6, Issue No. 104, pp. 521-4; Austro-Hungarian Competitions (Parliament Building in Budapest) *in:* Jg. xvii, 1883, Issue No. 38, p. 228; On the Replanning of the Karlsplatz in Vienna *in:* Jg. xxxviii, 1904, Issue No. 59, pp. 365-8, Issue No. 71, pp. 443-7 [Otto Wagner]; Ten Years of the Viennese School *in:* Jg. xxxix, 1905, Issue No. 71, pp. 430-2; The International Competition for the Palace of Peace in The Hague *in:* Jg. xl, 1906, Issue No. 44, pp. 309-10, Issue No. 49, pp. 344-5 [Otto Wagner], Issue No. 52, pp. 360-1 [Otto Wagner], Issue No. 58, pp. 396-8; Designs for the International Competition for the Palace of Peace in The Hague *in:* Jg. xli, 1907, Issue No. 22, pp. 154-6; Book Review of Die Grossstadt [The Big City] *in:* Jg. xlv, 1911, Issue No. 55, pp. 475-9; Otto Wagner's 70th Birthday *in:* Jg. xlv, 1911, Issue No. 55, pp. 474-5, Issue No 57, pp. 486-8; The Presentation of the great golden Salvator medallion to Oberbaurat Otto Wagner by the Municipality of Vienna *in:* Jg. xlv, 1911, Issue No. 64, p. 548; Review of Lux's monograph on Otto Wagner *in:* Jg. xlviii, 1914, Issue No. 53, pp. 525-7. — *Deutsches Biographisches Jahrbuch,* Überleitungsband ii [German Biographical Annual, Link Volume ii]: 1917-20, Stuttgart—Berlin—Leipzig 1928, List of the Dead 1918, p. 707. — *Deutsch-German, Alfred,* Wiener Portraits, Vienna 1903, pp. 27-32. — *Deutsch-Österreichisches Künstler-und Schriftstellerlexikon* [German and Austrian Artists' and Writers' Lexikon], Vol. i, Vienna 1902, p. 32. — *Dimitriou Sokratis,* Grossstadt Wien. Städtebau der Jahrhundertwende. [The Big City of Vienna. Municipal Building at the Turn of the Century.] *in:* der aufbau, Jg. xix, Vienna 1964, Issue No. 4/5, pp. 188-200. — *Dreger, Moritz,* Otto Wagner's Academy of Art *in:* Zeit, Vienna 1898, Issue No. 216. — *Dreger, Moritz,* The New School of Architecture *in:* Ver Sacrum, Jg. ii, Leipzig 1899, Issue No. 8, pp. 17-24. — *Du* (a magazine) Vienna 1900 to 1918, (Architecture and Crafts) *in:* Jg. xxiii, Zürich April 1963, pp. 2 ff.

Eggert, Hermann, The Competition for the New Reichstag Building, Berlin 1882, Special publication of the Centralblatt der Bauverwaltung, Jg. ii, Berlin 1882, Issues Nos. 26-32. — *Eggert, Hermann, ibid,* Section 7 [Otto Wagner] *in:* Centralblatt der Bauverwaltung, Jg. ii, Berlin 1882, Issue No. 32, pp. 291-2. — *Einstein, Albert,* Preface to Wahrheit — relativ oder absolut?, Zürich 1952. — *Eisenberg, Ludwig,* Das geistige Wien [Intellectual Vienna], Vienna 1893, p. 605. — *Eisenstein, Sergei,* Film Form, New York 1957. — *Eisler, Max,* Book Review of Die Baukunst unserer Zeit *in:* Der Architekt, Jg. xx, Vienna 1914-15, pp. 69-71. — *Eisler, Max,* Künstlerbriefe aus Österreich *in:* Österreichische Rundschau, Jg. ii, Vienna and Leipzig 1936, pp. 300-06.

Fassbender, Eugen, Grundzüge der modernen Städtebaukunde [Principal Features of Modern Municipal Building], Leipzig and Vienna 1912. — *Feldegg, Ferdinand von,* Artistic Competitions and How to Reform Them *in:* Der Architekt, Jg. vii, Vienna 1901, pp. 5-6, 20, 26. — *Feldegg, Ferdinand von,* On the Competition for the Emperor Francis Joseph Municipal Museum in Vienna *in:* Der Architekt, Jg. viii, Vienna 1902, p. 44. — *Feldegg, Ferdinand von,* The Closed Competition for the Emperor Francis Joseph Municipal Museum in Vienna *in:* Der Architekt, Jg. viii, Vienna 1902, Plate 66a. — *Feldegg, Ferdinand von,* Monumentality and Modern Architecture *in:* Der Architekt, Jg. ix, Vienna 1903, pp. 27-9. — *Findeis, Robert,* Die Wiener Eisenbahnverkehrsanlagen [The Viennese Railway Installations], Vienna 1945, p. 23 ff. — *Fischel Hartwig,* Otto Wagner *in:* Bildende Künstler, Vienna and Leipzig 1911, Issue No. 7 [Special Wagner Issue], p. 299-302. — *Fischel, Hartwig,* Otto Wagner *in:* Kunst und Kunsthandwerk [Art and Crafts], Jg. xxi, Vienna 1918, pp. 265-6. — *Frank, Ferdinand,* Fifty Years of the Viennese Stadtbahn *in:* Österreichische Gemeinde-Zeitung, Jg. xiv, Vienna 1948, Issue No. 17, pp. 19-25. — *Frankfurter Zeitung,* Obituaries on Otto Wagner, April 12, 1918 and April 19, 1918. — *Fremden-Blatt,* The House on the Michaelerplatz, Vienna May 14, 1911. — *Frey, Dagobert,* Otto Wagner. Some Reflections on the Past and Present *in:* Der Architekt, Jg. xxii, Vienna 1919, pp. 1-9. — *Frey, Dagobert,* Otto Wagner, An Epilogue. *in:* Otto Wagner, 'Einige Skizzen, Projekte und ausgeführte Bauwerke', Vol. iv, Vienna 1922, pp. 59-65. — *Frey, Dagobert,* Otto Wagner *in:* Neue Österreichische Biographie, Vol. i, Vienna 1923, pp. 178-87.

Die Gegenwart [The Present], Jg. xxxviii, Berlin 1909, Issue No. 32, pp. 571-3 [Criticism of the Judges' Decision in the Competition for the War Ministry Building]. — *Geretsegger, Heinz and Peintner, Max,* Otto Wagner and Present-day Architecture *in:* Der Bau, Jg. xviii, Vienna 1963, Issue No. 5, pp. 236-7. — *Giardi, Vittoria,* Commento a Otto Wagner *in:* L'architettura, Jg. iv, Milan 1958, Issue No. 32, pp. 118-23 (Dall'academia alla scuola moderna); Issue No. 33, pp. 192-7 (La Metropolitana di Vienna); Issue No. 34, pp. 264-9 (Alla svolta della Secessione); Issue No. 35, pp. 332-7 (La chiesa a Steinhof); Issue No. 36, pp. 408-13 (La Banca Postale a Vienna); Issue No. 37, pp. 482-5 (Una dignità creativa senza tramonto); Issue No. 38, pp. 550-5 (La conclusione meditata di un linguaggio). — *Giedion, Siegfried,* Space, Time and Architecture, Cambridge 1946, pp. 226, 238-43 [Otto Wagner and the Viennese School], 386, 506-08 [Otto Wagner's Faith in the Big City], 544. — *Glück, Franz,* Preface in the Catalogue for the 'Otto Wagner' Exhibition in the Historisches Museum der Stadt Wien 1963. — *Graf, Otto Antonia,* Otto Wagner's 'Haus der Kunst mcm-mm' *in:* Mitteilungen der Österreichischen Galerie, Jg. vi, Vienna 1962, Issue No. 50, p. 33. — *Graf, Otto Antonia,* Otto Wagner 1882, phil. diss. Vienna, Vienna 1963. — *Graf, Otto Antonia,* Otto Wagner *in:* 'Otto Wagner' Exhibition Catalogue, Historisches Museum der Stadt Wien 1963 and 'Otto Wagner' Exhibition Catalogue, Hessisches Landesmuseum in Darmstadt 1963. — *Guglia, Eugen,* Wien, Ein Führer durch Stadt und Umgebung [Guide to Vienna and the Surrounding Districts], Vienna 1908, pp. cxvi, 95, 126, 244, 307. — *Gurlitt, Cornelius,* Deutsche Kunst des 19. Jahrhunderts [German Art in the 19th Century], Berlin 1907, pp. 621 ff., 644.

Haberfeld, Hugo, Otto Wagner. On the International Congress of Architects in Vienna *in:* Illustrierte Zeitung, Leipzig

May 14, 1908. — *Haberlandt, Michael,* Österreich, Sein Land und Volk und seine Kultur [Austria, The Land, the People and the Culture], Weimar 1929, p. 413. — *Haendcke, Berthold,* 'Entwicklungsgeschichte der Stilarten' [History of Styles], Bielefeld and Leipzig 1924, pp. 559-61. — *Hamburg Rathaus Competition 1876:* Prize-winning Designs, Hamburg 1877. — *Hartmann, Karl O.,* Present-day Architecture. The Development of the Modern Style *in:* Der Architekt, Jg. XVII, Vienna 1911, pp. 92-3. — *Haussmann, Georges-Eugène,* Mémoires, Paris 1890-93, Vol. III, p. 55. — *Hennings, Fred,* Ringstrassensymphonie. Dritter Satz 1884-99 [Ringstrasse Symphony. Third Movement 1884-99], Vienna 1964, pp. 74-5. — *Hevesi, Ludwig,* A Modern Church [Währing] *in:* Kunst und Kunsthandwerk, Jg. II, Vienna 1899, pp. 450-2. — *Hevesi, Ludwig,* Österreichische Kunst im 19. Jahrhundert [Austrian Art in the 19th Century], Leipzig 1903, pp. 155-6, 286-8, 290, 306. — *Hevesi, Ludwig,* Church and Art *in:* Kunst und Kunsthandwerk, Jg. VII, Vienna 1904, pp. 513-4. — *Hevesi, Ludwig,* Otto Wagner's Modern Church [Steinhof] *in:* Zeitschrift für bildende Kunst, Jg. XVI, Leipzig 1905, pp. 236-7. — *Hevesi, Ludwig,* Acht Jahre Sezession [Eight Years' Secession], Vienna 1906, pp. 45, 67, 73, 97-100 [Otto Wagner's Academy Design], 138, 178, 198-9, 203-8 [Otto Wagner's Modern Church (Währing)], 272-82 [Otto Wagner], 288, 344, 348-51 [Emperor Francis Joseph Municipal Museum. Prior to the open Competition], 398-400 [Emperor Francis Joseph Municipal Museum (Closed Competition)], 436-9 [On the Emperor Francis Joseph Municipal Museum. The Models], 439-42 [The New Post Office Savings Bank], 490-4 [New Work by Otto Wagner (Steinhof)], 494. — *Hevesi, Ludwig,* Otto Wagner's Church [Steinhof] *in:* Pester Lloyd, Budapest Oct. 10 and Nov. 27, 1907. — *Hevesi, Ludwig,* A View of Cities. Vienna *in:* Jahrbuch der bildenden Kunst 1908-9 (Jg. VII), Berlin 1908, p. 12. — *Hevesi, Ludwig,* Altkunst-Neukunst [Old Art - New Art], Vienna 1909, pp. 58, 245-8 [The New Post Office Savings Bank], 249-54 [Otto Wagner's Modern Church (Steinhof)], 254-9 [Otto Wagner's Municipal Museum], 293-5 [On the Congress of Architects 1908], 295-9 [The New War Ministry Building], 314, 323, 333, 362. — *Hoffmann, Josef,* Stenographer's record of speech in which Hoffmann protested on behalf of the Artists' Association in the matter of the Municipal Museum designed by Otto Wagner for the Karlsplatz; speech delivered Jan 4, 1910 and printed in the Jahrbuch der Gesellschaft österr. Architekten 1909-10, Vienna 1910, pp. 55-66 and in Bildende Künstler, Vienna and Leipzig 1911, Issue No. 7 [Special Issue on Otto Wagner], pp. 332-42. — *Hofmann, Albert,* German Architecture at the Turn of the Century *in:* Jahrbuch der bildenden Kunst 1902, Berlin 1902, pp. 69-78 [Otto Wagner p. 75 ff.]. — *Hofmann, Albert,* Academy and Architecture *in:* Deutsche Bauzeitung, Jg. L, Berlin 1916, Issue No. 52, pp. 269-72. — *Hofmann, Albert,* Obituary on O. Kolomann Wagner *in:* Deutsche Bauzeitung, Jg. LII, Berlin 1918, Issue No. 44, pp. 189-90; Issue No. 45, pp. 197-9. — *Holey, Karl R.,* The Development of Viennese Architecture over the Past Fifty Years *in:* Technical Guide Through Vienna, Vienna 1910, pp. 247-55. — *Holey, Karl R.,* New Viennese Bank Buildings *in:* Der Architekt, Jg. XXI, Vienna 1916-18, pp. 1-4. — *Homlin, A. D. F.,* Otto Wagner on the Development of the Great City *in:* Architectural Record, Vol. XXXI, New York 1911, pp. 485-509.

Jahresbericht der Commission für Verkehrsanlagen in Wien [Annual Report of the Viennese Transport Commission], Vienna 1894 ff. — Jahresbericht 1906-07: The Lower Austrian Mental Hospitals and the Welfare Arrangements in the Province of Lower Austria for Mentally Defective Children. — *Joedicke, Jürgen,* Geschichte der modernen Architektur [History of Modern Architecture], Teufen (AR) 1958, pp. 10, 38, 40, 48 ff., 53-4, 214. — *Joyce, James,* Ulysses, London 1936. — *Juraschek, Fr. von,* The Expansion of the City of Vienna, of its Population and its Transport System between 1857 and 1894 *in:* Statistische Monatsschrift, Vienna 1896, pp. 329-44.

Kammerer, Marcel, On the Way in which Our Designs are Represented *in:* Der Architekt, Jg. XIV, Vienna 1908, pp. 41-2. — *Kammerer, Marcel,* Stenographer's record of speech in which Kammerer protested on behalf of the Artists' Association in the matter of the Municipal Museum designed by Otto Wagner for the Karlsplatz; speech delivered Jan 4, 1910 and printed in the Jahrbuch der Gesellschaft österr. Architekten 1909-10, Vienna 1910, pp. 28-43 and [in an abridged form] in Bildende Künstler, cont'd on p. 275a. Vienna and Leipzig 1911, Issue No. 7 [Special Issue on Otto Wagner], pp. 320-30. — The *Karlsplatz* and the Emperor Francis Joseph Municipal Museum. Resolutions passed by the Museum Building Committee based on the Proposals put forward by its own Subcommittee, Vienna 1907. — Statement issued upon completion of the Kirche am Steinhof by the Lower Austrian Landesausschuss [Provincial Council], Vienna 1907. — Die Kirche 'am Steinhof' [Pamhlet issued in connection with the consecration of the altar pictures. Contains comments on the altar pictures and windows and details of the techniques employed], Vienna 1913. — *Klasen, L.,* Grundrissvorbilder von Gebäuden aller Art [Groundplans in Buildings of Every Kind], Section 9, Leipzig 1887, pp. 832 ff. [Reichstag, Berlin]. — *Klein, Hugo,* The Secessionist Church *in:* Berliner Tageblatt, 1899, 615. — *Knaurs Lexikon der modernen Architektur,* Munich and Zürich 1963, pp. 290-2. — *Köller, Ernst,* His Work Is Still Controversial *in:* Salzburger Nachrichten, June 15, 1963. — *Koestler, Hugo,* The Viennese Stadtbahn *in:* Geschichte der Eisenbahnen der Österr.-ungarischen Monarchie [History of the Railways in the Austro-Hungarian Monarchy], Vol. I, Part 2, Vienna 1898, pp. 429-66. — *Kunstchronik,* Wiener Brief [Art Chronicle, Viennese Letter] *in:* Neue Folge, Jg. XXII, Leipzig 1911. Issue No. 33, pp. 516-9. — *Kunst und Künstler,* Jg. XVI, Berlin 1918, p. 357 [An Obituary of Otto Wagner]. — *Kuzmany, Karl Michael,* One of Otto Wagner's Churches *in:* Dekorative Kunst, Jg. XI, Munich 1907, pp. 106-14.

Die Wiener *Landes-Heil- und Pflegeanstalten* für Geistes- und Nervenkranke 'Am Steinhof' und in Ybbs an der Donau [The Viennese Provincial Sanatoria and Institutions for Mental and Nervous Diseases 'Am Steinhof' and in Ybbs on the Danube], Vienna 1934. — *Leixner, Othmar,* Wien, Ein Führer durch die Donaustadt [Vienna. A Guide to the City on the Danube], Vienna 1926. — *Leixner, Otto von,* Otto Wagner, the Architect *in:* Der Baumeister, Jg. I, Berlin 1903, Issue No. 5, pp. 49-54. — *Leixner, Otto von,* Otto Wagner. An Artistic Appreciation *in:* Zeitschrift des Österreichischen Ingenieur- und Architekten-Vereins, Jg. LXXI, Vienna 1919, pp. 2-5, 19, 25. — *Lichtblau, Ernst,* Preface to 'Wagnerschule, Arbeiten aus den Jahren 1905-

06 and 1906-07', Leipzig 1910. — *Loos, Adolf,* 'Trotzdem' [Nonetheless], Innsbruck 1931, p. 62 and 'Sämtliche Schriften' [Collected Writings], Vol. I, Vienna 1962, p. 322. — *Loos, Adolf,* 'Ins Leere gesprochen' [Talking to the Wind], Innsbruck 1932, p. 44 ff. — *Lützow C. von* and *Tischler, Ludwig,* (Eds), Wiener Neubauten [New Buildings in Vienna], Serie A [Private Buildings] Vol. I, Vienna 1876, p. 19, Plates 80-3 [Grabenhof]. — *Lux, Josef August,* Review of Modern Architecture *in:* Zeit, Vienna 1902, Issue No. 401. — *Lux, Josef August,* The Fight Over the New Viennese Museum *in:* Zeit, Vienna 1902, Issue No. 403. — *Lux, Josef August,* Die Wagnerschule 1902, Vienna and Leipzig 1903. — *Lux, Josef August,* On Modern Church Architecture *in:* Der Architekt, Jg. XI, Vienna 1905, p. 5. — *Lux, Josef August,* Artistic Problems Facing the Viennese Municipality. The Karlsplatz. *in:* Hohe Warte, Jg. II, Vienna 1905-06, pp. 4-6. — *Lux, Josef August,* The Masters of the Viennese Soil *in:* Wenn du vom Kahlenberg . . ., Vienna and Leipzig 1907, pp. 112-56. — *Lux, Josef August,* Otto Wagner, Munich 1914. — *Lux, Josef August,* Otto Wagner and the Viennese *in:* Persönlichkeit, Jg. I, 1914, pp. 81-96. — *Lux, Josef August,* In memoriam Otto Wagner, Vienna *in:* Deutsche Kunst und Dekoration, Vol. XLII, Darmstadt 1918, p. 198. — *Lux, Josef August,* Otto Wagner and the New Objectivity *in:* Deutsche Kunst und Dekoration, Vol. LXII, Darmstadt 1928, p. 203.

Malkiel-Jirmounsky, M., Les Tendances de l'Architecture Contemporaine, Paris 1930, pp. 24, 117-27 (Austria). — *Mayreder, Karl,* Municipal Development (Vienna) *in:* Technical Guide Through Vienna, Vienna 1910, pp. 52-60 [The period of municipal expansion], pp. 61-70 [The present]. — *Mc Coy, Esther,* Five California Architects, New York 1960, pp. 152 and 155. — *Meier-Graefe, Julius,* Entwicklungsgeschichte der modernen Kunst [History of Modern Art], Vol. II, Stuttgart 1904, pp. 689-98 [The New Vienna (Otto Wagner p. 696)]. — *Missong, Alfred,* Heiliges Wien. Ein Führer durch Wiens Kirchen und Kapellen [Sacred Vienna. A Guide Through Vienna's Churches and Chapels], Vienna 1933, pp. 171, 203-4. — *Moderne Architektur,* Prof. Otto Wagner und die Wahrheit über beide [Moderne Architektur and Prof. Otto Wagner and the truth about both]. Edited and published by Verlagsbuchhandlung Spielhagen and Schurich, Vienna 1897. — *Monatshefte für Baukunst* [Architectural Monthly], Jg. XXV, 1941, p. 278: [Otto Wagner 1841-1918]. — *Münz, Ludwig,* Adolf Loos, Milan 1956, pp. 7-8. — *Münz, Ludwig,* Introduction to the 'Adolf Loos' Exhibition Catalogue, Galerie Würthle, Vienna 1961. — Der Museumsbau auf dem Karlsplatz [The Museum Building on the Karlsplatz]. Pamphlet issued by the Association for the Preservation of Artistic Monuments in Vienna and Lower Austria, Vienna and Leipzig 1910, p. 10. — *Musil, Robert,* Der Mann ohne Eigenschaften, Hamburg 1958 [English translation by Eithne Wilkins and Ernst Kaiser, 'The Man without Qualities', London 1953]. — *Muthesius, Hermann,* Stilarchitektur und Baukunst. Wandlungen der Architektur im XIX Jahrhundert und ihr heutiger Standpunkt ['Style Architecture' and the Art of Building. Changes in architecture in the 19th century and its position today], Mühlheim-Ruhr 1902.

Neue Freie Presse, A Theatre Building by Otto Wagner [Wasagasse], Vienna April 13th, 1918. — *Neue Zürcher Zeitung,* Otto Wagner, April 17th, 1918. — *Neutra, Richard,* Meine Erinnerung an Otto Wagner [My Memories of Otto Wagner] *in:* baukunst und werkform, Jg. XII, Nuremberg 1959, Issue No. 9, p. 476. — *Neutra, Richard,* 'Life and Shape', New York 1962, pp. 62-8 [Section on reformers and municipal authorities].

Oerley, Robert, Stenographer's record of speech in which Oerley protested on behalf of the Artists' Association in the matter of the Municipal Museum designed by Otto Wagner for the Karlsplatz; speech delivered Jan 4, 1910 and printed in the Jahrbuch der Gesellschaft österr. Architekten 1909-10, Vienna 1910, pp. 20-8, and in Bildende Künstler, Vienna and Leipzig 1911, Issue No. 7 [Special Issue on Otto Wagner], pp. 304-10. — *Oerley, Robert,* Jahresbilanz [Annual Account] *in:* Jahrbuch der Gesellschaft österr. Architekten, 1909-10, Vienna 1910, pp. 87-8, 99. — *Oerley, Robert,* Otto Wagner's Personality *in:* Der Architekt, Jg. XXII, Vienna 1919, pp. 23-6. — Österreichisch-Ungarische Kunstchronik, Vol. IV, Vienna 1880, Issue No. 2, pp. 26-8: Works for the Festival Procession in the City of Vienna; Issue No. 9, pp. 129-30: The Francis Joseph Memorial at the Praterstern. — Österreichs Illustrierte Zeitung, Jg. X, Vienna 1900-01, Issue No. 41: Otto Wagner; Jg. XXII, Vienna 1913, Issue No. 32: Designs for the Emperor Francis Joseph Municipal Museum in Vienna (Opus IV). — *Ostwald, Hans,* 'Otto Wagner. Ein Beitrag zum Verständnis seines baukünstlerischen Schaffens' [Otto Wagner. An Attempt to Elucidate His Architectural Achievement], Diss. E. T. H. Zürich and Baden 1948.

Paulsen, Otto Wagner 1841-1918 *in:* Bauwelt, Jg. XXXII, Berlin 1941, Issue No. 36, p. 6. — *Pevsner, Nikolaus,* Pioneers of Modern Design, London 1960. — *Pirchan, Emil,* 'Otto Wagner, Der grosse Baukünstler', Vienna 1956. — *Planiscig, Leone,* Problemi d'architettura moderna: Otto Wagner *in:* Emporium, Vol. XXXII, Bergamo 1910, Issue No. 188, pp. 102-15. — *Platz, Gustav Adolf,* 'Die Baukunst der neuesten Zeit' [Architecture of Recent Times], Berlin 1927, pp. 25, 236-9. — *Plechl, Pia Maria,* Art Nouveau is on the Move *in:* Die Presse, Vienna Feb. 25, 1962. — *Poe, Edgar Allan,* The Philosophy of Composition *in:* 'The Centenary Poe', London 1949, p. 492. — The Imp. and Roy. *Post Office Savings Bank in Vienna,* Vienna 1908 and 1913.

Rainer, Roland, Otto Wagner *in:* der aufbau, Jg. XV, Vienna 1960, Issue No. 2, pp. 82-4. — *Rave, Paul Ortwin* and *Wirth, Irmgard,* 'Die Bauwerke und Kunstdenkmäler von Berlin, Bezirk Tiergarten' [The Buildings and Monuments in The Tiergarten District of Berlin], Berlin 1955, pp. 63-8 [Reichstag Building]. — 'Auswahl aus den Entwürfen zum deutschen Reichstagsgebäude 1882 (Ed. K. E. O. Fritsch) [Selection of Designs for the German Reichstag Building of 1882], Berlin 1883. — *Roessler, Arthur,* Oberbaurat Prof. Otto Wagner *in:* Bildende Künstler, Vienna and Leipzig 1911, Issue No. 7 [Special Issue on Otto Wagner], pp. 350-2 and *in:* Der Architekt, Jg. XVII, Vienna 1911, pp. 57-60. — *Roessler, Arthur,* Otto Wagner and His School *in:* Das Ehrenjahr Otto Wagners an der k. k. Akademie der bildenden Künste in Wien (Ed. Otto Schönthal), Vienna 1912, p. 1. — *Roessler, Arthur,* Oberbaurat

Prof. Otto Wagner *in:* Donauland, Jg. II, Ist half, May 1918, p. 354. — *Roessler, Arthur,* Schwarze Fahnen [Black Flags], Vienna 1922, pp. 118-26. — *Roller, Alfred,* Preface to Aus der Wagnerschule MCM *in:* Der Architekt, Supplementary Issue No. 6, Vienna 1901, pp. 5-7.

Schachner, Friedrich, Schachner oder Wagner. Zur Abwehr. Zum Wettbewerbe um den Bau des Kaiser-Franz-Josef-Stadt-Museums [Schachner or Wagner. A defence. Concerning the Competition for the Emperor Francis Joseph Municipal Museum], Vienna 1902. — *Schachtschabel, G.,* Automation in Wirtschaft und Gesellschaft, Hamburg 1961, p. 106. — *Scheuch, Manfred,* The Confirmation Candidate chose Architecture *in:* Arbeiter-Zeitung, Vienna June 30, 1963. — *Schmalenbach, Fritz,* Jugendstil [Art Nouveau], phil. Diss. Münster, Würzburg 1935, pp. 64, 112, 153. — *Schmidt, Justus,* 19th Century Viennese Churches *in:* Kirchenkunst, Jg. VII, Vienna 1935, pp. 35-6. — *Schmitt, Friedrich Josef,* Otto Wagner's Position in the History of Architecture *in:* Historisch-Politische Blätter für das katholische Deutschland, Vol. CLXII, Munich 1918, pp. 263-8. — *Schmutzler, Robert,* 'Art Nouveau-Jugendstil', Stuttgart 1962, p. 244. — *Schönthal, Otto,* Otto Wagner's Church [Steinhof] *in:* Der Architekt, Jg. XIV, Vienna 1908, pp. 1-5. — *Schönthal, Otto,* Otto Wagner's Church [Steinhof] *in:* Bildende Künstler, Vienna and Leipzig 1911, Issue No. 7 [Special Issue on Otto Wagner], pp. 342-4. — *Schönthal, Otto,* Otto Wagner's 70th Birthday *in:* Illustrierte Zeitung, Leipzig July 20, 1911. — *Schönthal, Otto* (Ed.), Das Ehrenjahr Otto Wagners an der k. k. Akademie der bildenden Künste in Wien. Arbeiten seiner Schüler, Projekte, Studien und Skizzen [Otto Wagner's Year of Honour at the Academy of Fine Arts in Vienna. Works by his Students, Designs, Studies and Sketches], Vienna 1912. — *Schuhmacher, Fritz,* 'Strömungen in deutscher Baukunst seit 1800' (Currents in German Architecture since 1800), Leipzig 1935, pp. 105, 111, 117, 130. — *Seligmann, Adalbert Franz,* On Otto Wagner's 70th Birthday *in:* Neue Freie Presse, Vienna July 13, 1911. — *Seligmann, Adalbert Franz,* Otto Wagner Obituary *in:* Neue Freie Presse, Vienna April 13, 1918. — *Setz, M.,* Sanatorium for Lupus Patients in Vienna *in:* Zeitschrift für Krankenanstalten, Jg. XI, 1915, p. 550. — *Sitte, Camillo,* Der Städtebau nach seinen künstlerischen Grundsätzen (The Artistic Principles of Town-Planning), Vienna 1889. — *Sitte, Camillo,* Preliminary Competition for the Emperor Francis Joseph Municipal Museum *in:* Allgemeine Bauzeitung, Vienna 1902, pp. 61-6. — *Sitte, Camillo,* Monumental Architecture and the Secession *in:* Neues Wiener Tagblatt, 1903. — *Sonnenschein, Sigmund,* The Viennese Stadtbahn *in:* Archiv für Eisenbahnwesen, Berlin 1894, pp. 825-69. — The Viennese Stadtbahn 1898-1908 [Publication issued by the Imp. and Roy. Railway Ministry], Vienna 1909. — Erection of the '*Staustufe Kaiserbad*' [Kaiserbad Dam] on the Danube Canal [Publication issued by the Commission for the Regulation of the Danube], Vienna 1910, first published in the Allgemeine Bauzeitung, Vienna 1910, Issue No. 1. — *Stephan, Paul,* Otto Wagner *in:* Neue Zürcher Zeitung, April 21, 1918. — *Strzygowski, Josef,* 'Die bildende Kunst der Gegenwart' [The State of the Fine Arts Today], Leipzig 1907, pp. 87, 238 ff. — *Strzygowski, Josef,* Otto Wagner *in:* Zeit, Vienna July 11, 1911. — *Strzygowski, Josef,* Otto Wagner Obituary *in:* Neue Freie Presse, Vienna April 12, 1918. — *Swoboda, Heinrich,*

The Church and Architecture *in:* Der Architekt, Jg. X, Vienna 1904, pp. 29-32.

Taussig, Sigmund, The Conversion of the Danube Canal into a Commercial and Winter Harbour and the Works at Nussdorf *in:* Danubius, Vienna 1894. — *Taussig, Sigmund,* On the Building Works for the Conversion of the Danube Canal into a Commercial and Winter Harbour *in:* Zeitschrift des Österr. Ingenieur- und Architekten-Vereins, Vienna 1897, Issues Nos. 14 and 15; cf. The Building Works on the Danube Canal *in:* Wiener Bau-Industrie-Zeitung, Jg. XIV, Vienna 1896, Issue No. 12, pp. 127-30. — *Taut, Bruno,* 'Bauen. Der Neue Wohnbau' [Building. The New Dwelling House], Berlin 1927, pp. 28, 48-9. — *Technischer Führer durch Wien* [Technical Guide through Vienna] (Eds.: Association of Austrian Engineers and Architects), Vienna 1910. — *Templ, Günter,* Otto Wagner's Villa Before It Is Demolished *in:* Die Presse, Vienna October 12-13, 1963. — *Thieme-Becker,* Allgemeines Lexikon der bildenden Künstler von der Antike bis zur Gegenwart, Vol. XXXV, Leipzig 1942, pp. 46-8. — *Tietze, Hans,* Otto Wagner, Vienna—Berlin—Munich—Leipzig 1922. — *Tischler, Ludwig,* (Ed.), Wiener Neubauten [New Viennese Buildings], Serie A [Private Buildings], Vol. III, Vienna 1891, p. 1, Plates 1-8 [Länderbank].

Die *Verkehrsanlagen in Wien* [Public Transportation in Vienna] (Published by the Viennese Transport Commission), Vienna 1900. — *Ver Sacrum,* Jg. I, Vienna 1898, Issue No. 2, p. 25: 'Der Architekt', Special Supplement containing book reviews of Aus der Wagnerschule; Jg. II, Leipzig 1899, Issue 8: The Hofpavillon on the Wiener Stadtbahn; Jg. III, Vienna 1900, Issue No. 11, p. 178: Commentary on the Resolutions passed at the 2nd Annual Meeting of the Art Council; Jg. III, 1900, Issue No. 12, pp. 189-95: The Exhibit for the Directors of the Imp. and Roy. Hofgarten at the Paris Exhibition; Jg. III, 1900, Issue No. 19, pp. 290-2: A Dwelling House near the Wienerwald by Otto Wagner; Jg. III, 1900, Issue No. 19, pp. 293-8: A Pied à Terre.

Wachsmann, Konrad, Wendepunkt im Bauen [Turning Point in Architecture], Wiesbaden 1959, p. 231. — *Wagner, Otto* (the younger), Das Haus des Kindes [The House for children] *in:* Der Architekt, Jg. XXII, Vienna 1919, p. 27. — Aus der Wagnerschule *in:* Der Architekt, Jg. I, Vienna 1895; Jg. II, 1896. — Aus der Wagnerschule MDCCCXCVII, Der Architekt, Supplementary Issue No. 1, Vienna 1897. — Aus der Wagnerschule MDCCCXCVIII, Der Architekt, Supplementary Issue No. 2, Vienna 1898. — Aus der Wagnerschule MDCCCIC, Der Architekt, Supplementary Issue No. 5, Vienna 1899. — Aus der Wagnerschule MCM, Der Architekt, Supplementary Issue No. 6, Vienna 1901. — Wagnerschule 01, Der Architekt, Supplementary Issue No. 7, Vienna 1902. — Wagnerschule 1902, Vienna and Leipzig 1903. — Wagnerschule: Works from the year 1902-03 and 1903-04, Leipzig 1905. — Wagnerschule: Works from the years 1905-06 and 1906-07, Leipzig 1910. — Otto Wagner's Year of Honour at the Academy ... See Schönthal, Otto. — Wasmuth's Lexikon der Baukunst, Vol. II, Berlin 1930, p. 560; Vol. IV, 1932, p. 674. — Wehr- und Schleusenanlage im Wiener Donaukanal bei Nussdorf [Nussdorf Dam] (Eds.: Commission for the Regulation of the Danube), Vienna 1911.

— Die Tiefbau-Arbeiten bei der Herstellung der *Wehr- und Schleusenanlage in Nussdorf* [Nussdorf Dam: Excavation works] (Published by the Contractors Redlich & Berger), Vienna 1920. — *Weyl, Th.,* Die Assanierung von Wien [The Sanitation of Vienna] *in:* Fortschritte der Ingenieurwissenschaften, Jg. II, Issue No. 9, pp. 80-9. — *Wick-Wagner, Luise,* 'Der Freiheit eine Gasse'. Versuch eines Porträts von Otto Wagner [One Path to Freedom. An Attempt at a Protrait of Otto Wagner] *in:* baukunst und werkform, Jg. XII, Nuremberg 1959, Issue No. 9, pp. 476-84. — *Wien* am Anfang des XX. Jhdts [Vienna at the Beginning of the XXth Century]. (Published by the Association of Austrian Engineers and Architects), Vol. I, Vienna 1905; Vol. II, 1906. — *Wiener Bauhütte,* Jg. II, Section I, Vienna 1874, Plates 74 and 82 [Casino]. — *Wiener Bauindustrie-Zeitung,* Jg. XIV, Vienna 1896, Issue No. 13, pp. 141-2: The projected installations between the Franzensbrücke and the Augartenbrücke in Vienna; Jg. XIV, 1897, Issue No. 25, pp. 281-2 and Issue No. 26, pp. 293-5: Review of 'Moderne Architektur'; Jg. XIV, 1897, Issue No. 27, pp. 307-9: Report of the enquiry set up to examine the designs for the regulation of the 1st district and the Karlsplatz; Jg. XIV, 1897 Issue No. 27, p. 34: The Erection of the Municipal Museum: (Supplement: 'Der Bauinteressent'), Jg. XX, 1902, Issue No. 5, p. 52: The Competition for the Cathedral of the Apostle Andreas in Patras; Jg. XX, Issue No. 18, 1903, pp. 137-9: From the Telegraph Office of 'Die Zeit'; Jg. XX, 1903, Issue No. 19, pp. 152-3: The Competition for the New Post Office Savings Bank in Vienna; Jg. XX, 1903, Issue No. 34, p. 274: Exhibition of Models for the Municipal Museum in Vienna; Jg. XXI, 1904, Issue No. 53 (Supplement: 'Der Bauinteressent'), pp. 441: The Kaiserbad Dam; Jg. XXIV, 1907, Issue No. 27, pp. 235-6: Competition for an Exhibition Building in Vienna (Zedlitzhalle); Jg. XXIV, 1907, Issue No. 20, pp. 168-9: Protest by a Committee of Architects against the Judges' Decision in the Competition for the Palace of Peace in the Hague; Jg. XXV, 1907, Issue No. 10 (Supplement: 'Der Bauinteressent'), p. 83: Comment on the Judges' Decision in the Competition for the Municipal Museum; Jg. XXV, 1907, Issue No. 11, p. 97 and Issue No. 12, pp. 109-10: Competition for the Erection of a New War Ministry Building in Vienna; Jg. XXV, 1908, Issue No. 14, p. 131: Association of Austrian Engineers and Architects [Report of Session of Dec. 21, 1907, which discussed Wagner's Municipal Museum]; Jg. XXVI, 1909, Issue No. 28, p. 239: Preliminary Competition for the Technical Museum for Industrial and Craft Products. — *Wiener Bauten* 1900 bis heute (Viennese Buildings from 1900 to the present day) (Ed. Schwanzer, Karl), Vienna 1964, pp. 5-9. — Architectur in *Wien* um 1900, Katalog der Ausstellung im Österr. Bauzentrum [Viennese Architecture at the turn of the century, Catalogue of the Exhibition in the Austrian Building Centre], Vienna 1964. — *Wiener, Norbert,* Mensch und Menschmaschine, West-Berlin 1958, pp. 44-5. — *Wolfbauer, Franz,* Otto Wagner *in:* Österreichs Illustrierte Zeitung, Jg. XX, Vienna 1911, Issue No. 45. — *Wurzbach, Constantin von,* Biographisches Lexikon des Kaiserthums Österreich [Biographical Lexicon of the Austrian Empire], Vienna 1885, p. 122. — *Wurzer, Rudolf,* The Siting of Schools as an Element in Town Planning *in:* der aufbau, Jg. XVIII, Vienna 1963, Issue No. 10, pp. 358 and 360.

Zevi, Bruno, Storia dell'Architettura Moderna, Turin 1955, pp. 91-9. — *Zimmermann, E.,* Otto Wagner and Modern Architecture *in:* Supplement to the Hamburger Nachrichten, 1902, Issue No. 40. — *Zuckerkandl, Berta,* Viennese Tastelessness *in:* Ver Sacrum, Jg. I, Vienna 1898, Issue No. 2, pp. 4-5. — *Zuckerkandl, Berta,* Zeitkunst 1901-7 [Contemporary Art], Vienna 1908, pp. 65-70 (Otto Wagner), 70-6 (The New Church), 77-81 (The Architectural Conscience).

AUTHORS' NOTE

THE ALIEN QUALITY ('alien' in the sense that all art is alien) which characterises much of Wagner's work has been largely responsible for the unthinking reverence which has all too often been paid to his creations. Such an uncritical approach is, quite simply, an example of the typical, self-justifying thoughtlessness of contemporary attitudes. It is an inadequate, even an insulting, response to the scope and complexity of Wagner's architecture and the principal reason for this book was the desire to rectify this situation. There were other reasons of course. But if we consider that a number of important Wagner buildings are now threatened with demolition, then—for purpose of this postscript—that is the only thing that matters. Many contemporary architects feel that the architectural polemics of the turn of the century, which were largely purposive and were consequently obliged to cater for the lowest level of intelligence in the enemy camp, established a completely self-contained system, which is now greatly admired for having 'anticipated' current modes of thought with such amazing accuracy. Consequently a building by Otto Wagner is regarded by these modern thinkers as an imperfect illustration of just such a 'system', which means that—for them—the tangible reality of the actual physical building constitutes no more than a number of individual acts of anticipation. And what is anticipated is of course the set of assumptions in current favour. Consequently, instead of a house, we are presented with a catalogue of stereotyped principles.

We are greatly indebted to the German publisher, Wolfgang Schaffler, for deciding to support our project at a very early stage. Without his co-operation this difficult, time-consuming and expensive undertaking could not have been brought to a successful conclusion.

It was Walter Pichler, who persuaded Wolfgang Schaffler to back our joint venture, and we wish to thank him both for this service and for his collaboration on the pictorial documentation.

We feel indebted to Richard Neutra, who has shown his interest in Otto Wagner on many occasions, for writing the introduction, in which he furnishes a new assessment of the architect's work and personality.

We also wish to thank Dr Josef Dapra, the photographer for the Residenz Verlag, Salzburg, Austria, who supplied nearly all the new photographs of Wagner buildings, for his generous co-operation and the printers, Friedrich Sochor in Zell am See, for the skilful way in which they overcame the problems presented by the variations in the pictorial material and the typographical difficulties to which this often gave rise.

Special thanks are due to Otto Wagner's daughters, Luise Wick-Wagner and Christine Lütgendorff-Gyllenstorm, for the active interest which they took in the production of this book, for many valuable items of information and for a few little-known or unknown snapshots, which have enriched the biographical section. Luise Wick-Wagner also placed at our disposal one of her father's sketchbooks dating from the year 1859 as well as her own personal papers, while Christine Lütgendorff-Gyllenstorm allowed us to consult Otto Wagner's unpublished diary.

We are indebted to Friedrich Reisser, the proprietor of the publishing house of Anton Schroll & Co, which has so often been associated with the works of famous Austrian architects, for permission to reproduce a large number of indispensable illustrations.

Numerous other persons, many of them representatives of public institutions, have helped to promote our project and have given us useful advice in both a private and an official capacity. Franz Dichck, the Director of the Museum der Stadt Wien, allowed us to reproduce a number of original documents in the possession of the Historisches Museum der Stadt Wien. Oberstaatsbibliothekar Dr Walter Ritzer, director of the library at the Technische Hochschule in Vienna, and Hofrat Professor Dr Siegfried Freiberg, who is in charge of the library and the collections of drawings and copper engravings at the Academy of Fine Arts in Vienna, kindly placed various documents at our disposal for photographic reproduction and helped us in every possible way within their working sphere. In the Austrian National Library we received considerable help from Staatsbibliothekar Dr Laurenz Strebel and in the library of the Federal Ministry for Trade and Reconstruction from Staatsbibliothekar Dr Bruno Zimmel, who furnished us with important material on the buildings on the Danube Canal. The vice-director of the Viennese Stadtwerke-Verkehrsbetriebe (Municipal Transport Works), Senatsrat Dipl.-Ing. Dr Erich Körber, granted us access to plans in the archives of the Hochbau (surface building) department and the drawing office of the railway construction department and to pictorial material from the photographic department of the Transport Works. We are also indebted to the head of the Transport Section of the Austrian State Archives, Oberstaatsarchivar Dr Paul Mechtler, for design material relating to the Stadtbahn. Other illustrations were obtained from: the photographic archives in the Austrian National Library; the director of the Graphische Sammlung Albertina, Dr Walter Koschatzky; Dr Hans Loibl, Techn. Oberamtsrat and head of the Office for Designs and Documents in the Magistrat der Stadt Wien; Dr Eduard Novey, Oberstadtbaurat and head of the Aussenstelle der Magistratsabteilung 37; Dipl.-Ing. Augustin Lang, Bauoberkommissär and head of an Aussenstelle; and Senatsrat Ing. Rudolf J. Boeck, head of Management Section III of the Office of Public Works in Vienna, who obtained access for us to the design archives of the Psychiatric Hospital on the Baumgartner Höhe. A number of photographs were provided by Lucca Chmel, Barbara Pflaum and Hannes Pflaum. Hofrat Dipl.-Ing. Erich Bayerl gave permission for the town plans of Vienna to be reproduced from the maps of the Federal Office for Land Surveys. Dr Robert Ritschel, the governor of the Austrian Post Office Savings Bank, kindly allowed us to take photographs in the Post Office Building, where we also received every assistance from Zentralinspektor Regierungsrat Hermann Herzan. We were given similar facilities in the Church Am Steinhof and the Lupus Sanatorium by Primarius Dr Otto Glück, Stadtrat and head of Geschäftsgruppe V in the Viennese Magistrat, and for the installations on the Danube Canal by Hofrat Dipl.-Ing. Josef Schmutterer, head of Department IV of the Federal Office for Riverside Buildings, who also gave us access to his official library. The information provided by Regierungsbauoberkommissär Dipl.-Ing. Bruno Gibisch in respect of the canal buildings was particularly helpful. Kommerzialrat Hans Gottlob and Dr Gerhard Hofner kindly allowed us to take photographs on the premises of Hüttelbergstrasse 26 and 28. The architect Hans Hollein provided us with important information and placed a number of special works from his own private library at our disposal, as did the architects Friedrich Kurrent and Hermann Czech.

Finally we wish to express our gratitude to Dr Franz Fuhrmann of the Salzburg Museum Carolino Augusteum for reading the German text in manuscript and the members of the staff of Residenz Verlag, Salzburg, for their generous assistance.

Heinz Geretsegger and Max Peintner

INDEX

Numbers in italics refer to illustrations. Buildings listed in the Index of Subjects are in Vienna unless otherwise stated.